Vince, by Ellen C. Patton. Acrylic on canvas, 2011. *Courtesy of the artist*

PULP
FICTI

Voyageur
Press

The Complete Story of Quentin Tarantino's Masterpiece

Jason Bailey

First published in 2013 by Voyageur Press, an imprint of MBI Publishing Company, 400 First Avenue North, Suite 400, Minneapolis, MN 55401 USA

Voyageur Press titles are also available at discounts in bulk quantity for industrial or sales-promotional use. For details write to Special Sales Manager at MBI Publishing Company, 400 First Avenue North, Suite 400, Minneapolis, MN 55401 USA.

To find out more about our books, visit us online at www.voyageurpress.com.

ISBN-13: 978-0-7603-4479-8

Library of Congress Cataloging-in-Publication Data

Bailey, Jason, 1975-
  Pulp fiction : the complete story of Quentin Tarantino's masterpiece / Jason Bailey.
    pages cm
   ISBN 978-0-7603-4479-8 (hardback)
  1. Pulp fiction (Motion picture) I. Title.
  PN1997.P85B35 2013
  791.43'72--dc23
                           2013012310

Editor: Grace Labatt
Design Manager: James Kegley
Designed by: Brad Norr Design

Printed in China

10 9 8 7 6 5 4 3 2 1

For Rebekah,
Miss Beautiful Tulip

BAD
A FILM BY QUENTIN TARANTINO
PULP
FICTION
MIRAMAX FILMS PRESENTS A BAND APART AND JERSEY FILMS PRODUCTION A FILM BY QUENTIN TARANTINO PULP FICTION MUSIC SUPERVISOR KARYN RACHTMAN
COSTUME DESIGNER BETSY HEIMANN PRODUCTION DESIGNER DAVID WASCO EDITOR SALLY MENKE DIRECTOR OF PHOTOGRAPHY ANDRZEJ SEKULA
CO-EXECUTIVE PRODUCERS BOB WEINSTEIN HARVEY WEINSTEIN RICHARD N. GLADSTEIN EXECUTIVE PRODUCERS DANNY DEVITO MICHAEL SHAMBERG
STACEY SHER STORIES BY QUENTIN TARANTINO & ROGER AVERY PRODUCED BY LAWRENCE BENDER WRITTEN AND DIRECTED BY QUENTIN TARANTINO
R RESTRICTED
SOUNDTRACK AVAILABLE ON MCA LP's, CASSETTES & CDs
DOLBY DIGITAL
MIRAMAX

Contents

Opposite:
Pulp Fiction, by
Adam Rabelais.
Digital art, 2011.
Courtesy of the artist

Prologue

The trailer, which unspooled in theaters and unreeled on VHS tapes in late summer 1994, begins with a fake-out. As stoic piano music plays, a solemn-voiced narrator reads the scrolling text with an excess of gravitas. "Miramax Films is proud to present . . . ," he begins portentously. To 1994 audiences, Miramax was the classy distributor of prestige pictures, the outfit behind the surprise hit *The Crying Game* and the previous year's multiple Oscar winner *The Piano*, whose somber score this trailer immediately recalls.

So what is Miramax Films proud to present this time? "One of the most celebrated motion pictures of the year," the narrator continues. Ah, very good. "The winner of the 1994 Palme d'Or, the Best Picture of the Cannes Film Festival." And just as the incantation of that prize is complete and the casual moviegoer has tuned out ("Uh-oh, this is gonna be one of them impenetrable, high-minded, subtitled 'art movies'"), the slow and delicate piano music is stopped cold by the blast of gunshots, which tear bullet holes into the screen. The classical score is replaced by

Cannes. © *Stephane Cardinale / Sygma / Corbis*

the furious guitar of surf rock king Dick Dale, and the imagery it accompanies is no less incongruent: cocked guns, fast cars, cool suits, and—wait, was that Bruce Willis?

The film was called *Pulp Fiction*, and it'd exploded across Cannes that May with similar brute force. Director Quentin Tarantino arrived at the prestigious international film festival with the swagger of a rock star. Though his first film, *Reservoir Dogs*, had underperformed in the States, it was a giant hit in Europe, its engagements in London and Paris running on for months, even years. When his new picture debuted late in the festival, it landed in the Palais des Festivals like a dirty bomb. This was something big, grand, loud, rude, and altogether thrilling.

Audiences and critics alike went wild for its heady brew of dark humor, pop-infused chatter, gangster cool, and narrative dexterity. It became Cannes' hottest ticket, and when the festival jury (headed by Clint Eastwood, star of Tarantino's favorite film, *The Good, the Bad, and the Ugly*) gathered to select the award winners, they handed *Pulp Fiction* the festival's highest honor. At the ceremony, an irate woman at the back of the auditorium disrupted the proceedings to shout "Scandal! Scandal!" in French. Tarantino responded by hoisting his middle finger. As the crowd cheered, he explained, "I don't make movies that bring people together. I make movies that split people apart."

Be that as it may, when the picture hit theaters that fall, it sure *felt* like a film that brought people together. Young audiences, intellectuals, cinephiles, and popcorn chewers alike were gripped by *Pulp* fever, buoyed by the film's cleverness, rocked by its bursts of violence, endlessly quoting its punchy dialogue. Tarantino had captured the early-nineties zeitgeist in his triptych of throwback crime stories, and audiences ate it up like a Royale with Cheese.

But back to that trailer. Down in my basement apartment in Kansas, I kept rewinding and re-viewing it, over and over again, intoxicated by its images, enraptured by its energy, enthralled by the promises it made—and would ultimately keep, the six times I watched the film during its original theatrical run (which was easier than it sounds; it ran nearly a full year in our market) and countless more once it hit VHS. Like so many other men my age, I didn't just *like* Quentin Tarantino, I wanted to *be* him, to parlay my own video store geekhood into a moviemaking career, and I was inspired by his success to make my own films. But they weren't my own, not really; they were my attempts to make Tarantino films, with wisecracking, pop culture–obsessed, pistol-packing cool cats in ties and sunglasses navigating painstakingly nonlinear timelines.

I couldn't recreate *Fiction*'s magic, of course. None of us could, not even the man himself. "I'm not the kind of guy that wants to put *Pulp Fiction* into perspective twenty years later," Tarantino said recently. But I do. What was it about that movie, at that moment, that was so powerful? The gunshots blazing through the screen in that first trailer were more than a shrewd marketing touch. They were the sound of a starter pistol, marking the launch of a new kind of director and a new type of picture, one that was a simultaneous snapshot of what film had been, what it was now, and what it could be. The movies never knew what hit 'em.

PART I

The Movie Geek

Quentin Tarantino: The Early Years

One usually has to dig deep into the subtext of Tarantino's films to find autobiography. He is, famously, an artist whose worldview is colored less by what he's lived than by what he's seen, and his films are often personal only inasmuch as they reflect the kinds of stories, imagery, and iconography that he likes. But there is one moment in *Pulp Fiction* that is very personal indeed. At the beginning of the film's second story, "The Gold Watch," we find young Butch watching television—an episode of the cheapo kiddie program *Clutch Cargo*, to be precise. But he's not just *watching* television; that's too passive a description. He's sitting directly in front of it, right up close, inches from the screen, drinking in everything that pours out of it.

"When I saw *Pulp Fiction*," said actor Steve Buscemi, who costarred in that film and *Reservoir Dogs*, "the little boy watching this big TV, being alone in the room, the TV being his friend—to me, that's Quentin."

Young Tarantino would spend much of his youth in that room, with his friend the television, consuming everything that appeared on the magic box, desperately wishing he could climb inside and go for a ride on the Partridge family's bus or have an adventure with Emma Peel. The only child of a young single mother, he was often left to entertain himself, and as he grew older, he would attend movies with the same intensity. "I didn't have any friends," he would say, "other than the other people in the theater."

Sixteen-year-old Connie Tarantino was living in Knoxville, Tennessee, when her son was born on March 27, 1963. His first name came from two sources: Quentin Compson, the central character of William Faulkner's *The Sound and the Fury* (one of her favorite books), and Quint, the handsome cowhand played by young Burt Reynolds on *Gunsmoke* (one of her favorite TV shows). In other words, from the moment he left the womb, young Tarantino was a creature of popular culture.

Much of that came from Connie, who shared with her son a love of television, comic books, and Elvis Aaron Presley. The duo moved to California when he was two and a half, landing roughly forty-five minutes from Hollywood, home of an industry in the midst of an upheaval. With viewers like Connie eschewing the cinema to stay at home and watch television, the big-budget, big-star movie model was failing, and studios were casting about for fresh approaches and new hooks. As the sixties came to a close, the film industry began to take risks, hiring young directors who took on adult subject matter in candid and challenging ways, thanks to the newly implemented Motion Picture Association of America (MPAA) ratings system.

Not that Connie—or later, Quentin's stepdad, Curt Zastoupil—paid much attention to

PULP FACT 1

Connie would later insist that the only film she ever had to take her son out of was Walt Disney's *Bambi*; little Quentin couldn't handle Bambi's mom dying.

[Exploitation Movies]

This catchall phrase describes low-budget films—usually genre pictures—that, lacking big stars or recognizable brands, have marketable or "exploitable" elements like sex, violence, drugs, rock music, or youth appeal. Though exploitation films date back to the thirties and forties (with cautionary tales like *Mom and Dad* and *Reefer Madness*), the golden age of exploitation movies was the mid-fifties through the seventies, when hucksters and showmen like William Castle, Samuel Z. Arkoff, and (most famously) Roger Corman churned out exploitation movies for the drive-in and grindhouse markets.

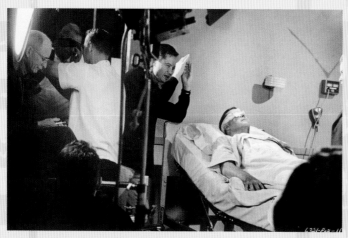

Roger Corman, king of the B movies and 2009 Honorary Academy Award recipient, on the set of *X: The Man with the X-Ray Eyes*, 1963.
Hulton Archive / Getty Images

ratings. They took Quentin to whatever movies they felt like seeing. At age eight, he saw Mike Nichols' fierce sex comedy *Carnal Knowledge*, and the following year, Tarantino took in a double feature of *Deliverance* and *The Wild Bunch*. Echoes of that fateful double bill would show up throughout his early works. The macho male codes of both appear in *Reservoir Dogs* (whose iconic opening title shots, *Variety*'s Todd McCarthy points out, find the title characters "emerging

from the restaurant like the Wild Bunch"), while the male rape of the former is explicitly recreated in *Pulp Fiction*. "Did I understand Ned Beatty being sodomized?" Quentin said later. "No. But I knew he wasn't having any fun."

From that early age, Tarantino was sowing something that went beyond a love for the cinema. It was an appetite, a voracious hunger for all that the movies had to offer. He was getting his cinematic education during one of the industry's richest eras, the New Hollywood of the 1970s, in which a generation of "movie brats," well-versed in movie history and fresh from hip film schools and apprenticeships with low-budget producers like Roger Corman, took over mainstream studio moviemaking with pictures that were both personal and popular.

Tarantino was no snob. He was as deeply enamored with the grindhouse as he was with the art house, and was as likely to become obsessed with a scuzzy exploitation cheapie as the latest from Francis Ford Coppola or William Friedkin. He would go to the cinema constantly, often by himself, which was his preference. The solitude of the experience allowed him to better focus on the movie, to memorize shots, dialogue, and names in the credits. It was all grist for the mill of his movie-mad mind.

Though his movie education was in full bloom, his conventional schooling was a bit more problematic. He was intellectually capable, with tests revealing an IQ near 160 (twice—he retook the test when school officials thought his high score was an error). But, as he later told *Vanity Fair*, "School completely bored me. I wanted to be an actor. Anything that I'm not good at, I don't like, and I couldn't focus at school." Frustrated by her son's aimlessness and truancy—he would frequently skip school to go to matinees—Connie ultimately granted his wish to drop out of school. Tarantino was sixteen.

He got his first real job, predictably enough, at a movie theater. Trouble was, the only operating cinema anywhere near his Torrance home was a rundown local franchise of the Pussycat, a

>>>> *Frame of Reference* <<<<

[Grindhouses]

The name *grindhouse* came from burlesque houses, whose performers would dance in a bump-and-grind style. In the 1970s, single-screen movie theaters and former burlesque houses in large urban hubs held on against multiplexes by booking increasingly extreme exploitation movies, often in daylong loops of several films in a row. The most famous concentration of grindhouse theaters in America was on 42nd Street in New York's Times Square, a block of rundown houses dubbed The Deuce.

The term *grindhouse* would come into the mainstream, relatively speaking, in 2007, when Tarantino and Robert Rodriguez teamed up to make *Grindhouse*, a throwback exploitation double-feature tribute.

Grindhouse theaters along Times Square, 1969. © Bettmann / Corbis

California porno chain. "Most teenagers would think, 'Cool, I'm in a porno theater,'" he said later. "But I didn't like porno. I liked movies." That said, his usher's job at the Pussycat put him in contact with the kind of colorful characters that would later turn up in his scripts. And it paid for his classes at the James Best Acting School in Toluka Lake, where he met other movie-crazy would-be actors and formed his first close friendships.

Finally, at eighteen, he quit the Pussycat, moved into a one-bedroom apartment in Harbor City, and nabbed a nine-to-five, suit-and-tie job that paid for his first VCR. But his closest video store was poorly stocked and lacked the kind of treasures he desired. So Quentin got in his beat-up Honda hatchback and drove the twenty minutes to Hermosa Beach, to a little specialty video store he kept hearing about called Video Archives.

THE Q. T. CANON
Tarantino's Favorite Films

FILM	Q.T. QUOTE	Q.T. INFLUENCE
Bud Abbott and Lou Costello Meet Frankenstein (Charles Barton, 1948)	"The Abbott and Costello stuff was funny, but when they were out of the room and monsters would come on, they'd kill people! When was the last time you saw anybody in a horror-comedy actually kill somebody? You didn't see that. I took it in, seeing that movie."	Tarantino's deft use of comedy to undercut horrifying or dramatic events and catch audiences off-guard is a constant throughout his work. (*Reservoir Dogs* leaps to mind, particularly Mr. Blonde's dialogue with the severed ear.)
Assault on Precinct 13 (John Carpenter, 1976)	"I'd follow *Assault on Precinct 13* wherever the hell it was playing. It was always great seeing it. It was neat."	Itself an homage to one of Tarantino's other favorite films, *Rio Bravo*, *Assault*'s claustrophobic, single-location intensity was duplicated in both *Reservoir Dogs* and *From Dusk Till Dawn*, in which young Scott wears a "Precinct 13" T-shirt.
Badlands (Terrence Malick, 1973)	"A religious experience. Great novelists wish they had written a novel as good as *Badlands* was a movie." 	This tale of young lovers on a crime spree was a model for both *Natural Born Killers* and *True Romance*—with director Tony Scott making the latter's debt even more plain by adding a female voice-over and a score echoing George Tipton's music for *Badlands*. **"I didn't have any qualms [about] wanting to pay homage to that film,"** *True Romance* **director Tony Scott said of** *Badlands*—**clearly in agreement with** *Romance*'**s author.** © *Photos 12 / Alamy*
Blow Out (Brian De Palma, 1981)	"Brian De Palma is the greatest director of his generation. This is his most purely personal and cinematic film."	Though other De Palma films are more explicitly quoted in Tarantino's work (*Carrie* in *Kill Bill*, for example), this one features a world-weary John Travolta performance that influenced Tarantino's desire to cast him in *Pulp Fiction*.
Breathless (Jim McBride, 1983)	"When I saw this in '83, it was everything I wanted to do in movies." Tarantino could reportedly recite its dialogue verbatim.	Early on, as a rockabilly soundtrack blasts, Richard Gere—driving in front of a black and white rear projection—tosses a gun on a comic book, an image that's like a preview of the entire Tarantino mythos. Later, Gere argues about the superhero Silver Surfer with a kid at a newsstand, a scene Tarantino later aped in the dialogue he wrote for Tony Scott's *Crimson Tide*.
Casualties of War (Brian De Palma, 1989)	"To me, the greatest war movie and the greatest indictment of rape ever captured. The Vietnamese girl's death walk has haunted me ever since."	The tenderness of feeling, and even some of the dialogue, between Sean Penn and his dying soldier buddy were an admitted influence on the scenes between Mr. White and the wounded Mr. Orange in *Reservoir Dogs*.
Django (Sergio Corbucci, 1966)	Tarantino placed *Django* third on the list of his favorite spaghetti Westerns and wrote of director Sergio Corbucci, "His West was the most violent, surreal, and pitiless landscape of any director in the history of the genre. His characters roam a brutal, sadistic West."	*Django* was such a hit that it inspired dozens, maybe hundreds, of unofficial sequels—including Tarantino's own *Django Unchained*. Corbucci's film also includes a young henchman named Ringo (as does *Pulp Fiction*), and a brutal ear-slicing scene (echoed in *Reservoir Dogs*).

FILM	Q.T. QUOTE	Q.T. INFLUENCE
The Good, the Bad, and the Ugly (Sergio Leone, 1966) 	"Probably the greatest example of reinvention of a genre on film. Horrible brutality, hysterical humor, blood, music, icons. What more could you ask for?" In a 2013 article he wrote for the *Daily Mail*, Tarantino declared, "The showdown at the end of *The Good, the Bad, and the Ugly* is, I think, the greatest moment of cinema since its invention." *Mary Evans / Arturo Gonzalez Producciones Cinematográficas / Constantin F / Ronald Grant / Everett Collection*	Aside from its obvious influence on *Django Unchained*, Leone's epic concludes with one of Tarantino's favorite climactic devices: the so-called Mexican standoff. In *True Romance*, when Clarence is describing the difference between films and movies, he notes, "*The Good, the Bad, and the Ugly*, *that's* a movie."
His Girl Friday (Howard Hawks, 1940)	"One of the things I'll do, if it's appropriate in a movie, is I'll just get the actors together and I show them *His Girl Friday*—just to show them not that we *have* to talk that fast in a movie, but you *can* talk that fast."	Tarantino ran *Friday* for the ensembles of *Four Rooms* and *Death Proof* and for Tim Roth and Amanda Plummer during *Pulp Fiction*. Its screenplay includes instructions to speak their opening dialogue in "a rapid-pace *His Girl Friday* fashion."
The Inglorious Bastards (Enzo G. Castellari, 1978)	"I think it's one of the best movies in all Italian exploitation. . . . It's terrific, it really is, really good, and the script is fantastic."	Another of the more obvious influences; Tarantino stole (and deliberately misspelled) the title of this film for his own 2009 men-on-a-mission World War II epic.
Le Doulos (Jean-Pierre Melville, 1962)	"*Les Doulos* has always been probably my favorite screenplay of all time—just from watching the movie. I just loved the wildness of watching a movie that up until the last twenty minutes I didn't know what the fuck I was looking at. And the last twenty minutes explained it all."	This "shoot first, ask questions later" approach has been central to the structure and chronology of all Tarantino's screenplays. Melville patterned his cool heroes on characters in American gangster pictures—which American filmmakers like Tarantino then reappropriated for their own works.
Rio Bravo (Howard Hawks, 1959)	"When I'm getting serious about a girl, I show her *Rio Bravo* and she better fucking like it." © *Pictorial Press Ltd / Alamy*	Male camaraderie in tight quarters, as in *Dogs*; Clarence's aforementioned speech in *True Romance* ("*Rio Bravo*, *that's* a movie"); the closing line of the *Killers* script ("Let's make a little music, Colorado," a reference to *Bravo's* singing cowboy, Colorado Ryan)—all are tributes to Hawks' classic film.
Rolling Thunder (John Flynn, 1977)	"To me, it's the greatest combo of action film and character study ever made. If you like revenge movies, this is the best revenge movie to see."	Major Charles Rane returns home from Vietnam in his dress blues—just like Captain Koons in *Pulp Fiction*. And *Thunder* contains a road movie element (in a convertible no less), with Linda Haynes playing a tough heroine like Tarantino's Alabama and Mallory.
Switchblade Sisters (Jack Hill, 1975)	"I've watched this with audiences all over the place. . . . At first, they're laughing *at* the movie. But then, as it goes on, you start laughing *with* the movie. And then a very strange thing happens . . . all of a sudden, you realize you actually *care* about these people. This crazy, hysterical movie, you've actually gotten invested in the characters."	The exploitation aesthetic of much of Tarantino's work is on full display here, while the warehouse setting of the gang's hideout and Hill's favored medium-wide compositions foreshadow *Reservoir Dogs*. But you also see the roots of Tarantino's love for tough female protagonists. The final knife fight feels like a warmup for Beatrix and Ellie's battle in *Kill Bill Volume 2*.
Taxi Driver (Martin Scorsese, 1976)	"It's just perfect."	The famous camera pan during the ear slicing in *Dogs* recalls Scorsese's dolly to an empty hallway in *Taxi Driver* (both allowing the audience to look away during painful moments), while Mr. Orange's mirror pep talk to himself is reminiscent of *Taxi Driver's* iconic "You talkin' to me?" scene—which is explicitly quoted by one of the hoods in *True Romance*. Scorsese's climactic overhead shot, showing the carnage of a bloody shootout, is quoted in *Django Unchained*.
Unfaithfully Yours (Preston Sturges, 1948) 	"I could listen to the dialogue—and especially the way Rex Harrison says it—all day long." *Everett Collection*	This late Sturges effort not only uses a three-story structure, but also navigates the line between genuinely dark fantasy and black comedy with a gracefulness that is central to Tarantino's style.

Video Archives: The Tarantino Film School

In this instant-streaming, torrent-downloading, on-demand era, it's difficult to imagine the nuclear impact that video stores had on film culture. But before the 1980s, opportunities to see classic movies were irritatingly limited: beat-up 16mm prints at campus film societies, revival house screenings, and the occasional appearance on late-night television (hacked to pieces, with commercial interruptions). Being a movie buff required more dedication and perseverance than the mere click of a mouse.

But as consumer VCRs dropped in price, mom-and-pop shops stocking VHS tapes began cropping up in strip malls and storefronts all over the country. Inside, the budding film enthusiast could find not only new hits and recognized classics, but also offbeat fare, obscure foreign titles, and genre efforts of all stripes. The video store revolution democratized film fandom, and not just because of the ease of access; it also placed classics and schlock side by side on the shelves, where they would be equally considered and equally consumed. The casual disregard of barriers would become key to the style of Tarantino, a moviegoer who always held popcorn movies and arthouse fare in the same regard.

He found plenty of both at Video Archives, where the shelves were stuffed with everything from Hong Kong action flicks to French New Wave classics to blaxpoitation throwaways to spaghetti Westerns, minded by a staff of equally knowledgeable—and equally passionate—film geeks. Tarantino found himself going there not just for the tapes, but also for the discussions; he'd spend hours talking movies with the Archives crew, chopping up subtext, ranking directors, taking down sacred cows, and talking up obscurities.

"It was like a clubhouse," recalled Roger Avary, the Video Archives employee who would later collaborate with Tarantino on *Pulp Fiction* and several other projects. "We'd have eight-hour conversations of film criticism, plus you'd have ten thousand films at your fingertips at any moment to prove a point. Each customer who walked through the door was a potential debate." And few customers provided more debates than Quentin, who was such a fast-talking film encyclopedia that Avary eventually talked the store's owners into offering him a job.

It was a steep pay cut for the twenty-two-year-old, from $1,200 a month to four bucks an hour, but the money was secondary; employees got free, unlimited movie rentals, and as far

>>>> *Frame of Reference* <<<<

[Film Geeks]

Tarantino explains the difference between film geeks and the more casual movie buff or intellectual cinephile: "The thing about film geeks is they have an intense love for film. Incredible love for film. Incredible passion. And they devote a lot of their time, they devote a lot of money, a lot of their life to the following of film. But they don't have a lot to show for this devotion, except . . . they have an opinion. A highly developed opinion." And this, he says, it what makes him unique among the polite wafflers of Hollywood: "I'm a film geek. My opinion is everything—you can disagree with me, I don't care! I know I'm right, as far as I'm concerned, and I'll argue anybody down."

as Quentin was concerned, that was priceless. With a film library for the taking and a crew of cinephiles to challenge him, Quentin would later note, "It ended up being like my college."

He spent most of the 1980s as either a customer or an employee of Video Archives, and in that time, it became a destination for movie geeks on both sides of the counter. Store hours were 10:00 in the morning until 10:00 at night, but the employees would come early and stay late, carefully curating and dissecting the endless loop of movies playing on the big-screen TV. No one would argue more fiercely or forcefully than Tarantino, who would spew lengthy monologues championing Fernando Di Leo's Italian crime picture *Wipeout!* or Andrew L. Stone's forgotten screwball comedy *Hi Diddle Diddle*. Some customers said his endorsements were more entertaining than the films themselves. "He was like, the star of the store," coworker Jerry Martinez would recall.

During his tenure at Video Archives, which ended in 1989, Quentin not only expanded his already exhaustive film knowledge; he decided he was as qualified as anyone to contribute to the art. He would write his first produced screenplays between shifts, his experiences at the store seeping into them—not just in the sundry references and homages to the films he'd seen there, but also in the characters, often inspired by the guys he worked and hung out with. In *True Romance*, for example, the Tarantino-esque Clarence works at a comic book store, where he hangs out in his off-hours. He notes, "Everybody who works here is my buddy," including his boss, Lance. (Video Archives was co-owned by Lance Lawson.) "It was like watching a big-budget

feature of your home movies," Quentin would say after the picture's release.

But that was all years away. In the meantime, Tarantino's home movies would be very low-budget indeed.

Early Films (and Missed Opportunities)

Tarantino started writing screenplays as early as the sixth grade, his initial efforts including a tribute to his preteen crush Tatum O'Neal and a *Smokey and the Bandit* rip-off called *Captain Peachfuzz and the Anchovy Bandit*. These were the early flirtations of an easily distracted kid. He'd often write them instead of paying attention in class. "I'd be doing my own writing of my own stuff," he said, "and not the schoolwork."

"When you start writing," he would later explain, "you think it's the greatest thing in the world and then twenty or thirty pages into that, you come up with another idea and it's 'Oh, I can't pay attention to that, this is so obviously better,' and you keep doing that." But once he'd immersed himself into the world of Video Archives, where it seemed everyone—employee or customer—wanted to direct, Tarantino got serious about his own filmmaking endeavors.

Lovebirds in Bondage

Little is known about this first, unfinished short film, which Tarantino cowrote and codirected in 1983 with Scott McGill, a Video Archives coworker. According to Tarantino, the dark comedy concerned a young man who gets himself committed so that he can be with his lover, who is brain-damaged after a severe auto accident.

(continued on page 23)

Film Geeks Turned Film GODS

Tarantino was neither the first nor the last enterprising movie buff to transform a fanatical love and devotion to the cinema into a career as a filmmaker.

Godard, left, with Truffaut on the set of *Fahrenheit 451*, 1966. *Mary Evans / Anglo Enterprises / Ronald Grant / Everett Collection*

Francois Truffaut, Jean-Luc Godard, Eric Rohmer, and many of their contemporaries in the French New Wave began as critics and theorists at the influential French film magazine *Cahiers du Cinéma*, where their appreciation of American genre filmmaking and journeymen directors of the studio system helped give birth to the auteur theory.

Martin Scorsese, asthmatic and unable to play with the neighborhood kids, spent all of his time indoors—at movie theaters and in front of his television, where the New York mainstay series *Million Dollar Movie* would run the same film continuously for a week. Scorsese would watch the films he liked over and over, studying their form and construction, and even drew storyboards for movies he hoped to eventually make.

Peter Bogdanovich worked as a film programmer for the Museum of Modern Art in New York, where his eloquent monographs for their retrospectives led to regular contributions to *Esquire*. Those pieces got the attention of B movie legend Roger Corman, who offered him the chance to make pictures of his own.

Paul Schrader was raised in the Calvinist church and was forbidden from even seeing films until he was seventeen. But he became entranced with cinema in college, earning an MA in Film Studies from UCLA (University of California Los Angeles) and writing criticism for the *Los Angeles Free Press, Cinema* magazine, and *Film Comment* before turning his attention to screenwriting (he penned two of Tarantino's favorite films, *Taxi Driver* and *Rolling Thunder*) and later directing.

Bogdanovich, programmer-turned-auteur, directing *Mask*, 1985.
© *Moviestore Collection Ltd / Alamy*

Kevin Smith based his first film, *Clerks*, on his experiences jockeying the counter of a New Jersey convenience store and its adjoining video shop. The 1994 film would benefit from press focusing on Smith and Tarantino's similar backgrounds—as well as the attachment of its trailer to prints of *Pulp Fiction*, which preceded it to theaters by less than a month.

Roger Avary, Tarantino's occasional collaborator (often without credit) called Video Archives "the greatest film school any of us could ever have." Though he never quite stepped out of Tarantino's shadow, he parlayed that connection into a debut feature, *Killing Zoe* (1993), which Tarantino and Lawrence Bender executive-produced, and had some success with his 2002 Bret Easton Ellis adaptation *The Rules of Engagement*.

TARANTINO,

It is fitting that the first time I heard the name Quentin Tarantino, I was standing behind the counter of a video store.

It was Sherman Oaks, it was 1990, and the store was a LaserDisc-only store, an industry favorite that was a secret for the most part, with a client list that was a who's who of Hollywood, in addition to having a hardcore film-nerd contingent with money to burn. I was a clerk there, and one night, an actor walked in the door about two hours before we were set to close. He had a script in his hand, and he looked around when he walked in. I recognized him from several movies, and when he turned and looked over at me, it seemed appropriate to lead with the title that leapt to mind most immediately. "Hey, Teen Wolf."

He laughed, and within a few minutes, I heard the backstory of the script he had with him and had given him advice for how to handle a specific professional challenge. The script was for an audition he was going to the next day, a low-budget independent crime film about a robbery that gets screwed up. He showed me the script.

"*Reservoir Dogs* by Quentin Tarantino."

It read like a mistranslation of both title and author, and right away, I was curious. The second page was a list of influences. Straight up.

"This movie is dedicated to these following sources of inspiration:
TIMOTHY CAREY
ROGER CORMAN
ANDRE DeTOTH
CHOW YUEN FAT
JEAN LUC GODDARD
JEAN PIERRE MELVILLE
LAWRENCE TIERNEY
LIONEL WHITE"

The actor wanted to know what those names meant and what he should be taking into the room with him, and I wanted to know who the filmmaker was who had the balls to make the actors do homework before they could walk into the audition on his first film as a director. I was impressed and entertained. The typos in the names above are his typos from his original script, and it's part of what I loved right away in that pre-Internet Movie Database age. He knew what he was talking about, spelling be damned, and if he was going to demand a certain amount of crime-movie literacy from his collaborators, then I was curious to see what he was going to do. I helped the actor prepare, sending him home with at least one rental to address each name on the list, and in exchange, I made him promise to bring the script back when he was done with it.

The Tarantino in its natural habitat.
© Alan Wylie / Alamy

FILM GEEK

By Drew McWeeny

He read for the role of Nice Guy Eddie. (Chris Penn played the part in the movie.)

A week later, I was fascinated by this script, amazed that this guy got someone to pay for it, jealous as shit that he was going to get to do it. I followed every bit of news about the film, was miserable when it played at Sundance and I wasn't there. The breathless reports about people freaking out during the ear scene had me giddy, because as it was written, it was pretty obvious what a clever beat it would be, and it was the sort of thing that didn't cost a dollar to do but that got audiences buzzing. That is exactly what you should be aiming for when making something like that.

When it opened in Los Angeles, my friends and I were there for the first public screening. We went back, too, and we supported it as best we could. I was flattened by how accomplished it felt, and how well it spent the little bit of money it took to make. I thought it was not just a good film, but a good model for how to do it. In general, Quentin understood what he needed to write if he was going to direct. It needed to cost nothing, and it needed to be fairly contained and simple. He wrote himself as smart a debut film as James Cameron had, for the types of filmmakers they respectively wanted to be. By the end of *The Terminator*, I had a pretty good idea that I'd be watching James Cameron movies that made me say "OH MY GOD" twenty times an hour for the rest of my life, and by the end of *Reservoir Dogs*, I had a feeling Tarantino would be sending people

scrambling to identify his influences even as they reacted involuntarily to his films as raw emotional experiences.

His films may have gotten bigger, but they haven't changed in their nature.

We were there on the opening night of *Pulp Fiction*, that October evening in Los Angeles, at the Chinese Theater in Hollywood, where a completely packed house full of young and curious filmgoers flipped their collective shit for the movie, cheering pretty much nonstop from the opening titles to the final reprise of that now-iconic surf guitar. It felt like a blockbuster, but there was nothing in there that Hollywood was offering—it felt like someone had committed a crime, slipped something completely subversive by the gatekeepers. Sure, that was John Travolta, and sure, that was Bruce Willis, but that movie was *insane*. That was the general takeaway, the instant word-of-mouth drumbeat that went out. "Oh, you have to see it. It's crazy. You can't believe what happens."

And again, there was a sense of play in terms of how nakedly Quentin's influences showed through. There was a LaserDisc I owned that had several short films by Martin Scorsese on it, and that same thing was available on video, and Quentin obviously saw the videotape at some point, because one of those short films is a documentary called *American Boy*, and in that documentary, Steven Prince tells the story that ended up being used as the scene involving Uma Thurman, the overdose, and that needle to the heart, almost beat for beat. And I didn't begrudge Tarantino that origin for a moment when I saw the film. I sure as hell noticed it, though, and it made me like him even more, knowing that he was the same sort of obsessive movie magpie that I was, that my friends were, that he collected moments and images that meant something to him, that stuck with him, that he couldn't help but use in new configurations, new contexts.

Pulp Fiction was the moment that changed everything for Quentin because of the groundwork laid by *Reservoir*. He had not only created a celebrated indie sensation, but he'd also weathered a controversy about the origins of his ideas and steered head-on into the conversation about how to handle violence in a film. *Pulp Fiction* was more ambitious, more entertaining, more aspirational, more outrageous, and there's a swagger to the filmmaking that immediately laid claim to an entire cinematic language. The more we saw people try to do what he did and fail, the more impressive his accomplishment seemed. And people definitely tried.

Many people tried to reproduce the success of *Pulp Fiction* but could not, because they didn't understand that the movie works not because of the nature of the stories—the violence, the lurid crime setting, the X-rated twist—but because of the way Tarantino takes a sad and even disheartening story of random violence and—by weaving it into a particular time-bent narrative—turns it into something that feels uplifting, even redemptive. All by turning our linear sense of cause and effect inside out. All for the happy ending of Vincent and Jules walking out

together, all for the way it works as a piece of music. All of the fetishes that Tarantino demonstrated in *Reservoir* were accentuated his second time out, and in every way, *Pulp Fiction* feels like a film made by someone who is committed completely to his point of view, his specific filter. It is a film made with complete control and a real command of tone and rhythm and language. *Pulp Fiction* is his announcement that this seen-everything-in-the-video-store approach to filmmaking is not just a valid way of learning the craft but also creates a sort of shared something between filmmaker and audience that actually deepens the connection. *Pulp Fiction* is the moment the postmodern truly went mainstream, when people felt the caffeine kick of his video-store vocabulary unleashed in full force. It remains the thing that most clearly defines him, the thing that his harshest critics cannot enjoy, and the thing that I think makes him one of the key film artists of our time.

From the moment the first video store opened, Quentin and his brand of filmmaking were inevitable, and he is the realization of what has to happen when you suddenly make it possible to mainline movies without any restriction. Can you think of any other currently working filmmaker who has rolled such a potent and immediate hand grenade into not only film but music and television and comedy and even literature?

From pastiche to iconic influence, Tarantino's voice has been consistent and clear.

Drew McWeeny has spent the better part of the last twenty years writing about films on the Internet—for Ain't It Cool News *and* Hitfix, *among others—or just plain writing films, and he has enjoyed watching the impact Tarantino has had on film, both good and bad.*

(continued from page 18)

"I played the guy," he recalled. "We never got as far as casting the girl, we only shot the guy stuff. It came out really good, and the next thing I knew [McGill] said his mom destroyed the footage. But later, I thought he had probably destroyed it himself."

My Best Friend's Birthday

Tarantino's next film, far more ambitious but also unfinished, was devised with acting school buddy Craig Hamann, who wrote the script's first draft before turning it over to Tarantino. The pair procured an old 16mm Bolex camera with a small canister that would only hold a few hundred feet—which was fine, since they were mostly using short ends—and shot the film in funding-challenged starts and stops over roughly three years. The cast and crew comprised coworkers, friends, and acting school classmates, and the money came mostly from Quentin's mother, Connie, his new stepdad Jan Bohusch, and Hamann's credit cards.

Their years of work and $5,000 investment were ultimately for naught; a power outage at the film-processing lab destroyed two rolls and three critical climactic scenes, which couldn't be reshot due to a lost location. The amateur auteurs couldn't figure out how to complete the film, and weren't happy enough with what they had to pursue it further. Tarantino wrote it off as a learning experience, regarding the project as "the best film school in the whole world" (and, compared to most, an inexpensive one).

It was more than a technical exercise, though. In the thirty-six-minute, rough-cut form that's readily available on YouTube, BitTorrent, and DVD bootleg sites, *My Best Friend's Birthday* not only includes elements Tarantino would reuse in his scripts for *True Romance* and *Natural Born Killers*, but also has thematic and aesthetic touchstones of his entire filmography. Tarantino's leading character is named Clarence, while the titular best friend is named Mickey; he would reapply those monikers to the protagonists of *Romance* and *Killers*. Clarence is dressed in the skinny-tie getup familiar from *Reservoir Dogs*, and his character harbors a fierce obsession with Elvis, expressed in an early prototype of the "If I ever had to fuck a guy" scene in *True Romance*. Misty, the prostitute that Clarence gets Mickey as a birthday present, is his first stab at *Romance*'s Alabama (Misty delivers a monologue in *Birthday*, later used in *Romance*'s screenplay but absent from

>>>> *Frame of Reference* <<<<

[16mm]

From the 1960s through the 1990s, 16mm was the format of choice for low-budget filmmakers. Grainier and less reliable than the 35mm stock used by major productions, but also cheaper to buy and develop, 16mm film was sometimes available even more economically in the form of short ends: unused pieces of film left over from other shoots, shorter bits at the end of an otherwise exposed roll.

the final cut, in which she attributes her career choice to worshipping Nancy Allen's high-class call girl in Brian De Palma's *Dressed to Kill*), and Clarence's Big Bopper–style "Hellllllo, baby" phone greeting from *Romance* first appears here. Clarence is a DJ on K-BILLY radio—alas, not during a "Super Sounds of the Seventies" weekend—while his first duet with Misty is done in a single, unbroken circling take reminiscent of the diner scenes in both *Reservoir Dogs* and *Death Proof*, as well as Django's scene with the mining company employees in *Django Unchained*. And the first sighting of a career-long preoccupation occurs as Clarence tells Misty about his old job in the women's shoe department at Kmart: "I have a foot fetish, so it kinda evened itself out."

True Romance

True *Romance* began as a short, *Badlands*-inspired script by Tarantino's Video Archives buddy Roger Avary, titled *The Open Road*. Tarantino fused Avary's tale with leftover elements of *My Best Friend's Birthday*, references to decades of lovers-on-the-run flicks, and echoes of autobiography to create his first screenplay of note.

His agent, Caryn James, thought the script was a knockout and sent it around to production companies and studios. The reception was unenthusiastic, in some cases borderline hostile. Most amusing was the response from Miramax, which would eventually become so identified with Tarantino that cofounder Harvey Weinstein

The set of *True Romance* (Brad Pitt, Michael Rapaport, Christian Slater, and Patricia Arquette). © *Warner Bros. Pictures / Sunset Boulevard / Corbis*

[Spec Script]

When a screenwriter pens a script of his or her own accord, without advance payment, it is known as writing on spec (on speculation of eventual sale), and the product of that process is a spec script. If a producer is interested in a spec script, he or she will obtain—usually for a nominal fee—an option from the screenwriter, which gives the exclusive right to shop it around and set up a production deal. Don Murphy and Jane Hamscher had a two-year option on *Natural Born Killers*; Tarantino gave Lawrence Bender only a two-month option on *Reservoir Dogs*.

would call his company "the house that Quentin built." But their representative was unimpressed with this early work, not even bothering with a rejection letter. Instead, the letter of introduction was returned, with a simple message scrawled across it with a black felt-tip pen: "UGH! HATED CHARACTERS."

"It just proceeded to completely stall for three years," Tarantino recalled, with the untested filmmaker's insistence on directing the film a possible roadblock. Tarantino eventually stepped aside and let the project proceed as a spec script for sale. It made its way to Tony Scott, a filmmaker whose big, glossy, smoky eighties style (harnessed in *Top Gun, Beverly Hills Cop II*, and the like) would seem distinctly at odds with Tarantino's. But the pair hit it off—Quentin was a big fan of Scott's critically drubbed 1990 Kevin Costner vehicle *Revenge*—and the British moviemaker's attachment to *Romance* got the film a green light at Warner Brothers. Tarantino pocketed the Writers Guild of America minimum of $50,000 for the screenplay.

Hollywood working at the snail's pace that it does, *True Romance* didn't begin casting until after *Reservoir Dogs* had transformed its unknown screenwriter into a hot commodity. On the strength of that film's hip factor, Scott assembled an enviable cast: Christian Slater and Patricia Arquette took the leads, while Dennis Hopper, Christopher Walken, Gary Oldman, Brad Pitt, Val Kilmer, Chris Penn, James Gandolfini, and (very briefly) Samuel L. Jackson filled out the supporting roles. The resulting film is a surprisingly successful hybrid of its director and writer's seemingly incompatible styles—Scott's slick and flashy, Tarantino's quirky and idiosyncratic. The director seems to fall in love with Tarantino's words, and while he amps up the action and the violence, he also applies his stylist's sense of film rhythm to all-talk scenes, like Gandolfini's monologue about his first kills, or the unforgettable interrogation of Clifford Worley (Hopper) by Vincenzo Coccotti (Walken).

No doubt Tarantino's version of *True Romance*, which he conceived as a million-dollar effort in the mold of the Coen Brothers' *Blood Simple*, would have been a very different one. (For one thing, his original screenplay was written in the timeline-leapfrogging, non-chronological style that would become his trademark.) But once he'd made *Reservoir Dogs*, he didn't want to go back to either *Romance* or the script that followed it. He explained: "I didn't want to do either one of them because they were both written to be my first film and by then I'd made my first film. I didn't want to go backwards and do old stuff. I think of them as like old girlfriends: I loved them but I didn't want to marry them any more."

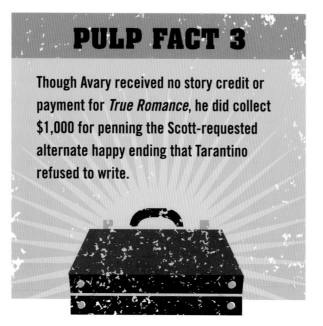

Natural Born Killers

Natural Born Killers, like *True Romance*, was a byproduct of Tarantino's *Open Road* rewrite, which included, according to Avary, "literally . . . everything he ever wanted to do . . . bits and pieces of *Reservoir Dogs, Natural Born Killers, Pulp Fiction*." Quentin's *My Best Friend's Birthday* collaborator Hamann, who was helping translate Tarantino's misspelled scrawlings into a proper typewritten screenplay, explained it thus: "Clarence, the lead character in *True Romance*, was writing a screenplay as all this was going on. What he was writing was *Natural Born Killers* with Mickey and Mallory." With Tarantino's opus weighing in at something like five hundred pages, he opted to split the script in two, and once he'd whipped *True Romance* into fighting shape, he turned to *Natural Born Killers*.

Tarantino's original *Killers* screenplay was a dark comedy with action beats. It was as focused on tabloid reporter Wayne Gale and his wisecracking crew (named after Video Archives employees) as it was on Mickey and Mallory Knox, the ostensible subjects. He wrote it from 1989 to 1990, and his agent was enthusiastic about this script, as she had been for *Romance*, but her pitches met with equal resistance from those who could make it happen. Again, Tarantino hoped to direct it himself, writing in notations for video and 16mm photography to keep the budget low.

The project ultimately fell into the hands of up-and-coming producers Don Murphy and Jane Hamsher, setting off a long, complicated, well-documented, he-said-she-said battle for control of the project between those producers, Tarantino's friend Rand Vossler, Tarantino himself, and Oliver Stone, who ultimately directed the film after the script was passed to him by Sean Penn. Stone revised the screenplay with writers David Veloz and Richard Rutowski, and though the option that Tarantino had sold to Murphy and Hamsher allowed the script to be altered with or without his participation, he was still steamed by the changes to his baby. "I wish [Stone] had just fucking ripped it off," he told a reporter, opting out of screenplay credit. He got a "story by" byline instead.

The two stubborn filmmakers traded harsh words in the press during their roughly concurrent *Killers* and *Fiction* press tours, with Tarantino dismissing Stone's lack of subtlety ("To me the best thing about him is his energy. But his biggest problem is that his obviousness cancels out his energy and his energy pumps up his obviousness. He's Stanley Kramer with style."), and Stone reprimanding Tarantino's poor form ("To be honest, it's just not done, a writer who

The road traveled by the *Natural Born Killers* recalls a certain briefcase's lock combination. *Argus / Shutterstock.com*

Tarantino was paid all of $1,500 for his eighty-eight-page draft of *From Dusk Till Dawn* and was glad to have it. The guys at KNB were equally happy with his screenplay and set about trying to get it made. But Kurtzman came up against the same funding trouble as his screenwriter: producers didn't want to take a risk on a first-time director. Kurtzman shopped it around for a couple of years, but (like Quentin) wasn't able to get it made until he was willing to turn it over to another director—and only then after his nobody writer had become a cinematic rock star.

becomes famous and then trashes his own movie. I feel like it's a code, it's a samurai code that you live with."). Upon its release, Tarantino claimed he tried to watch *Natural Born Killers* but walked out twenty minutes in. He's since said, "I'll catch it sometime when I'm in a hotel that has cable."

From Dusk Till Dawn

Just before Tarantino left Video Archives for good, he picked up his first, according-to-Hoyle paid writing gig. It came from KNB EFX Group, a special effects house whose founders wanted to create a film of their own, primarily as a showcase for their makeup and visual effects. So cofounder Robert Kurtzman and his writing partner John Esposito worked up a twenty-page treatment for a "gangster-vampire" movie set near the Texas-Mexico border, which Kurtzman would direct. The treatment in hand, they went looking for a writer who would work cheaply. Kurtzman read *True Romance* and *Natural Born Killers* and knew he had his man.

PULP FACT 4

One minor change of interest: instead of "Born Bad," Tarantino's script has Mallory warbling "Long Time Woman" in prison. The Pam Grier song is from her 1971 film *The Big Doll House*, which Tarantino would later use on the *Jackie Brown* soundtrack.

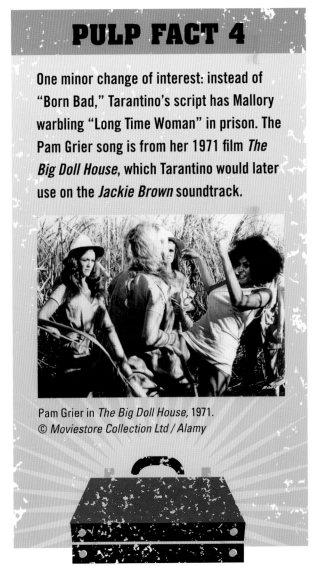

Pam Grier in *The Big Doll House*, 1971. © *Moviestore Collection Ltd / Alamy*

From Dusk Till Dawn.
© Moviestore
Collection Ltd / Alamy

From Dusk Till Dawn was finally released in 1996, with Tarantino in one of the leading roles, under the direction of his buddy Robert Rodriguez.

Past Midnight

Quentin's next paid writing job came in 1990 via a company called CineTel, which had briefly expressed interest in producing *True Romance*. An executive there, impressed by Tarantino's writing, hired him to do a dialogue polish on a forgettable cable thriller called *Past Midnight*, starring Rutger Hauer and Natasha Richardson. The job paid $7,000 and got Tarantino his first onscreen credit—but only as an associate producer. He insisted he'd penned "a page one rewrite. And then by the time they made the movie it became half of my rewrite and half of the original script." Among the half of his work that made it on the screen: a character wondering if perhaps Hauer's character "just isn't a natural born killer." Among the half that didn't: a creepy foot massage scene. "They didn't have the guts to go into it," he said later.

"They turned it into a back rub, which isn't the same thing." (But is it the same ballpark?)

Also in 1990, Tarantino attended his friend Scott Spiegel's Memorial Day barbecue and made one of the defining connections of his life. Lawrence Bender was an actor/dancer-turned-producer whose biggest credit to date was Spiegel's straight-to-video thriller *Intruder*. He and Tarantino hit it off right away, and when Tarantino told him about *Natural Born Killers*,

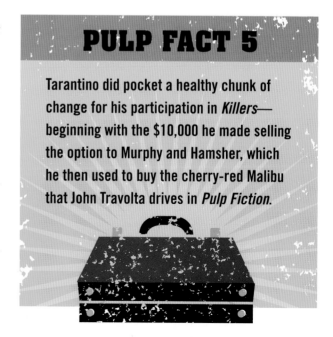

PULP FACT 5

Tarantino did pocket a healthy chunk of change for his participation in *Killers*—beginning with the $10,000 he made selling the option to Murphy and Hamsher, which he then used to buy the cherry-red Malibu that John Travolta drives in *Pulp Fiction*.

Tarantino with longtime friend and collaborator Robert Rodriguez at ShoWest in Las Vegas, 2007.
S_bukley / Shutterstock.com

Bender was discouraged to hear that the option was unavailable. Tarantino, unfazed, pitched him a new idea (off the top of his head, legend has it) for a script he hadn't yet written about a heist gone awry. Bender liked the idea, and the intimate scenario—mostly confined to a single location—sounded like the kind of thing that could be made on the cheap. He asked Quentin to let him see it once the script was written.

Why Am I Mr. Pink? by Joey Tolomei. Canvas, acrylic, and oil paint, 2012. *Courtesy of the artist*

So for three weeks over that summer, Tarantino holed up in his dumpy apartment in a sketchy area of Hollywood, the sounds of wailing sirens and street thugs wafting in through his windows, mixing with the resin of twenty-plus years of rabid pop culture consumption: tough-talking gangsters, enigmatic antiheroes, bloody violence, and Madonna records. In that three-week burst, Quentin Tarantino crafted his finest work to date. He called it *Reservoir Dogs*.

Reservoir Dogs

I get a kick out of heist pictures," Tarantino would later explain, "so I thought I'd write one. I'd had the idea in my head about a film that doesn't take place during the robbery, but in the rendezvous afterwards." When he worked at Video Archives, he took home heist movies by the handful. "I wrote it real quick," he said of the *Reservoir Dogs* script, "but that's slightly deceptive, simply because I had done so much homework on it before."

True to his word, Tarantino showed the finished script to Bender, who was confident he could get the live-wire picture made. But the filmmaker, disillusioned from years of shopping his screenplays around and hanging his hopes on near-misses before handing them off to other directors, wasn't going to dance that dance again. The logistical simplicity of *Dogs* meant that he could make it on the cheap, guerilla-style, 16mm, with actor friends filling out the roles. He'd use the $50,000 he'd just made for selling *True Romance* to pay for it. After all, he'd written the funniest role, Mr. Pink, for himself. Bender pleaded with him; the script was too good to not at least *try*. Tarantino bent, but only slightly: he gave Bender a ridiculously short two-month window to raise funds, and made him promise that if (and, Tarantino figured, when) it

didn't happen, Bender would play Nice Guy Eddie for him.

Yet Bender got it done. A friend of a friend passed the screenplay to Monte Hellman, the cult director of *Two-Lane Blacktop* and *Cockfighter*, who took on an executive producer/godfather position. In that role, he got the script to executives at LIVE Entertainment, which mostly produced films for the home video market. Meanwhile, Bender's acting coach slipped a copy of the screenplay to Harvey Keitel, who wanted to meet the man who wrote it. Keitel recalled, "I said, 'How'd you come to write this script? Did you live in a tough-guy neighborhood growing up?' He said no. I said, 'Was anybody in your family connected with tough guys?' He said no. I said, 'Well, how the hell did you come to write this?' And he said, 'I watch movies.'" Keitel decided he not only wanted to be in the film—he wanted to help get it made.

"Harvey had been my favorite actor since I was sixteen years old," Tarantino said, while noting, "I didn't write the part for Harvey because I thought it'd probably be, you know, my Uncle Pete." Instead, Uncle Harvey came on as a coproducer; he financed Tarantino and Bender's casting trip to New York (where they added Steve Buscemi to the team); and he got his *Thelma and Louise* costar Michael Madsen to sign on as Mr. Blonde. Keitel's attachment to the project upped LIVE's budget commitment to the neighborhood of $1.5 million.

Shot in five weeks with a crackerjack ensemble cast that also included Tim Roth, Chris Penn, legendary onscreen tough guy Lawrence Tierney, and Tarantino himself (in the smaller role of Mr. Brown; Buscemi ended up

PULP FACT 6

Among *Reservoir Dogs'* voluminous influences: French heist pictures like *Rififi* and *Bob Le Flambeur*, Stanley Kubrick's *The Killing* and John Huston's *The Asphalt Jungle*, the 1974 action flick *The Taking of Pelham 123* (with its color-coded criminal aliases), the portraits of workaday thieves in the 1978 Dustin Hoffman vehicle *Straight Time* (from the book by Eddie Bunker, who would play Mr. Blue in *Dogs*), and the Hong Kong action movies *A Better Tomorrow Part II* and *City on Fire* (the latter film's influence, some would later contend, crossing the line from homage to outright theft).

© Palomar Pictures, United Artists, AF Archive / Alamy

City on Fire, 1987. Tarantino included *Fire* star Chow Yun-Fat in his dedicatory list of influences on the first page of the *Reservoir Dogs* script. © Moviestore Collection Ltd / Alamy

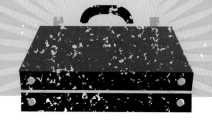

playing Pink), *Reservoir Dogs* was an electrifying debut for the filmmaker, not yet thirty years old. From its virtuoso seven-and-a-half-minute opening sequence, in which the gruff, sharp-suited badasses debate pop songs and the necessities of tipping, the film announced Tarantino as a new and fresh voice of American vernacular dialogue, a deliciously skillful practitioner of Mamet-esque gutter poetry. His characters were funny, literate, tough, and hard-edged. Tarantino showed us moments that most movies left out: the agonizingly protracted bleeding of a gunshot wound, the euphemistically sensitive hoods arguing over aliases, the undercover cop workshopping his background story with the focus and intensity of an acting class assignment (shades here of Tarantino's own thespian training).

Mr. Orange's commode story sequence elevates the film's innovative, hopscotching chronology to a point of near absurdity: in the most elementary terms, by the time we're in the bathroom with Mr. Orange, we're in a flashback to a flashback to a flashback of a thing that didn't happen. Tarantino's direction is equally confident and nimble. Beginning with the smash cut from the cool visuals and music in the opening to Orange screaming bloody murder in the back seat, he expertly intercuts long takes and oblique angles with kinetic violence and slambang action, varying the tempo in a manner that leaves its audience exhausted but exhilarated.

Before postproduction was even complete, word was getting out that this scrappy, bloodstained indie was something special. *Reservoir Dogs* sailed into the Sundance Film Festival in January of 1992 and became that fest's hot ticket—to the immense satisfaction of Tarantino,

Dogs street art in Newtown, Australia. *Mark Higgins / Shutterstock.com*

who'd had a less-than-encouraging run with it at the Sundance Institute's filmmaker workshop the year before (the industry professionals advising Tarantino told him bluntly to ditch the long takes and shoot conventional coverage). As Peter Biskind would later write in *Down and Dirty Pictures*, his history of the nineties indie scene, *Dogs* "marked a seismic change in the direction of indie film, which was rapidly moving toward a more genre-influenced cinema—albeit with a transgressive and ironic, postmodern spin."

Miramax Pictures paid $400,000 for theatrical distribution rights after Sundance and took the film to Cannes, where it went over like gangbusters. Its initial theatrical run was less impressive, taking in only $2.8 million domestically in a release that, at its widest, hit sixty-one screens. Reviews were mostly positive, however. *Entertainment Weekly*'s Owen Gleiberman called it "a dizzying entry in the 'fuck you!' school of macho bravura," Vincent Canby of the *New York Times* dubbed it "a small, modestly budgeted crime movie of sometimes dazzling cinematic pyrotechnics and over-the-top dramatic energy," and the *Chicago Reader*'s Jonathan Rosenbaum proclaimed it "a stunning debut" that "sets off enough rockets to hold and shake us for every one of its 99 minutes."

Variety's Todd McCarthy, while praising the film, added a careful caveat: "As accomplished as all the individual elements are, however…[*Dogs*] feels like the director's audition piece, an occasion for a new filmmaker to flaunt his talents." It sounds like a backhanded compliment, but in retrospect, it's a workable premise. Maybe *Reservoir Dogs* was his audition. Now it was time for the big show.

PART II

The Script That Changed Everything

"A Magazine or Book Containing Lurid Subject Matter": Screenplay Origins

Spanish poster for *Black Sabbath* (1963), the inspiration for *Fiction*'s three-part structure. *Everett Collection*

As with so many truly innovative works of art, *Pulp Fiction* was born not out of inspiration, but out of necessity. It was fall of 1990, and Tarantino was frustrated by his inability to raise funds for either *True Romance* or *Natural Born Killers*. His Video Archives buddy and fellow would-be filmmaker Roger Avary was having no more luck with his own endeavors. For both men, the hiccup was a dearth of prior directorial experience, so they hit on the idea of crafting a snazzy, impressive short film (which would be easier to finance anyway). But the problem with shorts was that they were an end unto themselves, of use only as a calling card, impossible to market or sell.

So the idea evolved into something more ambitious: a trio of shorts, one by Tarantino, one by Avary, and one by another director. (Exactly who was never quite settled.) They'd produce the first section as a short, they figured, and then (as Jim Jarmusch had done with 1984's *Stranger Than Paradise*) use that short to raise funds to make the rest of the film.

Their structural inspiration was Mario Bava's horror triptych *Black Sabbath*. For the

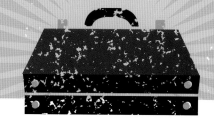

PULP FACT 7

Though *Pulp*'s debt to *Sabbath* would grow muddier as it evolved, Tarantino nonetheless paid tribute to Mario Bava by naming a brand of heroin after him in Lance and Vincent's bedroom scene.

[Pulp]

It would seem sacrilege not to merely quote the screenplay on this one. To wit:

PULP [pulp] n.

1. A soft, moist, shapeless mass or matter.
2. A magazine or book containing lurid subject matter and being characteristically printed on rough, unfinished paper.

American Heritage Dictionary: New College Edition

subject matter, Tarantino and Avary unsurprisingly chose the world of crime. The tentative title was *The Black Mask* after the pulp magazine famed for publishing the works of Raymond Chandler, Dashiell Hammett, Erle Stanley Gardner, and others. The idea was to acknowledge those roots and then go bananas with them. "The stories are completely separate, and they're the same stories you've heard a zillion times," Quentin explained in 1992. "You know, the staples of the genre, but hopefully taken where you've never seen them before." He and Avary worked out the chestnuts they would spring from: the gangster who takes out the big boss's wife, a boxer who's paid to take a dive, a heist that goes awry.

That third idea, of course, became *Reservoir Dogs.* Avary would similarly take the boxer story and expand it into its own feature

The original title for the film came from the classic pulp magazine *Black Mask,* founded in 1920 by H. L. Mencken and drama critic George Jean Nathan.

screenplay, which he titled *Pandemonium Reigns.* Tarantino started writing the first story but never finished it, and that was the uncertain point *Pulp Fiction* was at in the summer of 1991, when he met Stacey Sher at the premiere of *Terminator 2: Judgment Day.* Sher had just joined actor-producer Danny DeVito and producer Michael Shamberg to start Jersey Films, and the fledgling production company was looking for projects. *Reservoir Dogs* hadn't yet been released, but its buzz was deafening, and Sher had a hunch that whoever locked down Tarantino's next project was going to look very smart, very soon.

She asked Quentin what he was working on, and he pitched her *Pulp Fiction* (possibly because he hadn't had a moment to figure out something new). Sher, intrigued, introduced

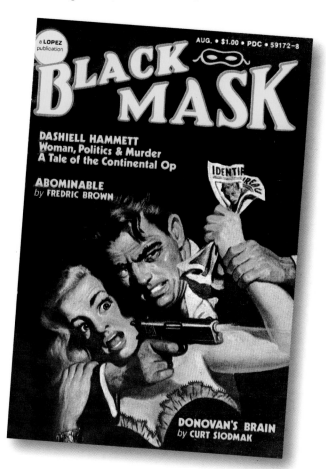

Tarantino to DeVito. "I listened to him for about ten minutes, thinking, I may be meeting someone who talks faster than Martin Scorsese," DeVito recalled. "I said, 'I want to make a deal with you for your next movie, *whatever* it is.'" A few weeks later, Jersey Films signed Tarantino and Bender—under the banner of their new production company, A Band Apart (named after the phonetic pronunciation of Godard's *Bande à Part*)—to a development deal. Sher then set up *Pulp Fiction* at TriStar Pictures, landing Quentin a cool $900,000 to write and direct. With the first installment of that considerable payday in hand, he went off to pen the script.

Tarantino got his first taste of life outside the United States in 1992, while touring the international festival circuit with *Reservoir Dogs*. His favorite city was Amsterdam, where he could see movies in English, smoke out in the city's famed coffee shops, and generally disappear. He knew he couldn't get any real work done back in L.A., where the phone was ringing with nonstop calls from friends, fans, and industry

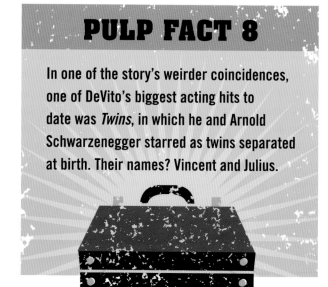

PULP FACT 8

In one of the story's weirder coincidences, one of DeVito's biggest acting hits to date was *Twins*, in which he and Arnold Schwarzenegger starred as twins separated at birth. Their names? Vincent and Julius.

types. So he packed a suitcase full of crime novels and notebooks and split town.

He got a little apartment in Amsterdam. There he played music, drank beer, smoked weed, watched French gangster movies from a nearby video store, and wrote. "I had this very cool writing existence," he recalled. "I didn't have to worry about money. Through luck and happenstance, I found an apartment to rent right off a canal. I would get up and walk around Amsterdam, and then drink like twelve cups of coffee, spending my entire morning writing."

He was amused by the slight variances in everyday European life—"little differences," as *Pulp Fiction* character Vincent Vega would call them. In a 1992 interview with Peter Brunette to promote *Reservoir Dogs*, he explained those anomalies, spouting what would become his most famous dialogue scene in an embryonic form: "I'd never been to other countries before this year, but I've now been to other countries, and I love going into McDonald's. The difference? In Paris McDonald's, they serve

>>>> *Frame of Reference* <<<<

[Development Deal]

A development deal is an agreement between an artist and a production company, or a production company and a studio, or an artist and a studio, to put a project together. In Tarantino's case, Jersey Films signed him for a deal to develop *Pulp Fiction*, which they could then shop to studios.

Pulp Fiction: The Musical, in the country where Tarantino wrote the screenplay: the Netherlands. The production took place during the 2012 Lowlands Music Festival. *Photo by Dimitri Hakke / Redferns via Getty Images*

beer. And they don't call it a Quarter Pounder, because they have the metric system there: Le Royale with Cheese! They don't know what a fucking Quarter Pounder is!''

In an interview with Charlie Rose two years later, Tarantino explained how an old idea merged with what he was experiencing while writing it. "I can have an idea in my head for five, six, seven years," he noted. "And I've kind of, little by little, been working it out, different things

about it. The day that I sit down to do it, whatever is going on with me at the time will find its way into the piece. It has to, or the piece isn't worth making.''

Quentin ultimately spent more than a year on *Pulp Fiction*'s first draft, which would come in at a hefty five hundred pages. Part of that bulk was a result of his continued insistence on writing in longhand. "It's always a big deal for me when I'm going to write a new script,

SCRAPS

"Basically, I don't come up with any new ideas," Tarantino modestly confessed in 1993. "I always start with scenes I know I am going to put in and scenes from scripts I never finish. Every script I have written has at least twenty pages that are taken from other things I've done." In his first few screenplays, certain concepts and key phrases recur (see "I've Been Sayin' That Shit for Years" on page 76), indicating both what the writer calls a "stockpile of ideas" and his refusal to let a good one go to waste. In other words, since he didn't know if any of those scripts were going to be produced, it wouldn't do any harm to put something in another screenplay that might get made first. *Pulp Fiction* would ultimately become a clearance of the old inventory; as Roger Avary later explained, "We essentially raided all of our files, and took out every great scene either of us had ever written, put them on the floor, started lining them up and putting them together." From the works that were produced—and not produced—before it, we can assemble something of a genealogy of the *Pulp* script, determining what came from where.

From *My Best Friend's Birthday* (unfinished film, circa 1987):

- Clarence is the victim of a prank by a radio station coworker, who buys itching powder at a novelty store and passes it to Clarence, claiming it's cocaine. This confusion (played here for broad laughs rather than possible death) foreshadows Mia's mistaking of heroin for coke in *Fiction*.
- Mention is made of the Rockabilly Burger restaurant, which sounds similar to Jackrabbit Slim's.

From *True Romance/The Open Road* (original Avary screenplay, circa 1987):

- This contains early versions of Marvin's grisly gunshot death on wheels and the fourth man emerging from the bathroom and emptying his gun, yet landing none of his shots.

From *From Dusk Till Dawn* (original screenplay, 1990):

- In Tarantino's original script, doubting pastor Jacob (played in the eventual 1996 film by Harvey Keitel) recites the Biblical passage Ezekiel 25:17—significantly rewritten by Tarantino—while fending off vampire demons with a cross.

From *Past Midnight* (uncredited rewrite, 1992):

- Tarantino originally wrote an unsettling foot massage sequence (shades of Tony Rocky Horror), but it was changed by the film's director to a back rub.

From *Reservoir Dogs* (1992):

- In a scene cut from the final version, while Nice Guy Eddie, Mr. Pink, and Mr. White are driving back to the rendezvous, Eddie tells Mr. White that he's arranged for Bonnie to take care of Mr. Orange: "Sweet broad, helluva broad, and a registered nurse," just like Jimmie's wife in *Pulp Fiction*. When Mr. White expresses his doubts, Eddie notes, "I am personally leaving myself vulnerable with this Bonnie situation."

to go into the stationary store and buy the notebook. I've really romanticized it. I buy the three red ink pens I'm going to use, and the notebook. 'This is the notebook I'm going to write *Reservoir Dogs* with,' I say. It's a big ritual." (In the *Kill Bill* movies, he gives The Bride this same ritual, as she drafts her "kill list" in a spiral notebook with colored pens.)

The finished product is, he admits, rife with spelling and grammatical errors, the byproduct of his abbreviated schooling. "My stuff is unreadable. So when I've finished, I try to give it to friends of mine to type it for me." For *Pulp Fiction*, that friend was Linda Chen, a typist and unofficial script consultant for *Chinatown* scribe Robert Towne, among others.

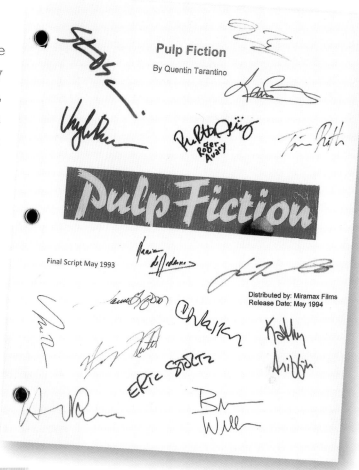

The final script, signed by the cast.

>>>> *Frame of Reference* <<<<

[Screenplay Miscellany]

Tarantino's first draft was the initial assemblage of the screenplay. Every time a writer revises a script, that is a new draft. When revisions are done, the final shooting draft is used, with page and scene numbers locked in and remaining the same even if there are revisions during the shoot.

Five hundred pages was massive, even for a first draft. Screenplays usually average out to about a page per minute, with a 90-page script running about an hour and a half, a 120-page script two hours, and so on. At that rate, *Pulp Fiction*'s first draft would have run over eight hours.

"His handwriting is atrocious," Chen remembered. "He's a functional illiterate. I was averaging about nine thousand grammatical errors per page. After I would correct them, he would try to put back the errors, because he *liked* them."

As he worked on the script, the initial concept of a standard anthology evolved into something a bit more sophisticated. "What I really wanted," he later explained, "was to make a novel on the screen, with characters who enter and exit, who have their own story but who can appear anywhere." Here he took a page not from *Black Mask*, but from J. D. Salinger: "When you read his Glass family stories, they all add up to one big story. That was the biggest example for me." And it was within this new conceptualization

[Back End and Residuals]

These are methods of paying a writer, director, actor, or other technicians for their work if the film is a hit. "Back end participation" is a formula for receiving a portion of the film's profits once the studio or producers have made back all the money spent on the project—which can be a tricky proposition, thanks to creative Hollywood accounting. Residuals are a small royalty payment to the creative personnel (usually arranged through their union), paid out of ancillary revenues from secondary markets like DVD sales and television broadcasts.

that he came up with a third story to fill that *Reservoir Dogs*–size hole in the original blueprint. He'd introduced Jules and Vincent, the chatty hit men, early in the film. "While rewriting the story of the boxer," he recalled, "I said to myself, 'Why not end the morning with Jules and Vincent instead of having them separate after the shooting?'"

The full range of Avary's contribution to the *Pulp Fiction* screenplay remains a matter of debate. "When we originally ventured into *Pulp Fiction*, the agreement was that we would split the writing part of the back-end participation, as well as the screenplay credit," Avary would later say, and with that agreement in place, he traveled to Amsterdam to work with Quentin on the script. "We went back and we got *Pandemonium Reigns* and we squashed it back down and it became 'The Gold Watch.'" Avary also says that two set pieces he'd written for what became *True Romance*—one about a head being blown off inside a car, another concerning a gunman emerging from hiding in a bathroom and emptying his gun, yet landing none of his shots—made their way into the script, along with "things that Quentin had written for other movies. . . . We just kind of rushed everything together." After that initial work, Avary left Amsterdam to start *Killing Zoe*, his feature directorial debut, which Tarantino's name (as executive producer) had helped get made.

(continued on page 44)

Roger Avary.
Trago / Getty Images

PUTTING THE PULP IN *PULP*

By Adam Rosen

Quentin Tarantino, it can be reasonably observed, has a thing for Americana. While his style influences have come from all ends of the Earth, the subject matter of his films has been almost entirely domestic. Western folklore, Greatest Generation mythology,

Pulp Fiction, by Matt Warren. Pencil on paper, 2012.
Courtesy of the artist

blaxploitation, plain old exploitation, pulp fiction—all have been remade in Tarantino's image throughout the course of his career.

Accordingly, a lot is inevitably discarded in the evolution from popular culture artifact to Tarantino production. We would be left with a period piece, not a Tarantino film, if Tarantino just copied the above genres wholesale. For his films to endure, mannerisms, values, and other era-defining elements must give way to cinematic concerns of style and commentary.

It's worth considering what's been left out. (And, what's been left in.) In the case of *Pulp Fiction*, this means sleuthing around the world of lowercase pulp fiction, the cheap fiction magazines printed in the United States from the very end of the nineteenth century until the middle of the twentieth and the titular inspiration for Tarantino's 1994 release. By making acquaintance with pulp history, we may get a hint at where pulp fiction ends and *Pulp Fiction* begins.

Fiction called pulp was named for the inexpensive, wood pulp–based paper it was printed on. Literally disposable—and maybe culturally, depending on your perspective—pulp magazines were meant to be thrown away after a few passes among friends. (The good stuff, cotton and linen, was reserved for serious reads such as *Harper's* and *The Saturday Evening Post*.) Covers were engineered to titillate, and nearly always depicted libidinous young women, violent scenes, or libidinous young women in violent scenes. Inside, stories featured skulking criminals, duplicitous females, mad doctors, and other characters drawn to appeal to readers' less noble instincts.

Unsurprisingly, parents and other polite members of the republic considered pulps "exploitative, unsophisticated, violent, and sexist," wrote pulp historian Peter Haining. Even less surprisingly, this sort of material was extremely popular. The creation of a new publishing process reflected demand; as an increasingly literate nation clamored to fill its entertainment needs, paper production was forced to get quicker and cheaper.

Likewise, the public's growing appetite for cheap reads meant that more stories had to be fashioned. Waves of writers, many of them college graduates and/or journalists, found their way to New York to slog for magazines with names like *Dime Detective*, *Gangster Stories*, and *Black Mask*, arguably the most important publisher of crime fiction in American history. It was, predictably, a hack's life. Manuscripts numbering in the tens of thousands of words, due by the end of the week, were not uncommon, and many pulp writers weren't too far removed from the alcoholic, rough-and-tumble lives they wrote about.

Despite its modern association with crime or mystery, the term *pulp* actually referred to any story printed on pulp paper. The original pulps, in fact, were written "for family consumption," says Ed Hulse, a pulp historian and publisher of the modern pulp magazine *Blood 'n' Thunder*. However, by the 1920s the market had exploded, compelling publishers to put out increasingly sex-tinged, crime-saturated, or bizarre stories in order to survive. Among other genres that crystallized at this time, there were sci-fi pulps (Ray Bradbury published some of his earliest stories in *Weird Tales*) and, if those weren't creepy enough, "shudder" pulps, which married sex and horror in stories like "Eye of the Fiend," "Black Pool for Hell Maidens," and "Pawn of Hideous Desire." In time, *pulp* transitioned from the description of a medium to shorthand for a specific style.

Pulp writers were inspired, if we can call it that, by the roiling cities of post–World War I America, which provided a never-ending parade of corruption, decadence, and violence. "Pulps dealt with the 'strange' way of living in big cities"

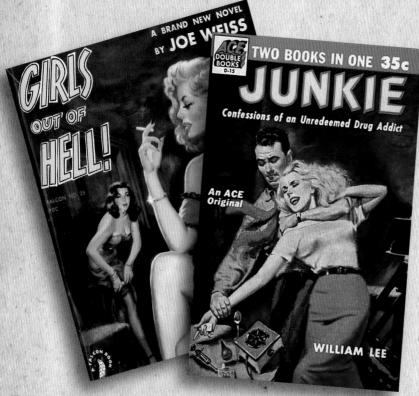

and "urban disturbance," says literary critic and *Cult Fiction* author Clive Bloom. "America is a young country, and [at the time of pulps], so many people were living in cities who may have never lived in a city." Prohibition, which brought the country the infamous Chicago Mob battle called the Saint Valentine's Day Massacre, simultaneously amplified the country's fears about city-spawned crime and whetted its appetite for tales about the underworld. The sense of dread was overwhelming; *Black Mask* titles from the day include "The Shrieking Skeleton" (1924), "Murder in the Ring" (1930), "Diamonds Mean Death" (1936), and similar stories on unnatural human expiration.

Under these circumstances, flowery prose simply wouldn't do. Pulp writers had no use for Thomas Hardy, much less Sherlock Holmes: "Dissatisfaction with the Victorian rhetoric and polite exposition," wrote Haining, "was nowhere more strongly felt than among the writers of private eye stories." Though pulp journeyman Hank Searls had attended Stanford, his *Black Mask* story "Drop Dead Twice" is decidedly short of high-art garnish. It opens thusly:

> It was a very nice job—definitely professional. And final. The blonde lay across the hotel bed lengthwise, a gleam of golden flesh showing above her stocking, but otherwise perfectly presentable. A white linen handkerchief was clutched in her hand. She had been mugged—strangled—throttled. Whatever you wanted to call it, the killer had quite thoroughly known his business.

Before you could say "blueberry pie," an American trope was born. Thank Searls, Carroll John Daly, Dashiell Hammett, Raymond Chandler, and countless other laboring pulp authors for the modern crime thriller formula. Tough guys had been around forever, but never before had they been so damn pithy. Or, if you like, hard-boiled.

The country wouldn't be the same. Leggy femme fatales; wisecracking dicks; menacing foreigners; violence just 'cause—every enduring trope in paperbacks, film, and television owes its debt to the crime stories of the pulp heyday. This development, much like the recent mania for vampires, was driven by commercial interests. "To reach a wide audience [pulp authors] had to stereotype, and use certain formulaic means of understanding," Bloom says. "The 'nasty black man,' 'dangerous Chinaman,' etc., quickly became recognizable," thus lowering the barrier to sales. Without the pulps there could be no James Bond, and most certainly no Arnold Schwarzenegger. Neither, of course, could there be a Butch Coolidge, a double-crossing boxer on the run, nor a Marsellus Wallace, a Mob boss willing to go all the way to Indochina to exact revenge on a motherfucker.

Tarantino has acknowledged as much, telling *Vanity Fair* in 2013 that his intent with *Pulp Fiction* was to comment on the cliché "you've seen a zillion times—the boxer who's supposed to throw a fight and doesn't, the Mob guy who's supposed to take the boss's wife out for the evening," and so on. Glancing at Hollywood or TV

history, a zillion may seem only a minor exaggeration. A 2007 story in the satirical newspaper the *Onion* gets right at the matter: "Entire Precinct Made Up of Loose Cannons."

While pulp types populate *Pulp Fiction*, their connection to the golden age of pulp literature is often superficial. The movie's California setting is fitting. Hammett's *The Maltese Falcon*, arguably the most famous pulp of all time (and

originally serialized in *Black Mask*), was set in San Francisco, and Los Angeles is as much a primary character in Chandler's stories as any human. But the movie's inclusion of California surf rock, twist dancing, and classic Chevrolets is, historically speaking, a generation too late.

Indeed, *Pulp Fiction* almost seems to suggest that the pulp heyday was the fifties and sixties—which is neither wrong (it's a judgment, after all), nor remotely out of bounds for any filmmaker, especially one whose calling card is pastiche. It has, though, led many viewers to conflate the term *pulp* with the flourishes of *Pulp Fiction*, to the frustration of Hulse and other pulp purists. "We've reached a point where almost anything can be called pulp fiction," Hulse says. "If anything is 'pulp fiction,' nothing is pulp fiction."

Whatever the debate over Vincent and Jules' skinny ties, *Pulp Fiction*'s dialogue and narrative are unambiguously Tarantino. Pulp's market was working- and middle-class men (and inevitably, teens) who had neither the time nor the inclination to unravel artfully mangled plots nor five-minute dialectics on the pros and cons of consuming pork. In pulp, a straightforward narrative was everything. Even a middling drudge could make a career out of pulp so long as he could keep a story going. *Pulp Fiction*'s plot zoomed ahead, but it made lots of talkative pit stops along the way.

As well, Tarantino's multiracial cast of scoundrels is certifiably postpulp. In the pulp era, nonwhites were nearly always villains, or at the least, they were collateral damage. This was partially due to prejudice and partially due to Americans' sense of post–World War I vulnerability. (There's an entire book devoted to the latter theme, *Anti-Foreign Imagery in American Pulps and Comic Books, 1920–1960*.) *Pulp Fiction*'s equal-opportunity vice, however, offered little consolation for feminist writer bell hooks, who called the movie "multiculturalism with a chic neofascist twist" in one of the movie's most high-profile critiques.

Though intended as a rebuke, this line probably describes *Pulp Fiction* in a way Tarantino would find acceptable. Making things chic has always been his goal, and the throw-away fiction magazines of the interwar period, stocked as they were with worn-out, all-American motifs, provided endless opportunity to do so. Transforming low culture into celluloid gloss is not just what Tarantino does best. It's simply what he does. We've seen it a zillion times.

Adam Rosen is an editor at Soomo Publishing in Asheville. He founded the Non-motivational Speaker Series in New York.

(continued from page 38)

Tarantino's recollection differs. "I had said, 'Let me buy *Pandemonium Reigns*, I'll do a first pass, incorporate it into my material, and then you can come in, and we can do another pass on it.' Well, that second pass never happened, because I pretty much did it all on the first pass. There was no reason to bring him in anymore." Of the Avary script, Tarantino would later say, "I just liked the basic idea of it, and a couple of incidents, and threw the rest away." He would elaborate in other interviews: "There are a bunch of ideas that belong to him: the hillbillies, the pawnbroker. He had invented the watch, for example, but I had to make up the history of this watch. I also made Fabienne into a French woman."

Whatever the case may be—and the disagreement over how much of *Fiction* was Avary's work led to a lengthy falling-out between the two friends—Avary received only the Writer's Guild of America (WGA) minimum of $30,000 for his work on the film. Avary would later tell author Peter Biskind that during *Pulp*'s postproduction, Tarantino persuaded him to forfeit his screenwriting credit for the "stories by" byline that appears in the film. He claimed he was offered a cash payment, as well as an adjustment in residuals and back-end participation. Strapped for cash, he agreed, and Tarantino was credited as writer/director. (Recently, Avary told *Vanity Fair* he "doesn't recall any of this." His final summary: "I love the movie. I'm delighted with my contribution. That is enough. And I love Quentin. He's like a brother.")

Tarantino managed to wrestle the script down to two hundred pages by the third draft— still hefty, by Hollywood standards. "The script itself weighed about fourteen pounds," Eric Stoltz (Lance the drug dealer) recalled. "It was a novel!" Tarantino delivered it to TriStar (a month late), and waited. He wasn't sure what the suits would think, but he was happy with what he'd come up with, and unconcerned with living up to expectations. "As far as some people were concerned," he would later tell *Playboy*, "*Reservoir Dogs* was as good as it was going to get. This poor, silly boy is trying to follow up *Reservoir Dogs*?"

But he had. He'd topped it, concocting a screenplay that was smart, funny, warm, and groundbreaking, though he'd disagree with the latter assessment. "If somebody had asked me what ground was being broken in *Pulp Fiction*, I'd have said none," he claimed. "It's just what I wanted to see in a movie, what I thought would be cool."

Signatures:
The Mexican Standoff

One of Tarantino's favorite cinematic tropes is the so-called Mexican standoff—familiar from such films as *The Good, the Bad, and the Ugly* and *Hard Boiled*, in which two or more characters have guns pointed at each other and seemingly no way out. "When you're doing a gangster film, the Mexican standoff is like the modern equivalent of a Western showdown," he has said, noting that part of his interest in the device came from wanting to see the logical conclusion that seldom came to pass: everyone just firing their guns and shooting each other. Some of his standoffs have gone that way. Some haven't.

Reservoir Dogs: Early on, Mr. Pink and Mr. White's fisticuffs lead to a John Woo–style point-blank two-man standoff, broken up by the unexpected arrival of Mr. Blonde. The real action comes later, when Joe Cabot takes aim at Mr. Orange, which prompts Mr. White to take aim at Joe, which prompts Nice Guy Eddie to take aim at Mr. White, which prompts the shooting of all three men.

True Romance: While Clarence is in the can, cops bust in on his drug deal with Lee Donowitz. Donowitz's bodyguards point their guns at the cops, escalating the situation, which is further exacerbated by the arrival of Blue Lou Boyle's men, themselves pointing guns at everyone. After much shouting, a flurry of gunfire and bloodshed erupts.

Natural Born Killers: Mickey Knox, armed with a shotgun he's nabbed from a guard, bursts in on Jack Scagnetti assaulting his beloved Mallory, and the two men draw down on each other. "Looks like we got us a Mexican standoff," Mickey announces, a line present both in Oliver Stone's film and Tarantino's original script.

Pulp Fiction: In the climactic restaurant scene, Jules painstakingly choreographs the particulars of this standoff: Vincent's gun's on Honey Bunny/Yolanda, whose gun is on Jules, whose gun is on Pumpkin/Ringo.

Kill Bill Volume 2: The Bride's hit, Karen Wong, arrives at her hotel room just as The Bride has discovered she is pregnant. Their guns drawn on each other, The Bride explains her predicament and proposes they walk away from the situation and leave each other be.

Inglourious Basterds: After Archie Hicox accidently reveals that he is not a German while undercover at La Louisianne Tavern, Dieter Hellstrom reveals that he has a gun pointed at Hicox's testicles. Hicox says that he is doing the same, as is his associate Hugo Stiglitz. It doesn't end well for Hellstrom—nor for the others, since Staff Sergeant Wilhelm is one of the few left standing after the resulting melee. Aldo Raine, waiting outside the tavern with grenades at the ready, tries to make a deal with Wilhelm, noting that "A Mexican standoff ain't trust . . . no trust, no deal!"

After the
Mexican
standoff in
Reservoir Dogs.
© Pictorial Press
Ltd / Alamy

Shaking Up the Structure

"I remember my mom saying, 'Why didn't they put the movie together right?'"
—Samuel L. Jackson

Jackson's mother wasn't alone. When *Pulp Fiction* opened in October 1994, its unconventional chronology was one of its most discussed (and later, imitated) elements. "Every once in a while, films don't play by the rules," Tarantino explained in 2012. "It's liberating when you don't know what's happening next." In 1994, audiences felt that liberation, responded to it, and were electrified by it.

Tarantino wasn't the first filmmaker to play with narrative linearity. The list of practitioners is long and distinguished, from Akira Kurosawa (*Rashomon*) to Alain Resnais (*Last Year at Mirenbad*) to Mario Bava (*Four Times That Night*) to Nicolas Roeg (*Don't Look Now*) to Woody Allen (*Annie Hall*). *Pulp Fiction* wasn't Tarantino's first crack at the form—it was, even at this early point, a trademark, present in *Reservoir Dogs* and the original scripts of *True Romance* and *Natural Born Killers*. Tarantino considered it more a literary device than a cinematic one. "When you read a good novel, and it starts in the middle of the story, then jumps back in time, you don't think it's any big deal. It's all part of an unfolding narrative. I'm not against a linear structure, it's just that it's not the only game in town."

Editor Sally Menke recalled that the first time they screened a rough cut of the finished film, "I remember the projectionist saying, 'Did I get the reels mixed up?'" It's not an unreasonable question, considering that the film's top-billed star is gunned down halfway through the film, only to reappear, alive and well, some twenty minutes later.

But what Tarantino does in *Pulp Fiction* is quite different structurally from *Reservoir Dogs* or *Kill Bill*, which hopscotch between the present and (for lack of a better word) flashbacks that go back weeks or even years. *Pulp Fiction's* timeline is compact, taking place over only a few days, and with the exception of Butch's dream/memory of Captain Koons delivering the watch, free of the kind of character background bits we get in *Dogs* or *Bill* (there is no vignette of Vincent at work in Amsterdam, for example, or of Butch and Fabienne's first date). He's not telling a wide-ranging story; he's merely dispensing with the conventional 'A-leads-to-B-leads-to-C-leads-to-D chronology that moviegoers are most familiar with and organizing his story in a manner that heightens the drama.

PULP FACT 9

The literary influence on Tarantino's films can be further seen by his use of chapter titles, which are employed implicitly in *Reservoir Dogs* and *Pulp Fiction* and explicitly in *Inglourious Basterds* and the *Kill Bill* movies (*Volume 1* featuring the rather comical intertitle "Chapter One: 2.")

So let's clarify the terms. If *Pulp Fiction* were organized into the aforementioned A-B-C-D order (which it has been, often by Internet video editors with some time on their hands), it would go something like this:

A. Many years ago, Captain Koons gives young Butch his family's "war watch."

B. The present day. Jules and Vincent drive to Brett's building, retrieve the briefcase, and kill Brett and Flock of Seagulls.

C. A fourth man emerges from the bathroom, emptying his pistol towards Jules and Vincent, but leaving them standing. They kill the man. Driving away, Vincent accidentally shoots Marvin in the face. Jules drives to Jimmie's, where the Wolf helps them dispose of Marvin's body and the car.

D. Jules and Vincent go to breakfast and discuss Jules' future.

E. At the same coffee shop, Honey Bunny and Pumpkin discuss their own future, and decide to rob said coffee shop.

F. Jules interrupts the robbery, saves the briefcase, and sends the lovers on their way.

G. Jules and Vincent take the briefcase to Marsellus' club, where he is paying off Butch to throw the Wilson fight.

H. A day or more passes. Marsellus goes out of town. Vincent takes Mia out to Jackrabbit Slim's. Afterwards, she accidentally ODs on his heroin. Vincent and his dealer Lance barely manage to save her life.

I. A day or more passes. Marsellus returns from his trip. In the big-money bout, Butch kills Wilson in the ring and makes his getaway, with the help of Esmerelda Villalobos. He goes to the motel, gives Fabienne oral pleasure, showers, and goes to sleep.

J. The next morning. Butch realizes Fabienne left his watch in his apartment. Butch goes there, retrieves the watch, and kills Vincent. While driving back, he encounters Marsellus, and hits him with his car. The two men end up in the pawnshop, where they are tortured and Marsellus is raped before Butch gets free and saves Marsellus. Butch returns to the motel, gets Fabienne, and they ride off into the sunset on Zed's chopper.

Tarantino takes this series of events and reorganizes it, from A-B-C-D-E-F-G-H-I-J to E-B-G-H-A-I-J-C-D-F. "It has an end but, because it goes back to the beginning, you kind of realize that you've seen a complete circle," he explained. "A circle doesn't have an end, but it doesn't continue either." It's like how people used to see movies back in the days of the double feature on a loop—they'd leave when they got to the part where they came in.

But why does he tell his story that way? To some extent, it is simply because he *can*. In America, Tarantino explained in 1992, "Movies have got to be linear: if you begin a scene at the beginning of a race, you have to end it at the end of a race. I prefer what Sergio Leone does in *Once Upon a Time in America*, which is true of all his films: 'Answers first, questions later.'" So part of his aim is to confound those A-B-C-D expectations, to battle the predictability so embedded in mainstream moviemaking (particularly coming out of the 1980s). "Pretty much nine out of ten movies you see let you know in the first ten minutes what kind of movie it's going to be," he noted, "and I think the audience subconsciously reads this early ten-minute message and starts leaning to the left when the movie is getting ready to make a left turn; they're predicting what the movie is going to do. And what I like to do is use that information against them."

The filmmaker's critics have called *Pulp*'s construction a gimmick, employed to be cute, or clever, or showy. In his book *The Blood Poets*, critic Jake Horsley contends that "Tarantino rearranges the order of the scenes in much the same way a good lawyer shuffles the evidence: not for coherence but for resonance; for effect." Aaron Barlow takes issue with this idea in his book *Quentin Tarantino: Life at the Extremes*: "[A] good courtroom lawyer is also a good storyteller, and effect is an important part of any successful narrative. Tarantino, understanding this, would never denigrate the importance of 'effect,' as Horsley does."

And Barlow is right. Watching *Fiction* as it is, it's impossible to imagine it ending any other way than with Jules' redemption (and Pumpkin's). Butch and Fabienne's ride into the sunset may be the proper conclusion chronologically, but Jules and Vincent's stroll out of the Hawthorne Grill is the right one emotionally. Eschewing traditional structure gives Tarantino the freedom to tell his story how he wants to tell it, to jump from highlight to highlight, to skip the dull stuff, to play with connections and textuality, to keep from having to choose the perfect opening by using three (in

the diner, in the car after the credits, and in the club after the first chapter title) and letting them fight it out. He trusts the viewer—and knows that we, like him, have seen enough movies (not as many as he has, he probably thinks, but enough) to know which parts fit where and to fill in the blanks ourselves.

As Randall A. Auxier surmises in *Quentin Tarantino and Philosophy*, "He wants us to piece the actual temporal sequence together. He dares us to do it. Why? Because it's fun." The audience becomes a collaborator and partner as much as an admirer. "He wants us to *experience* what that is like for him to have that freedom, so that we can appreciate the decisions he made and share his playful delight at the effects. Yes, he is playing with us, but he is not *toying* with us; he is toying with the three unities for our edification."

That seems as good an explanation as any. *Pulp Fiction* is, from an architectural point of view, a puzzle film, inviting its audience to play along, make connections, and grin appreciatively as they put it all together—when the fade-up reveals Jules and Vincent in those incongruent "volleyball game" outfits, or when a cutaway interrupts their diner dialogue to disclose that this is, in fact, the very place where that prologue we forgot about (it was two-plus hours ago, after all) was set, and that those lovey-dovey robbers and these two hit men are about to crash into each other. The joy Tarantino has clearly taken in breaking it apart and putting it back together with us is reminiscent of another great puzzle film: *Citizen Kane*, whose creator Orson Welles famously called film "the biggest toy train set a boy ever had."

Opposite:
Pulp Fiction, poster by Jacob Wise.
Courtesy of the artist.
© *Jacob Wise*

(continued on page 56)

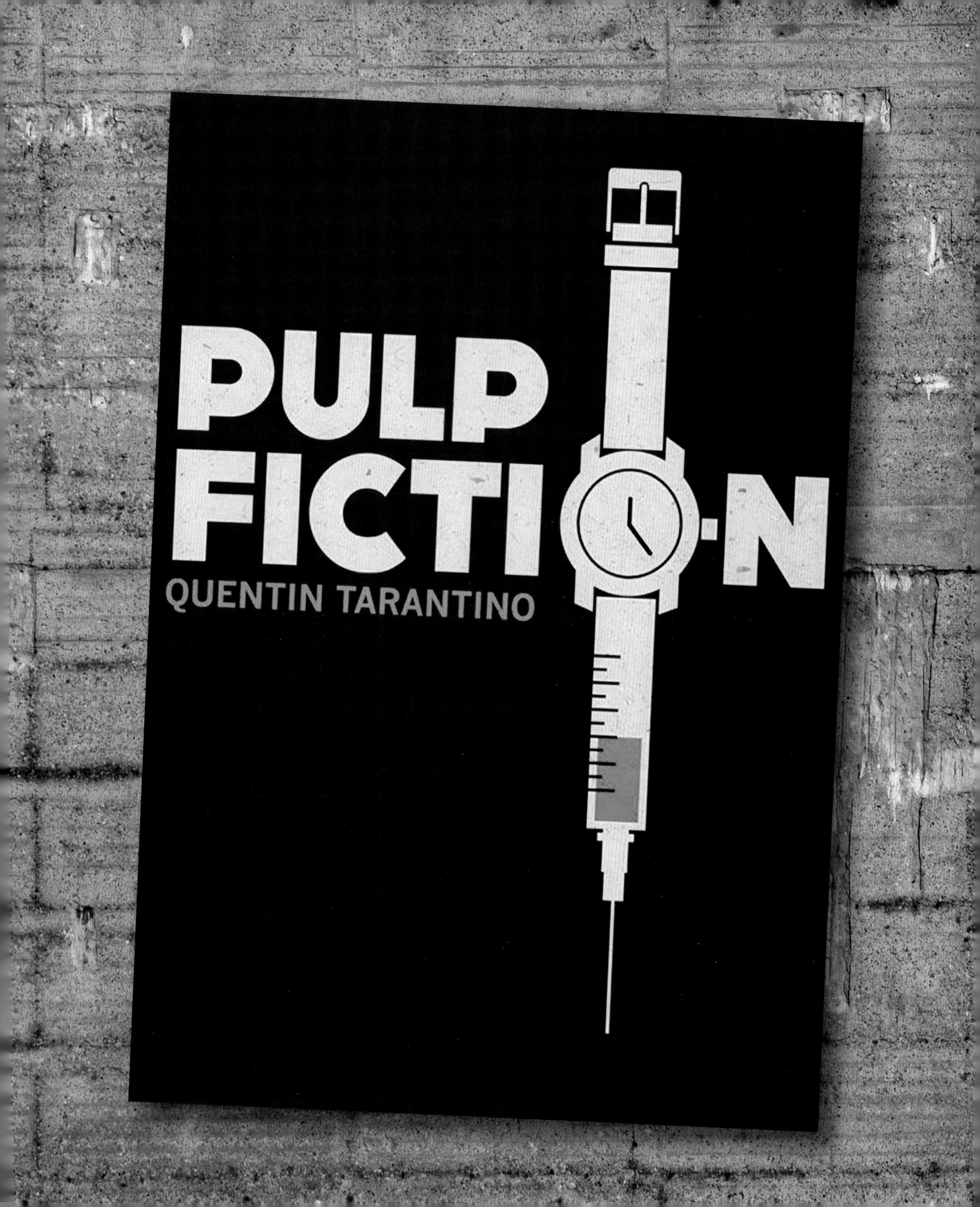
PULP
FICTI·N
QUENTIN TARANTINO

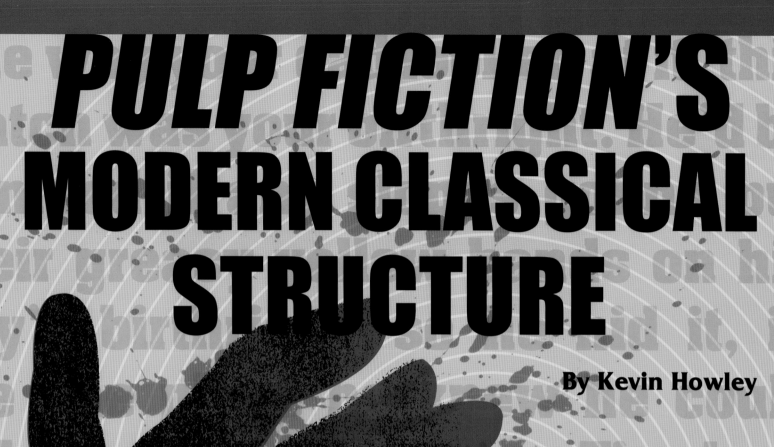

PULP FICTION'S
MODERN CLASSICAL
STRUCTURE

By Kevin Howley

"Any time of the day is a good time for pie."
—*Fabienne, Pulp Fiction*

Like premature reports of Mark Twain's demise, news of the death of classical narrative is greatly exaggerated. Rather, like generic conventions—the Western's climactic showdown, film noir's mysterious femme fatale, or the horror film's monstrous "other"—story structure itself, including the treatment of narrative and temporal relations is undergoing some (radical, perhaps) reinterpretation. This reworking of story causality and linear narrative does not, however, represent a rejection of the principles of classical filmmaking; indeed, flashbacks and narrative ellipses are common storytelling devices in classical filmmaking. Rather than rejecting the principles of Hollywood classicism, the narrative and stylistic innovations prevalent in contemporary American movies constitute what film historian David Bordwell calls "intensified continuity."

Tarantino and Avary's script for *Pulp Fiction* is an exemplar in this regard. As the screenplay's subtitle, "Three stories . . . About one story," suggests, Tarantino and Avary are interested in exploring the intersections and interpenetrations between people, places, and actions: precisely those ingredients that Pauline Kael suggests are the "stuff" of movies. In this essay, I want to suggest that *Pulp Fiction*'s emphasis on story and storytelling indicates a discernible interest in time or, more precisely, different aspects of time in cinema. With its fractured narrative structure, *Pulp Fiction* exploits film's unrivaled facility for temporal construction and (re)ordering.

Although screenwriters often follow the three-act narrative structure championed by Syd Fields in his industry standard text *Screenplay*, the tripartite formulation does not hold up very well either in practice or under critical scrutiny. Kristin Thompson suggests a four-part invention that offers a more robust model for understanding how Hollywood films are structured and how they operate. This model consists of: (1) the set up; (2) complicating action; (3) development; and (4) a climax, followed by an epilogue. This formulation is neither fixed nor rigidly determined; its flexibility invites variation and affords filmmakers an opportunity to create individual and distinctive works within a hierarchical and disciplined regime of production: the hallmark of classical Hollywood cinema. Despite its playful, but by no means inconsequential, disregard for narrative chronology, *Pulp Fiction* fits Thompson's four-part structure quite well.

The film's prologue, which includes the opening scene in which Pumpkin and Honey Bunny contemplate holding up the diner and concludes with Vincent and Jules rubbing out

a couple of would-be criminals, provides the setup for *Pulp Fiction*. Typically, the setup establishes an initial situation and provides expository information related to characters and their relationships to one another. In addition, the setup either establishes the main characters' goals or provides the viewer with enough background information to understand the circumstances under which the film's protagonists define these goals. Likewise character traits are established and clearly defined in these opening scenes. Finally, the setup is important inasmuch as it sets the tone for the entire film.

The conversation between Pumpkin and Honey Bunny is emblematic of the stance Tarantino is taking toward his story and his audience. At first, the viewer seems privy to a quiet conversation between a young couple whose thoughts, quirks, and mannerisms are well known to each other. They appear to be bickering, albeit in a playful, teasing tone that indicates shared affection. For anyone who has been in a long-term relationship, it is a familiar enough conversation.

When audiences see a caper film, their expectations consist of witnessing a group of hardened criminals discussing the intricate details of some fabulous scheme for a big score, not a couple of lovebirds discussing the benefits of robbing a diner, where they will catch patrons "with their pants down"—an allusion to Vincent Vega's poorly-timed bowel movements—let alone a couple of hit men talking about fast food, television sitcoms, or the gender politics of foot massage.

Pulp Fiction employs dialogue and visual motifs throughout the setup that provide narrative clarity and unity along the lines associated with classical Hollywood cinema. The dialogue in the coffee shop is precisely the sort of conversation that pervades *Pulp Fiction* and indicates that the film has much more to do with the mundane aspects of a life of crime than it does with the glamour, danger, and intrigue typical of thrillers or film noir. That is to say, *Pulp Fiction* deals with the unimportant or empty moments that more conventional crime stories, noirs, and thrillers omit. And yet, this small talk is not inconsequential. In keeping with classical narrative structure, this conversation establishes character and character relations early in the film and in a thoroughly entertaining and engaging fashion.

Following the four-part structure described above, *Pulp Fiction*'s next section, titled "Vincent Vega and Marsellus Wallace's Wife," serves as the film's complicating action. Complicating action provides a shift in action or, more typically, provides an obstacle of some sort that the protagonist must overcome on his or her way to achieving a particular objective. This section achieves both these ends. Whereas the prologue focused on the hit and the retrieval of Marsellus' enigmatic briefcase, this next section shifts the action to Vincent's interaction with Mia Wallace. The section opens with a close-up of Butch Coolidge, who will feature prominently in the film's third section. Butch's appearance here, in particular his brief but hostile confrontation with Vincent, foreshadows their fatal meeting in the film's middle passage. Suffice it to say that Marsellus Wallace plays a pivotal role in stitching together the narrative threads between this section and the next. Marsellus is ground zero of the relationship between Vincent and Butch and Vincent and Mia.

Blissed out on some recently acquired heroin, Vincent Vega arrives at Mia Wallace's home only to be confronted by the disembodied voice and preying eyes of his dinner companion. In an homage to Anna Karina, Jean-Luc Godard's one-time wife and muse, Mia spies on Vincent while she powders her nose with a few lines of cocaine. Their respective drugs of choice and general demeanor suggest that this simple dinner date may be a bumpy ride, indeed the perfect recipe for some complicating action.

And yet, by the end of the evening, Mia and Vincent appear to getting along just fine, having won first prize in the dance contest at Jackrabbit Slim's. But in Tarantino's universe, things change quickly; as we later learn, you can be dead in the time it takes to toast a couple of Pop-Tarts. Just as the surf music that accompanies the film's opening credits is jarringly interrupted by the sounds of Kool and the Gang, so too the tranquility of Vincent and Mia's evening is shattered when Mia mistakes Vincent's heroin stash for cocaine and goes into cardiac arrest. Here, another music cue provides ironic comment on time. As Mia lies dying of an overdose, the soundtrack plays Urge Overkill's rendition of the Neil Diamond hit, "Girl, You'll Be a Woman Soon."

In a tour de force sequence reminiscent of Hitchcock's finest moments—excruciating scenes of tension mixed with macabre humor—Vincent manages to save Mia. These bravura set pieces are integral to the drama—after all, Vincent is racing against time to keep Mia from dying. Furthermore, these sequences are emblematic of intensified continuity. That is to say, despite the scene's accelerated pace, the shot length, picture composition, camera movement, image, and sound editing all adhere to established techniques associated with Hollywood classicism. For instance, as Vincent races toward Lance's suburban home, wide shots of Vincent's car racing down deserted city streets are intercut with point-of-view shots taken from Vincent's perspective of the dying mobster's moll and close-ups of Vincent on his cell phone. In turn, these shots cut to images of Lance doing his best to ignore Vincent's desperate call and finally to shot-reversal shots as the two argue over whose "problem" Mia really is.

Likewise, handheld camera movements following the action as Vincent pulls up on Lance's lawn, point-of-view shots as the drug dealer and his wife search for the cardiac kit, and finally, Vincent plunging the hypodermic into Mia's chest all follow the rules associated with traditional continuity editing. As David Bordwell points out, "When shots are so short, when establishing shots are brief or postponed or nonexistent, the eyelines and angles in the dialogue must be even more unambiguous, and the axis of action must be strictly respected." Throughout this harrowing sequence, Tarantino adheres to these conventions, albeit in an accelerated and intensified fashion.

The "Vincent Vega and Marsellus Wallace's Wife" section of the film ends with the two agreeing not to tell Marsellus anything about what has happened. This bond between Mia and Vincent is not at all unlike the bond that will develop between Butch and Marsellus in the film's next section. Here again, Tarantino's "fractured" narrative is actually a very tightly woven tale, stitched together by the formal elements and stylistic devices associated with classical Hollywood narrative.

The story of Butch's watch is the centerpiece of *Pulp Fiction*'s overarching narrative. More important, for purposes of this discussion, this tale fits quite neatly into Thompson's four-part structure. By the time we get to *Pulp Fiction*'s next story, "The Gold Watch," a number of crucial plot lines, character traits, and expectations have been firmly established. Like all classical narratives, *Pulp Fiction*'s characters are goal-oriented. Vincent and Mia have agreed to keep their little adventure quiet; Marsellus has been

clearly established as someone you don't mess with. Butch is determined to beat Marsellus at his own game and is obsessed with retrieving his father's watch. And Marsellus, keen to make a killing on a prizefight, tutors Butch on how best to throw his upcoming bout:

> **Marsellus: In the fifth, your ass goes down.**
> **Butch nods his head.**
> **Marsellus: Say it!**
> **Butch: In the fifth, my ass goes down.**

This third section of the film shifts the action from Vincent and Mia to Butch and Marsellus. Having agreed to take a dive, Butch has different plans. He double-crosses Marsellus and literally beats his opponent to death. As Marsellus, accompanied by Mia, realizes he has been had, he instructs his crew, including Vincent, to "scour the Earth" for Butch. Jules is conspicuously absent from this scene, yet another device to keep the audience guessing.

The search for Butch is a crucial turning point in the film's action and leads to an extended sequence of events, including Butch's flight from the boxing arena; a phone call to his friend, who has helped engineer Butch's plan; a rendezvous with Butch's girlfriend, Fabienne (Maria de Medeiros); the search for the missing gold watch; Vincent's murder; and a confrontation between Marsellus and Butch that culminates in the infamous rape sequence in the basement of the Mason-Dixie Pawn Shop. The development section ends with Butch and Fabienne riding away on a chopper.

In terms of narrative chronology, this is the end of the story. Butch has successfully retrieved his father's gold watch, reconciled with Marsellus, and is free to live happily ever after. However, one major plot point remains unresolved. What are the mysterious contents of Marsellus' briefcase? When Vincent examines the contents of the briefcase, we have some clues. The combination is 666, the mark of the beast. Moreover, when he first lays eyes upon it, he is quite literally speechless. And for film aficionados, it is difficult to miss the reference to Robert Aldrich's cold war-period thriller *Kiss Me Deadly*, in which an equally mysterious briefcase contained the "atomic whatsit." Still, the audience is left wondering what exactly is in Marsellus' briefcase. In fact, we never find out. As it turns out, the briefcase and its contents are what Hitchcock would refer to as a McGuffin, a plot device that keeps the audience's attention and provides narrative cohesion, but is ultimately unimportant to the overall story.

Tarantino's Hitchcockian ruse is not an anomaly in this regard. Throughout the film, he employs several classical techniques to unify his plot or signal spatial and temporal changes in the narrative. He uses one very old device, the title card, throughout the film, ensuring that temporal shifts are not nearly as jarring or confusing as they might have been.

Jules' deadly monologue is yet one more device Tarantino uses to give unity and clarity to his narrative, very much in the tradition of classical Hollywood storytelling. As we know from the earlier scene, this distinctive and exceedingly disarming monologue immediately precedes certain death for anyone who hears it. Thus, Jules' quotation of scripture provides a narrative link between the earlier scene and this flashback. Significantly, we will hear this passage again in the film's epilogue, when Jules explains to Pumpkin and Honey Bunny his reluctance to exact vengeance upon them.

Pulp Fiction's temporal disorder and character quirks might best be understood in terms of those stylistic assimilations Hollywood classicism has made over the years to appropriate innovative techniques that do not conform to the principles of story causality, goal-oriented characters, and narrative unity. The film's epilogue succinctly encapsulates this notion. Having diffused a potentially lethal situation and successfully retained Marsellus' briefcase, Jules and Vincent exit the coffee shop triumphantly; notwithstanding the fact that Vincent was killed by a fatal shotgun blast in the previous reel. No doubt acknowledging his audience's nostalgic attachment to John Travolta while simultaneously revealing his own soft spot for the popular actor, Tarantino resurrects the beloved star of *Welcome Back Kotter*, *Saturday Night Fever*, and *Grease*. Thus, by rearranging the temporal order of his stories, and especially with Vincent's dead-man-walking routine that closes the film, Tarantino treats his audience to that most time-honored of Hollywood conventions: the happy ending. Viva Vincent Vega!

Kevin Howley is Associate Professor of Media Studies at DePauw University. He is the author of *Community Media: People, Places, and Communication Technologies* (Cambridge, 2005) and editor of *Understanding Community Media* (Sage, 2010) and the forthcoming *Media Interventions* (Peter Lang). This essay has been excerpted from a longer article in the May 2004 issue of *Scope* Magazine, entitled "Breaking, Making, and Killing Time in *Pulp Fiction*."

(continued from page 48)

The Welles comparison is not new. *The Independent*'s Jon Ronson wrote in 1995, "Not since *Citizen Kane* has one man appeared from relative obscurity to redefine the art of moviemaking." But it's not just the youth of the moviemaker, or his impact. *Citizen Kane*, in addition to being a great film, is a great *showoff* film. Of it, Pauline Kael perceptively wrote, "It is Welles' distinctive quality as a movie director—I think it is his genius—that he never hides his cleverness, that he makes it possible for us not only to enjoy what he does but to share his enjoyment in doing it."

Pulp Fiction is in that great tradition of showoff films, and Tarantino's script pulses with the thrill of trying things out and knowing, as he would later say, that for the first time "what I was writing was going to get made." That excitement is ever-present in the script, and in the film, and in the films that followed. "Hey, look," he seems to whisper to us, with a grin. "Look what I can make this thing do."

Signatures:
Non_{linear} Chronology

"One of the main things I like to do with my scripts is monkey with structure a little bit," Tarantino said back in 1993, and he's certainly held true to that promise. His trademark shuffling of time and events can be seen in nearly every film he's written, either for himself or for other directors, though we do see a pattern of less time play later in his filmography:

Reservoir Dogs: This film starts in the middle, with its crew of thieves on the way to the centerpiece robbery, then flip-flops between the aftermath and the events leading up to the job.

True Romance: Tarantino's original script opens as the final film does, with Clarence talking about Elvis and trying to pick up a girl. It then jumps ahead to young lovers Clarence and Alabama meeting Clarence's dad, following them to Hollywood with Coccotti in hot pursuit. Once in Hollywood, Dick Richie asks how Clarence and Alabama met, which kicks off a long flashback of their first date and the subsequent murder of Drexl, bringing us up to speed.

Natural Born Killers: The original screenplay begins with married serial killers Mickey and Mallory Knox's spree in progress, and a bloodbath in a diner. (Oliver Stone's eventual film version opens the same way.) Tarantino then jumps ahead to find Mickey and Mallory in prison, with warden McCluskey convincing Scagnetti the cop to transport (and presumably kill) the couple. Meanwhile, TV host Wayne Gayle talks Mickey into a live-from-prison interview. The couple's previous rampage is seen mostly in documentary clips from Wayne's show, leading up to the prison interview, riot, and escape of the film's climax.

Jackie Brown: Tarantino's adaptation of Elmore Leonard's *Rum Punch* unfolds mostly chronologically, but the film's climactic handoff/switcheroo of a bag of stolen money is seen three times from three different perspectives, each revealing a bit more of what went down.

Kill Bill Volume 1: The first half of Tarantino's revenge epic begins with a brief pre-title sequence, showing Bill's attempted murder of The Bride. It then jumps to the middle, as The Bride offs the second person on her kill list, before going back to reveal her four years in a coma, escape from the hospital, and journey to Okinawa to procure a samurai sword. The Bride then goes to Tokyo to kill the first person on her list, and the film has caught up with itself.

Kill Bill Volume 2: After an establishing prologue, we go to the scene of the crime: the massacre at The Bride's wedding rehearsal. From there, the film jumps back to where we left off in *Volume 1*, and the chronology is roughly linear, with one notable exception: after Budd buries The Bride alive, there is an extended flashback to her training with Pai Mei—training that allows her to escape from that buried coffin.

Death Proof: This film unfolds chronologically, though the presence of the Blocks at the hospital indicates that the first half of this film takes place before *Planet Terror*, which precedes it on the *Grindhouse* double bill.

Inglourious Basterds: *Basterds* is mostly straight ahead, although the Basterds' backstory is filled in via flashback, and the roughly concurrent progressions of the Basterds' Operation Kino and Shosanna Dreyfuss' plan to torch her theater are seen one at a time, in alternating chapters.

Django Unchained: Tarantino's most straightforward work to date, with Django's journey given only sparse flashbacks to his torture and separation from Broomhilda, and the ride of the pre-Klan raiders interrupted by a comic scene of their preparations and in-fighting a few minutes earlier.

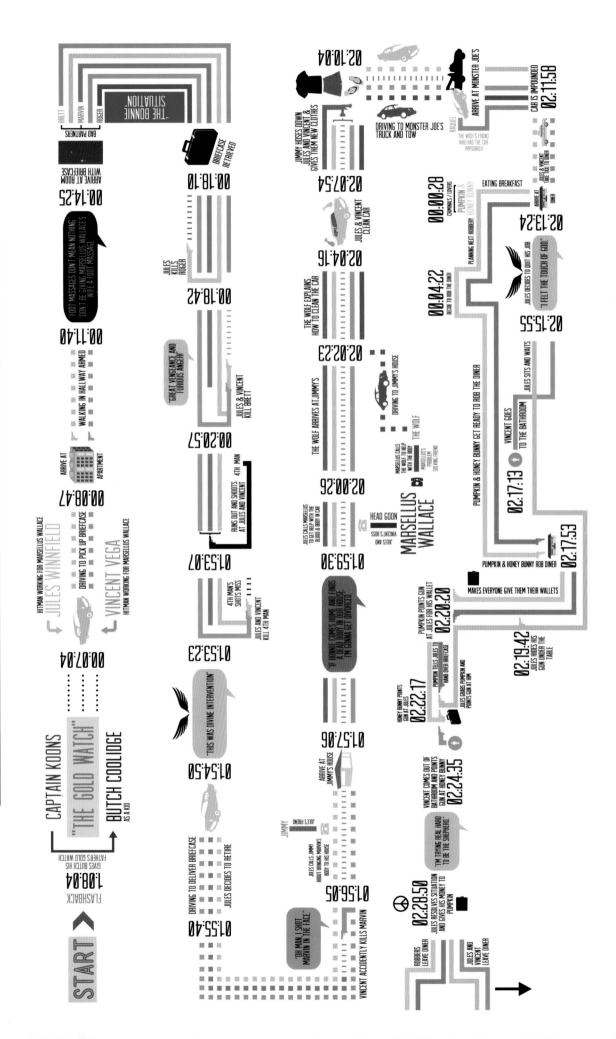

PULP FICTION *The* CHRONOLOGICAL ORDER

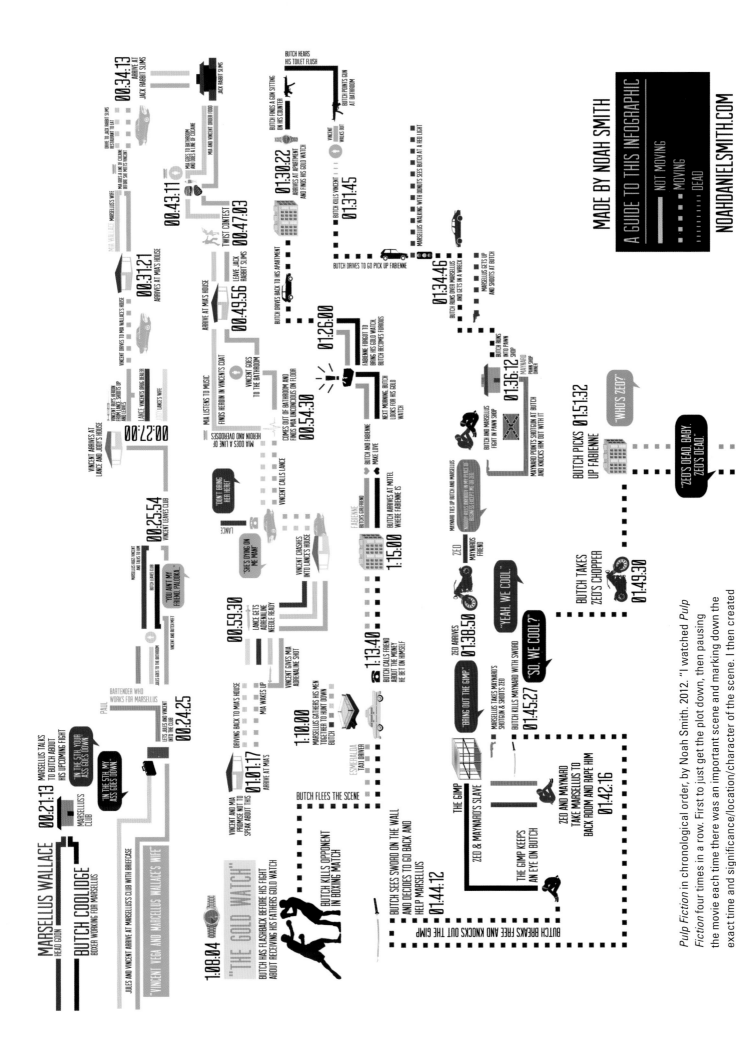

MARSELLUS WALLACE
HEAD GOON

BUTCH COOLIDGE
BOXER WORKING FOR MARSELLUS

"THE GOLD WATCH"

BUTCH HAS FLASHBACK BEFORE HIS FIGHT
ABOUT RECEIVING HIS FATHERS GOLD WATCH

1:08:04

JULES AND VINCENT ARRIVE AT MARSELLUS'S CLUB WITH BRIEFCASE

"VINCENT VEGA AND MARSELLUS WALLACE'S WIFE"

MARSELLUS WALLACE
MARSELLUS TALKS TO BUTCH ABOUT
HIS UPCOMING FIGHT

00:21:13

"IN THE 5TH YOUR ASS GOES DOWN."

"IN THE 5TH MY ASS GOES DOWN."

MARSELLUS'S CLUB

PAUL
BARTENDER WHO WORKS FOR MARSELLUS

LETS JULES AND VINCENT INTO THE CLUB

00:24:25

VINCENT AND BUTCH MEET

JULES GOES TO THE BATHROOM

BUTCH LEAVES CLUB

"YOU AIN'T MY FRIEND, PALOOKA."

MARSELLUS HUGS VINCENT AND TALKS TO HIM

VINCENT LEAVES CLUB

00:25:54

VINCENT ARRIVES AT
LANCE AND JODY'S HOUSE

00:22:00

LANCE
VINCENT'S DRUG DEALER

VINCENT BUYS HEROIN FROM LANCE AND LEAVES

LANCE'S WIFE

VINCENT DRIVES TO MIA WALLACE'S HOUSE

00:31:21
ARRIVES AT MIA'S HOUSE

MIA WALLACE
MARSELLUS'S WIFE

ARRIVE AT MIA'S HOUSE

MIA LISTENS TO MUSIC

VINCENT GOES TO THE BATHROOM

VINCENT CALLS LANCE

"DON'T BRING HER HERE!"

"SHE'S DYING ON ME, MAN!"

LANCE

MIA DOES A LINE OF
HEROIN AND OVERDOSES

MIA DOES A LINE OF COCAINE
BEFORE SHE MEETS VINCENT

00:34:13
ARRIVE AT
JACK RABBIT SLIMS

DRIVE TO JACK RABBIT SLIMS
RESTAURANT TO EAT

JACK RABBIT SLIMS

00:43:11

MIA AND VINCENT ORDER FOOD

TWIST CONTEST
00:47:03

LEAVE JACK RABBIT SLIMS
00:49:56

FINDS HEROIN IN VINCENT'S COAT

COMES OUT OF BATHROOM AND
FINDS MIA UNCONSCIOUS ON FLOOR

00:54:30

LANCE GETS ADRENALINE
NEEDLE READY

00:59:30

VINCENT GIVES MIA
ADRENALINE SHOT

VINCENT AND MIA
PROMISE NOT TO
SPEAK ABOUT THIS

01:01:17
ARRIVE AT MIA'S

VINCENT CRASHES
INTO LANCE'S HOUSE

DRIVING BACK TO MIA'S HOUSE

MIA WAKES UP

1:10:00
MARSELLUS GATHERS HIS MEN
TOGETHER TO HUNT DOWN
BUTCH

ESMERALDA
TAXI DRIVER

BUTCH FLEES THE SCENE

BUTCH KILLS OPPONENT
IN BOXING MATCH

BUTCH CALLS FRIEND
ABOUT THE MONEY
HE BET ON HIMSELF

1:13:40

1:15:00
BUTCH ARRIVES AT MOTEL
WHERE FABIENNE IS

FABIENNE
BUTCH'S GIRLFRIEND

BUTCH AND FABIENNE
MAKE LOVE

FABIENNE FORGOT TO
BRING HIS GOLD WATCH.
BUTCH BECOMES FURIOUS

NEXT MORNING, BUTCH
LOOKS FOR HIS GOLD
WATCH

01:26:00

01:30:22
ARRIVES AT APARTMENT
AND FINDS HIS GOLD WATCH

BUTCH DRIVES BACK TO HIS APARTMENT

BUTCH FINDS A GUN SITTING
ON HIS COUNTER

BUTCH HEARS
HIS TOILET FLUSH

BUTCH POINTS GUN
AT BATHROOM

MIA GOES TO BATHROOM
AND DOES A LINE OF COCAINE

01:31:45
BUTCH KILLS VINCENT

VINCENT
WALKS OUT

MARSELLUS WALKING WITH DONUTS SEES BUTCH AT A RED LIGHT

BUTCH DRIVES TO GO PICK UP FABIENNE

01:34:46
BUTCH RUNS OVER MARSELLUS
AND GETS IN A WRECK

MARSELLUS GETS UP
AND SHOOTS AT BUTCH

BUTCH AND MARSELLUS
FIGHT IN PAWN SHOP

BUTCH RUNS
INTO PAWN
SHOP

01:36:12

MAYNARD
PAWN SHOP
OWNER

MAYNARD POINTS SHOTGUN AT BUTCH
AND KNOCKS HIM OUT WITH IT

MAYNARD TIES UP BUTCH AND MARSELLUS

NOBODY KILLS ANYBODY IN MY PLACE OF
BUSINESS EXCEPT YOU OR ME

ZED
MAYNARD'S FRIEND

ZED ARRIVES
01:38:50

"BRING OUT THE GIMP."

THE GIMP
ZED & MAYNARD'S SLAVE

THE GIMP KEEPS
AN EYE ON BUTCH

01:42:16
ZED AND MAYNARD
TAKE MARSELLUS TO
BACK ROOM AND RAPE HIM

BUTCH BREAKS FREE AND KNOCKS OUT THE GIMP

01:44:12
BUTCH SEES SWORD ON THE WALL
AND DECIDES TO GO BACK AND
HELP MARSELLUS

01:45:27
BUTCH KILLS MAYNARD WITH SWORD

MARSELLUS TAKES MAYNARD'S
SHOTGUN & SHOOTS ZED

"SO, WE COOL?"

"YEAH, WE COOL."

"WHO'S ZED?"

BUTCH TAKES
ZED'S CHOPPER
01:49:30

BUTCH PICKS
UP FABIENNE 01:51:32

"ZED'S DEAD, BABY.
ZED'S DEAD."

END

MADE BY NOAH SMITH

A GUIDE TO THIS INFOGRAPHIC

NOT MOVING
MOVING
DEAD

NOAHDANIELSMITH.COM

Pulp Fiction in chronological order, by Noah Smith. 2012. "I watched Pulp
Fiction four times in a row. First to just get the plot down, then pausing
the movie each time there was an important scene and marking down the
exact time and significance/location/character of the scene. I then created
the graphic off of my notes in forty-eight hours without sleeping." —Smith.
Courtesy of the artist. www.noahdanielsmith.com

"A Community of Characters": The Archetypes of *Pulp Fiction*

In *Pulp Fiction*, Quentin Tarantino constructs a three-story narrative wherein a character may be the focus of one story, a supporting player in another, and a background player in the third (as Vincent is); may pop in periodically in all three (as Marsellus does); or may function merely as a special guest star in one (like, say, Captain Koons). The script's first page brands the picture as "THREE STORIES . . . ABOUT ONE STORY...," which he explained in a 1994 interview. "When I finished the script I was so happy because you don't *feel* like you've seen three stories—and I've gone out of my way to make them three stories, with a prologue and an epilogue! They all have a beginning and an end. But you feel like you've seen one story about a community of characters, like *Nashville* or *Short Cuts*, where the stories are secondary. This is a much different approach—the stories are primary, not secondary, but the effect is the same."

Tarantino's characters are performers. If, as Richard Greene and K. Silem Mohammad assert in the introduction to their collection *Quentin Tarantino and Philosophy*, his films are "texts" that "flaunt their knowing enmeshment in and dependence on a multilayered network of texts," then the audience (and Tarantino himself) "must deal not only with what the characters think, say, and do, but with the way in which

they recall similar characters who have thought and said and done it all before."

So his characters are archetypes, but there is more to it than that—they're *self-aware* archetypes, conscious of their status as exemplars, and choosing to act in ways that either bolster or subvert that image. This awareness is a key component of the Tarantino playbook, which perches precariously between reality and performance. We don't tend to think of Tarantino's films as being all that naturalistic—which is not to say that they aren't *believable*. But his

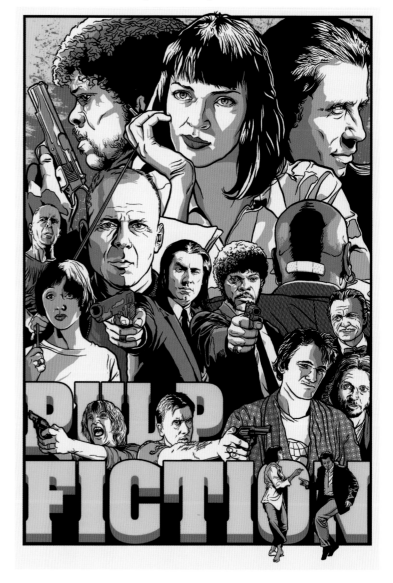

Pulp Fiction, by Joshua Budich. Screenprint, 2011. *Courtesy of the artist*

A *Community* of characters. *"Pulp Fiction?* Yeah, I saw it on an airplane. It's cute. It's a thirty-minute film about a group of friends who like cheeseburgers, dancing, and the Bible."—Community's Shirley, aka "Jules" (with Britta/Mia, Chang/Butch, and Annie/Yolanda). *Photo by Lewis Jacobs / NBC / NBCU Photo Bank via Getty Images*

aesthetic, a mosaic of callbacks and style and carefully studied cool, feels less like documentary than presentation, and the most relatable (and, on a personal level, authentic) moments in his films are those in which common concerns encroach on cinematic situations—for example, how *do* you dispose of a body and clean up the car it has sullied, on a practical, logistical level? (Not coincidentally, those moments are also his funniest.)

In other words, as a writer/director, Tarantino is also a performer—not surprising, considering that he was trained not as a filmmaker, but as an actor. That biographical fact would also seem to explain the wealth of performers in his films. From his first feature (*Reservoir Dogs*, with its extended acting class for undercover cop Freddy/Mr. Orange) to his most recent (*Django Unchained*, in which Dr. King Schultz carefully explains to his new partner Django that their work as bounty hunters involves "playing a character," and "during the act, you cannot break that character"), his creations are aware of their roles, and play them.

Vincent Vega: The Tough-Guy Softie

ARCHETYPAL PREDECESSORS: Ah Jong (Chow Yun-Fat) in *The Killer*; Charlie (Lee Marvin) in *The Killers*; Billy Score (Henry Silva) in *Sharkey's Machine*

What I'm always trying to do," Tarantino explained in 2012, "is get you to kind of like these guys, despite onscreen evidence that you shouldn't. Despite the things they do and say and despite their agenda." Nowhere in *Fiction* is this more evident than in the character of Vincent Vega, an unrepentant hit man and heroin addict who is nevertheless possibly the most sympathetic character in the film.

"What knocks me out," Tarantino noted, "is when people say to me, 'Oh, Travolta is so sweet, so lovable,' and I'm thinking to myself, *What?* I mean, he starts off the film by blowing these guys away and not giving a damn." In another interview, Tarantino expanded on this notion: "He's first presented as a hit man and that's never taken back. He is what he is, he is shown plying his trade, but then you get to know him above and beyond that."

And that's the key to Tarantino's approach to the character—and to all of his characters, who are presented within the crime film frame as (traditionally) cruel and sinful, but are revealed to possess great compassion and morality. For Vincent, that morality manifests itself in the key concepts of loyalty and honor to one's friends and employer, a notion he feels so strongly about that (in the abstract, at least) the punishment doled out to Tony Rocky Horror seems extreme, but acceptable. That abstract notion is put to the test by the undeniable chemistry he feels with Mia and is explicitly articulated in the pep talk he gives himself in the mirror of Mia's bathroom.

Vincent Vega, by James
Purcell. Acrylic, 2012.
Courtesy of the artist.
www.percyfunke.com

It's a test he passes. When he comes out of that bathroom, before he sees his date overdosed on the floor, he has already begun the process of excusing himself for the evening. That's when the night goes up in flames, sure, but perhaps to Vincent's ultimate benefit. "Mia takes Vincent on an emotional ride," Tarantino explained, "not just the fact that he's got to save her, but it's conceivable that, in a small way, Vincent's not quite the same guy after having lived through that night."

Jules Winnfield: The Badass

ARCHETYPAL PREDECESSORS: John Shaft (Richard Roundtree) in *Shaft*; Tommy Gibbs (Fred Williamson) in *Black Caesar* and *Hell Up in Harlem*; Frank Webster (Woody Strode) in *Man Hunt* (*La Mala Ordina*)

Tarantino's protagonists are always cool," writes James H. Spence in *Quentin Tarantino and Philosophy,* "much cooler than we are. They are confident, calm under pressure, articulate, and well dressed. Usually they are criminals." No Tarantino protagonist has fit this description as snugly as Jackson's Jules Winnfield, who is such a bad motherfucker that he even has a wallet identifying himself as such. He is a distinctly modern hit man (Lee Marvin and Charles Bronson certainly didn't have girlfriends who made them into de facto vegetarians), but a hit man nonetheless, and one who does his job with the flair and flourish of a great theatrical actor.

Jules is himself—jovial, personable, funny— in the post-credit sequence, as he and his partner Vincent drive to their assignment, gossiping and chitchatting on the way. But once it's time for the job to be done, he must don the persona

Jules' predecessor: Shaft. *Everett Collection*

Vincent and Jules take aim. *Courtesy of Miramax*

of the badass, and he cues Vincent to do the same with one of the film's most iconic lines: "C'mon. Let's get into character." Once they've entered the apartment of Brett and the gang, Jules delivers a carefully calculated performance. It begins on a note of painstakingly false friendliness, in which he's laying it on too thick, and he knows it, and he knows that they know it. Smiles and forced pleasantries are exchanged, food and drink are sampled, though with a force that seeps from hospitality into intimidation. That menace is made plain by the sudden volume and power of his blunt "I don't remember

asking you a goddamn thing!"—and though he immediately backs away from that fury, he has made it clear to the room what he is capable of. And in a few minutes, he will deliver on that promise.

To understand the degree of performance in this scene, it is instructive to observe the behavior not only of Jules, but of Vincent. He says few words in the scene, and the director mostly keeps him in the background, out of focus. Vince knows his role in this little playlet, and that role is to hang back. But watch what he does once Jules introduces Ezekiel 25:17 to the conversation: behind Brett, Vincent—taking the biblical attribution as a cue, as any good actor would—comes out of the kitchen, hits his mark behind the target, and cocks his pistol in anticipation of his next cue. As he waits, Jules' speech becomes more theatrical, taking on the cadences and musicality of a Baptist preacher, and when he reaches his conclusion ("I lay my vengeance upon thee"), Vincent takes his second cue, and joins Jules in blowing Mr. Big Brain Brett to high heaven.

More than any other character, this killer—and killer actor—will transform over the course of *Pulp Fiction*, the moments that follow this final performance of his Ezekiel scene transforming him from a cog in Marsellus' machine (and Tarantino's) to a free spirit. But we'll return to that later.

Say What Again, by JJ Adams. Acrylic on canvas, 2012. "The first time I saw *Pulp Fiction* I was high; I didn't understand a single word. Every word came out as a "blah" and I was glued to my seat. The Kahuna Burger scene lasted two hours and almost killed me. The second time I saw the film sober and it changed my life. Pure absolute genius." —Adams. *Courtesy of the artist and Art Rebellion*

Lost in Translation

The best-selling *Pulp Fiction* screenplay published by Miramax Books and Hyperion in December 1994 is pointedly dated and labeled "May 1993, Last Draft." But such a thing just plain doesn't exist; even with a film as impeccably scripted as this one, changes are made on set and in the editing room. The latter deviations are detailed in Part V, but a script-to-screen comparison reveals not only the expected rewordings and shortened exchanges, but several major alterations to *Pulp*'s "last draft."

- **Vincent and Jules at the door:** In the midst of the existing dialogue about Vincent's night with Mia, in which he insists it's "not a date" but merely "good company," in the screenplay he and Jules get into a rather heated discussion about his focus on the job at hand, with Jules imploring his partner to "stop thinkin' about that ho, and get yourself together like a qualified pro."

- **Opening hit, extended:** In the screenplay, Jules and Vincent's visit to Brett and the boys goes on much longer than in the final cut, where their execution of Brett fades out to the strains of "Let's Stay Together." The script continues through the emergence of the "fourth man" from the bathroom, blasting his "hand cannon" at Jules and Vincent and getting blown away. As a result, we rejoin the scene slightly later in "The Bonnie Situation," immediately before the recitation of Ezekiel 25:17. (Incidentally, the third story bears a different title in the screenplay: "Jules, Vincent, Jimmie, and the Wolf.")

- **Vincent visits Marsellus:** Somewhere between script and screen, Tarantino decided to add Jules ("our man in Inglewood") to the scene where Vincent delivers the briefcase to Marsellus and discusses his date with Mia with "English Bob"

(aka "Paul, and this shit's between y'all."). Jules isn't there in the scripted version, apparently having decided to start walking the earth *immediately*. The script also describes Vincent arriving for the meeting in his Malibu and parking it right next to Butch and Fabienne's Honda—raising the possibility that the "dickless piece of shit" who keyed the Malibu was, in fact, Butch (with whom Vincent would have just had the "you ain't my friend, palooka" confrontation).

- **Vincent's arrival:** The business with Mia and the intercom is not in the script. Instead, Mia greets Vincent through a crack in the door to her bedroom, where she is still dressing. Her full entrance is still carefully primed, though— the screenplay indicates that she is "naked with her back to us" during their brief conversation, and she is only seen in close-up glimpses as Vincent "contemplates what's on the other side of the door."

- **Ed Sullivan:** The faux-Sullivan maitre d' of Jackrabbit Slim's is nowhere to be found in the script—the scene begins, after (presumably) some establishing shots, with the two of them at their booth and Buddy taking their order. The twist contest that he hosts is also missing in action. Instead, Mia merely announces that she wants to dance, so they hit the floor among several other couples.

- **Jody:** She doesn't appear in the Vincent/Lance drug deal scene, and her button for the adrenaline shot is not "That was fuckin' trippy," but the far less memorable "Anybody want a beer?"

- **After the Fight:** The script includes a brief exchange between Esmerelda and Butch when he gets in the cab ("Are you the man I was supposed to pick up?") and some business with Marsellus and opposing fighter Floyd Ray Willis' trainer. Mia is present in the scene, but her dialogue thanking Vincent for dinner was apparently added in or ad-libbed.

- **French dialogue:** At the end of Butch's phone call with Scotty, he says to himself, in French with English subtitles, "Fabian my love, our adventure begins." (Fabienne's name is misspelled this way throughout the script.) While this was cut, it mirrors the subtitle-free dialogue she mutters later in the final cut, while Butch is giving her oral pleasure: "Butch my love, the adventure begins."

- **Butch's soliloquy:** Between the motel and his apartment, Butch gets out of the Honda and delivers a long monologue to himself, working through his decision to go back for the watch. "This is my war," he says. "The watch is a symbol. It's a symbol of how your father, and his father before him, and his father before him, distinguished themselves in war. And when I took Marsellus Wallace's money, I started a war." And so on. Tarantino seems to have wisely realized that this sort of thing is better left unsaid.

- **Racists at the pawnshop:** Intriguingly, none of the references to Marsellus as a "nigger," in either the Butch-Marsellus fight scene or during the Zed-Maynard strategizing, are in the script. Neither is Butch's echoing of Marsellus' "That's pride, fuckin' with you" speech during their fistfight.

- **Foreshadowing the Wolf:** At the end of the scripted version of the pawnshop basement scene, after Marsellus has sent Butch on his way, he picks up the phone, dials a number, and says, "Hello Mr. Wolf, it's Marsellus. Gotta bit of a situation."

- **More fun with Marvin:** In the script, Vincent first accidentally shoots Marvin in the neck, but wounds him so badly that he decides "the right thing to do" is to shoot him in the head and put him out of his misery. "I just want to apologize," he tells Marvin, before pulling the trigger again. "I want you to know I think it's fucked up."

- **A direr Bonnie situation:** On the phone with Jules, Marsellus indicates that there may be a need to "speak the unspeakable" if they don't hit their morning deadline, and Bonnie reacts badly. Jules isn't hearing it: "If push met shove, you know I'll take care of business. But push ain't never gonna meet shove."

- **Photo op:** The scenes at Jimmie's house end with an extra bit of business when Jimmie insists on taking a photograph of his three guests as a memento. "It's the only thing I asked," he says, insistent, and the trio obliges—with caveats. "I don't smile in pictures," the Wolf says.

- **Diner cuisine:** In the script, Vincent offers Jules some of his sausage, leading to the "pigs are filthy animals" conversation. For reasons unclear, his offer is changed to bacon.

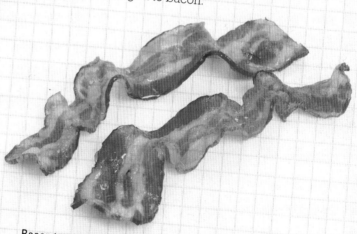

Bacon tastes good. *ElliotKo / Shutterstock.com*

- **Dream flash:** Between Pumpkin counting "two" and "three" in the Mexican standoff, the script indicates a *Reservoir Dogs*–style "everyone gets shot" outcome, which is then revealed to be Jules imagining how it could go. "Jules' eyes, still closed, suddenly open," reads the script, and the scene proceeds. Tarantino later said that he decided not to shoot this because he wanted to keep audiences anticipating such an outcome.

Mia Wallace: The Femme Fatale

ARCHETYPAL PREDECESSORS: Phyllis Dietrichson (Barbara Stanwyck) in *Double Indemnity*; Kitty Collins (Ava Gardner) in *The Killers*; Gilda (Rita Hayworth) in *Gilda*

Not since Harry Lime in *The Third Man* has a character been given so carefully prepared an entrance as Mia Wallace's. Vincent and Jules spend several minutes discussing how her feminine wiles spelled doom for Antwan Rockamora, and Vincent's continued insistence that his evening out with Mia is "not a date" is met with a cynical "Have you met Mia?" from English Bob, and cackling laughter from Jules. By the time *we* meet her, she'd better be something.

Ava Gardner as Kitty Collins, classic femme fatale—emphasis on the *fatale*. She declares, "I'm poison, Swede, to myself and everybody around me!" *John Kobal Foundation / Getty Images*

Miss Wallace, by Isabelle Dillard. Watercolor, gouache, and ink, 2012. *Courtesy of the artist.* ldillard.etsy.com

When she's finally introduced, Tarantino still holds back. Instead of revealing her face, he unveils her in tight close-ups—her back, her lips, and her feet, those troublesome, controversial feet. But the most intriguing close-up of her first scene is that of her hand on the joystick of her in-home surveillance system, about as broad a phallic symbol as you're going to encounter here. This is a woman who is accustomed to controlling her men as smoothly as that joystick, and usually via a similar apparatus.

The character of the married femme fatale who manipulates and ends the poor schmuck with the misfortune to fall for her is, true to Tarantino's initial equation, one of the oldest chestnuts in the book. But he doesn't write her with the purring slinkiness of those characters. She's more interesting than that, wielding her sexuality not as a weapon but as a matter of fact, less as currency than as a burden to bear, at least when it comes to the nattering of "you little scamps" that it provokes. She is one of Tarantino's richest characters, and one he was anxious to write after the estrogen-free *Reservoir Dogs*. While promoting that film, he promised reporters at the Toronto International Film Festival, "The script I'm doing now has probably the best character I've ever written, this female character who I'm proud of."

He was right to take that pride—Mia is a fast-talking, self-aware, rowdy firecracker, easily transcending her vampy setup. But let's not forget: she also could have put Vincent in the ground, and not just if that shot to the heart hadn't worked. Their evening was going in a very different direction before then, and any questions of Mia's receptiveness to those notions can be answered by one of the last things she says to Vincent: "I can keep a secret if you can."

Tarantino met Uma Thurman at Toi's restaurant on Sunset to discuss *Pulp Fiction*. Within moments of meeting her, he knew he'd found his Mia. *Courtesy of Miramax*

Butch Coolidge: The Boxer

ARCHETYPAL PREDECESSORS: Stoker (Robert Ryan) in *The Set-Up*; Billy Tully (Stacy Keach) in *Fat City*; Charley Davis (John Garfield) in *Body and Soul*

The first time we see down-and-out boxer Butch Coolidge, as he listens to Marsellus Wallace lecture him on his career and the fall he is going to take, he is lit in a manner that indicates a duality: half of his face in sharp, defined light, half in the dark. It's not the only time we see him like that; later in the film, when Tarantino flashes back to his childhood and shows us young Butch listening to another man's lengthy monologue, the sharply divided lighting scheme is replicated. We can presume this was done to connect us (at least subconsciously) to the character we've already met. But why is he lit like that in the first place?

The persona of Butch Coolidge, the heartless fighter, is one of (in Quentin's words) "a complete fucking asshole . . . I wanted him to be a bully and a jerk, except that when he's with his girlfriend Fabienne, he's a sweetheart." The contrast is sharp. His feelings about life and death are, to put it mildly, cavalier; he couldn't care less about the death of his opponent Floyd Wilson in the ring, guns down Vincent without a moment's thought, and is fully prepared to murder Marsellus with either his car (on the

Butch (Bruce Willis) and Fabienne (Maria de Medeiros). Said Willis, "Frankly, and I think all the actors would agree, we worked very hard to serve the original script, which is the complete opposite of what normally happens in films. Actors always try and change their lines." *Courtesy of Miramax*

PULP FACT 10

The film's main boxing bout is Wilson versus Coolidge—a match with a remarkably presidential ring, though Calvin Coolidge and Woodrow Wilson never faced each other in an election. The undercard match is Vossler versus Martinez, a reference to Tarantino and Avary's Video Archives coworkers, whose roommate fights were legendary at the store.

COOLIDGE VS WILSON

"THE MOMENT OF TRUTH"

THURS, JULY 16 DOORS OPEN 8PM

LOS ANGELES ARENA

"It's time, Butch." Butch Coolidge (Bruce Willis) is summoned to the ring by his trainer, Klondike (Sy Sher). *Courtesy of Miramax*

street) or Marsellus' pistol (in the pawnshop), in spite of the fact that he has wronged his potential victim. That's a different guy than the whisperer of lovey-dovey endearments who shares Fabienne's bed, and his double-cross is an attempt to leave Butch the jerk behind. "When he walks into that hotel room and closes that door," Tarantino would explain, "he's closing it on Butch forever, but she leaves that watch and it's like, 'I've got to be Butch one more time.'" He removes the button-up, collared shirt that he'd put on in anticipation of his and Fabienne's blueberry pancake breakfast (in the script, she instructs him to wear it with dress pants) and

returns to Butch's wardrobe (costume?) of jeans, jacket, and plain white T-shirt.

But in that one last run, Butch changes. His kindhearted and coldhearted selves merge, and the split personality is no longer necessary. In contrast to his murder of two men in the previous twenty-four hours, Butch performs an act of mercy and saves the life of Marsellus, a man who, just minutes earlier, he'd tried to kill. What happens? Perhaps it is merely the product of equalization; in a film filled with beholden relationships, matters of duty and obligation and debt, Butch and Marsellus are no longer servant and master, but are on equal footing and united against the

Butch's weapon of choice. *Vudhikrai / Shutterstock.com*

common enemy of their kidnappers. Or it could be a changing understanding of his world—in that moment of truth at the pawnshop door, with the Tennessee license plate on the wall behind him (and with his awareness of what it represents, as Knoxville is his rendezvous point with Scotty), Butch's idea of freedom changes. His getaway is no longer clean.

And it is in that moment that the true meaning of the gold watch that led him there comes into focus. Like his father, grandfather, and great-grandfather before him, Butch is now in a war, and in a war, you do not leave a man behind. As Jim Smith writes in his book *Tarantino*, Butch is "a man in a long line of self-sacrificing heroes. This means not only that the audience anticipates his later heroism but that the audience would be disappointed if it did not come about, and thus doubly rejoices when it does." Their excitement

Butch. From the series *Does he look like a bitch?*, by Jessica Gonzalez. Digital painting, 2012. *Courtesy of the artist. www. jessicaspitsfire.com*

is heightened by Butch's careful selection of the weapon for his quest, a choice summarized by Tarantino as: "I'm going to be a hero, which hero am I going to be? Who am I going to walk through the door as?" He first picks up a hammer, but that's not dramatic enough. Next he tries out the props of *Walking Tall*'s Bufurd Pusser (baseball bat) and *Texas Chainsaw Massacre*'s Leatherface (chainsaw), before settling on the samurai sword. "I'm gonna be Takakura Ken in *The Yakuza*," Tarantino-as-Butch explained. "That's the most honorable, and that's who I'm going to be." And that's what honor and morality are for Butch, and for all of Tarantino's characters: a choice, merely waiting to be made.

Taking Dictation: The Tarantino Dialogue

In 1992, talking about *Reservoir Dogs*, Tarantino described his writing process with words culled not from a writer's vocabulary but an actor's: "The characters improvise, and I'm like a court reporter writing it down. I get a chance to be both an actor and a director. As an actor I get to play all the characters, get them to work filmically, be rid of the extraneous stuff." In other discussions of the film, he drew the contrast between his experiences and those of other up-and-coming screenwriters more explicitly. "Look, I never went to writing school," he explained, "'Write a Screenplay in 27 Days,' Robert McKee or any of that nonsense. Everything I learned as an actor I completely applied to writing, and one of the things you get taught as an actor is, when I'm writing, I just get the characters talking to each other—whatever happens is what happens and what they say is what they say."

Butch 'n' Marsellus,
by Andrea Barbieri.
Digital art, 2012.
*Courtesy of the
artist,* © *2012
Andrea-barbieri.
artistwebsites.com.
All rights reserved.*

The approach makes sense, considering that Tarantino's first serious writing was scenes for his acting class. It's also part of why actors respond to his work with such enthusiasm and vie for the opportunity to say his words. "He has a great facility for writing natural dialogue," noted Samuel L. Jackson, who should know—he's mouthed Quentin's dialogue in six films and counting. "Even though these people are killers or misfits in society, they have real conversational things going on in their lives—like normal guys, normal people." Eric Stoltz echoed Jackson's endorsement of Tarantino's naturalistic dialogue: "The words just come out like real people talking, which is a relief, as an actor."

But it's not that simple, not exactly. On a *Siskel and Ebert* episode devoted to Tarantino's post-*Pulp* influence on cinema, Roger Ebert compared Tarantino's dialogue to David Mamet's, noting that both "superficially *sound* like realistic dialogue, but the closer you listen to it, the more you realize it's *written* dialogue. It's not recorded off the street; it's created as an imaginative work." In other words, Quentin's characters talk like real people—but better, more imaginatively, with more wit.

The impact of *Pulp Fiction* on American movies has been such that it's hard to gauge how subversive it seemed at the time. But as Ebert noted during that show, normal action movie dialogue of the era (for example, in the films of Sylvester Stallone, Arnold Schwarzenegger, and even *Pulp* star Willis) served one purpose and one purpose only: to advance the plot, preferably in as few words as possible, so the films were more easily exportable to lucrative international markets.

Tarantino's plots, though vital and carefully worked out, are not his primary concern. He is predominately interested in his characters.

His attitude towards them echoes the "cardinal principle" of the *Black Mask* magazines that provided *Pulp Fiction*'s inspiration, as articulated by founding editor Joseph Shaw in a 1946 anthology of stories from the publication. His writers "did not make their characters act and talk tough; they allowed them to. They gave the stories over to their characters, and kept themselves off the stage, as every writer of fiction should." Tarantino's attitude echoes this notion. "People come up to me and say, 'You write great dialogue,'" noted the normally immodest scribe, "and I feel like a fraud taking credit for it. It's the characters who write the dialogue. I just get them talking and I jot down what they say."

This loosey-goosey attitude also explains one of the trademarks of his writing. "As long as I care about the people and I know them," he explained, "they just go off. And that's why my dialogue is about things that don't have anything to do with anything. They'll go off and talk for ten minutes about Pam Grier. Or ten minutes about Madonna, or Coca-Cola, or macaroni and cheese. Like the conversations I have in real life."

He attributes this element of his writing to the oft-invoked influence of Elmore Leonard. "His books were the first books I ever read where the characters referred to other movies," he said in 1998, while promoting his Leonard adaptation *Jackie Brown*. "You know, two black guys in the welfare office talking about the movie they saw last night—they don't think they're doing a commentary on pop culture but they are." What was a minor touch for Leonard became a guiding principle for his young disciple. "People say, 'You talk about pop culture all the time,'" Tarantino said while promoting *Pulp Fiction*. "Well, it's a shared language that we all have. If you go to the movies over the weekend, when you come back in to work on Monday, you talk about what you saw."

Or you talk about what you observed in Amsterdam, and your upcoming date with the big man's wife. *Pulp Fiction*'s most famous dialogue scene, by a long shot, is the post-title sequence, with Jules and Vincent's celebrated

>>>> *Frame of Reference* <<<<

[Robert McKee]

Robert McKee is a screenwriting guru (played by Brian Cox in Spike Jonze and Charlie Kaufman's *Adaptation*) whose three-day Story Seminars attract legions of would-be screenwriters who plunk down big money for his guidance, in spite of the fact that his writing credits include one TV movie, a handful of television episodes, and no feature films. His books *Story* and *The Screenwriter's Problem Solver* emphasize the importance of formula and traditional structure, and the allegiance to this kind of gospel are why so much of modern studio filmmaking is so banal and predictable. In other words, it's the kind of thing *Pulp Fiction* flew in the face of, and part of why audiences responded to its freshness.

discussion of Amsterdam hash bars, Parisian McDonald's restaurants, and foot massages. It is not the kind of thing moviegoers were used to seeing from crime figures. Normally, two hit men on their way to execute a room full of men who'd crossed their boss would discuss the job at hand—what offense had been committed, how they were going to even the score, their thirst for revenge. These two barely touch on the specifics; we're left to piece together what's going on from throwaway mentions of "our guy"

I Can Keep a Secret if You Can, by Audrey Pongracz. Oil on canvas, 2011. *Courtesy of the artist*

and the insufficient firepower on hand. They're engaging in water-cooler talk. They're punching the clock with the same indifference as Ralph Wolf and Sam Sheepdog in the old *Looney Tunes* short.

That comic incongruity is present throughout Tarantino's writing. His lifelong interest in showing the scenes that other movies leave out translates to the juxtaposition of common human reactions with dramatic or cinematic situations. As a younger man, he watched *The Taking of Pelham 123* and wanted to see the scene where its crooks parceled out their color-coded nicknames; in *Reservoir Dogs*, he gave us that scene instead of showing the heist they pulled. Perhaps he watched *GoodFellas*, saw the aged enforcers pop Joe Pesci in the head, and wondered who had to clean up that mess; in *Pulp Fiction*, he made that kind of busywork the centerpiece of the third act. And he knows that the potential overdose of a gangster's wife would cause chaos in a drug dealer's household, but not so much that the dealer wouldn't argue with his wife over the location (and necessity) of a medical book, or that the dealer wouldn't apply pretzel-like logic to pass off the job of an adrenaline injection to the man who brought her there, or that said man might figure he should mark the location of her heart with a "big, fat Magic Marker," just to be safe. Whether we like to admit it or not, those might be our own reactions to finding ourselves in a situation as improbable as this one—and that may be why his dialogue *seems* so natural, because when we hear it, the visceral placement of ourselves (or people like us) into dangerous and charged scenarios like these is complete.

I've Been Sayin' That Shit For Years | Frequently Recurring Phrases

Additional unnecessary bathroom information
"I gotta take a squirt." (Mr. Pink, *Reservoir Dogs*) "I'm gonna take a piss"/ "I gotta take a shit." (Vincent Vega, *Pulp Fiction*) "I gotta drain the lizard." (Earl McGraw, *From Dusk Till Dawn*) "I'm just gonna go pee." (Simone, *Jackie Brown*)

Batman and the Riddler
"Riddle me this, Batman. If you're all so much in love with each other, what are you doing here?" (Clarence, *True Romance*) "Well, riddle me this, Batman. How do you feel about the fact that you're never gonna see Mallory again?" (Wayne Gayle, *Natural Born Killers*, original screenplay)

Childhood games made chilling
"Eanie, meanie, minie, mo, catch a redneck by the toe…" (Mallory Knox, *Natural Born Killers*, original screenplay) "Eanie, meanie, minie, mo, catch a nigger by his toe…" (Zed, *Pulp Fiction*)

Coasters for tasty beverages, by Kelly Puissegur. *Courtesy of the artist. retrowhale.com*

Drinks, Tasty
"You mind if I have some of your tasty beverage to wash this down with?" (Jules, *Pulp Fiction*)
"Whadaya say about the tasty beverage?" (Chester, *Four Rooms*)
"Now is that a tasty beverage or is that a tasty beverage?" (Warren, *Death Proof*) "Can I get you a tasty refreshment?" (Calvin Candie, *Django Unchained*)

Forward momentum of ramblers, The
"Okay ramblers, let's get ramblin'. Wait a minute, who didn't throw in?" (Joe Cabot, *Reservoir Dogs*) "Okay ramblers, let's get ramblin'." (Seth Gecko, *From Dusk Till Dawn*)

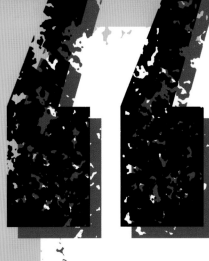

Go-to Madonna reference

"I like her early stuff. You know, 'Lucky Star,' 'Borderline'. . . ." (Mr. Blue, *Reservoir Dogs*) "I have a bit of a tummy, like Madonna when she did 'Lucky Star,' it's not the same thing." (Fabienne, *Pulp Fiction*)

Hey, that'd make a good movie title!

"I realized for the first time my one true calling in life. I'm a natural born killer." (Mickey Knox, *Natural Born Killers*, original screenplay) "Maybe Jordan isn't a natural born killer." (Lee Samuels, *Past Midnight*) "I'm calling you a killer. A natural born killer." (Bill, *Kill Bill Volume 2*)

A favorite of Mr. Brown's—and a favorite reference of Tarantino's. *Photo by Time Life Pictures / DMI / Time Life Pictures / Getty Images*

Mickey Knox (Woody Harrelson), a natural born killer.
© *DPA / Courtesy Everett Collection*

Hoyle

"Believe me when I tell you, it is in Mickey Knox's own best interest to play this game according to Hoyle." (Wayne Gayle, *Natural Born Killers*, original screenplay) "Whether or not what we experienced was an according-to-Hoyle miracle is insignificant." (Jules, *Pulp Fiction*)

Joe, diddle-eyed

"Grab yourself an egg roll. We got everything here from a diddle-eyed Joe to a damned-if-I-know." (Drexel Spivey, *True Romance*) "I'll bet you everything from a diddle-eyed Joe to a damned-if-I-know that in Milwaukee they got a sheet on this Mr. White motherfucker's ass." (Holdaway, *Reservoir Dogs*)

Importance of being cool

"I need you cool. Are you cool?" (Mr. White, *Reservoir Dogs*) "And that's what we're gonna be. We're gonna be cool." (Jules, *Pulp Fiction*) "Everybody be cool, this is a robbery!" (Pumpkin, *Pulp Fiction*) "Everybody be cool. You. Be cool." (Seth Gecko, *From Dusk Till Dawn*)

Importance of rule comprehension

"Rule number one: no noise. . . . Now are you absolutely, positively clear about rule number one?" (Seth Gecko, *From Dusk Till Dawn*) "Rule number one: no punching her. . . . Now, are we absolutely, positively clear on rule number one?" (Buck, *Kill Bill Volume 1*)

Lord's name in vain

"Don't blaspheme! . . . I said don't do that!" (Jules, *Pulp Fiction*) "Ain't no way I'm doing Ship's Mast. . . . Don't blaspheme!" (Kim, *Death Proof*)

Lost in chatter

"What the fuck was I talking about?" (Mr. Brown, *Reservoir Dogs*) "What the fuck was I saying?" (Chester, *Four Rooms*)

Names, Christian

"Under no circumstances do I want any one of you to relate to each other by your Christian names." (Joe Cabot, *Reservoir Dogs*) "If I had to guess, I'd say Beaumont's his Christian name." (Ordell, *Jackie Brown*)

Questions of pots and disposal

"I don't have a pot to piss in or a window to throw it out. All I've got is Floyd." (Dick Richie, *True Romance*) "Before I set that nigga up, he didn't have a pot to piss in or a window to throw it out." (Ordell, *Jackie Brown*)

Professionalism among thieves

"You're acting like a first-year fucking thief. I'm acting like a professional." (Mr. Pink, *Reservoir Dogs*) "This is not me! I am a professional thief." (Seth Gecko, *From Dusk Till Dawn*)

Sexual clarification

"Do I look like a beautiful blonde with big tits and an ass that tastes like French vanilla ice cream? . . . Then why are you telling me all this bullshit, huh? You wanna fuck me?" (Clarence, *True Romance*) "What does Marsellus Wallace look like? . . . Does he look like a bitch? Then why'd you try to fuck him like a bitch, Brett?" (Jules, *Pulp Fiction*)

Shit, repugnant

"I will never forgive your ass for this shit. This is some fucked-up, repugnant shit!" (Jules, *Pulp Fiction*) "Damn, girl, how you live like this? This some repugnant shit!" (Ordell, *Jackie Brown*)

Thirsts quenched

"That hit the spot!" (Jules, *Pulp Fiction*, after a long drink of Sprite) "That really hit the spot." (Luis, *Jackie Brown*, after a quick round of sex)

Giclée art print, 2012, by Amanda Maldonado of The Pressing Pigeon. *Courtesy of the artist*

PART III

Making *Fiction*

"An Epic in Everything but Budget"

In 1992, while promoting *Reservoir Dogs*, Quentin Tarantino talked about shooting one of the film's kinetic action sequences, in which Mr. Pink (Buscemi) runs from police, steals a car, and speeds away. "For a chase like that, you need to close down the street," he explained. "But we didn't have the money to do that." He walked Buscemi through the action thus: "Okay, what's going to happen is you're going to take the gun, you're going to empty it on the cops, you're going to jump in the car, and, if the light is green, you're going to drive away."

>>>> *Frame of Reference* <<<<

[Turnaround]

When a studio decides not to make a script or project that they've been developing, they will usually seek to sell it to another studio or production company and recover some (if not all) of their investment. The decision to pass on a film and shop it around—or allow its producers to do so—is called putting a project in turnaround.

"If the light is *green*?" Buscemi responded, incredulously.

Tarantino told the story with a grin and a shrug. "Hopefully, on the next movie we'll have more money."

With Tarantino's $900,000 fee for *Pulp Fiction* approaching the entire *Dogs* budget, more money was a pretty safe bet. What was less certain was that it was going to come from TriStar. Two days after Tarantino delivered his two-hundred-page opus, he was called in for a meeting with studio head Mike Medavoy and several junior executives. They weren't wild about the script, which Tarantino wanted to make for $8 million, "and they really couldn't lose on the film," he later surmised. "But they would have rather had me come to them with a star-driven piece of material that they could do for $25 million. I don't think they wanted to make a movie unless they thought it was going to make $100 million"—which, ironically enough, *Pulp* eventually would.

But the TriStar suits read the big set piece with Tarantino's protagonist lovingly shooting heroin, and they balked. The writer/director tried to assure them that the film would be funny, and fast, and hip, but they couldn't see

[Term Sheet]

A term sheet is something of a precontract for the negotiations of a movie deal (or any business deal, really), in which each party's terms are outlined and either negotiated or agreed upon. In the movie business, this is where preliminary financial details and overall creative power are (hopefully) settled.

it. Medavoy told his staff that the film was "too demented," and put it in turnaround.

Luckily, there was a receptive party on deck. Bender put the script in the hands of their old friend and *Reservoir Dogs* executive producer Richard Gladstein, who had left LIVE Entertainment for a post as head of production at Miramax. Gladstein read it and gave it to his boss, Harvey Weinstein, who was about to board a plane back to New York from Los Angeles. Weinstein called Gladstein three times from the plane as he worked his way through the screenplay, growing increasingly excited about it on each call. On the third, before he'd even finished, Weinstein gave word: "Buy the script, I'm making the movie."

Miramax had nearly made *True Romance* with Tony Scott, bailing when the budget got too high for their tastes (Weinstein and his brother, Bob, are credited as executive producers), and they had handled theatrical distribution for *Reservoir Dogs*. On that film, they'd seen the financial possibilities of being in what Harvey

Weinstein dubbed "the Quentin Tarantino business." Sure, the domestic grosses had underwhelmed, but it did bang-up business overseas, and Tarantino was proving a savvy self-marketer.

But first, the deal had to be made. Guaranteeing the film's $8 million budget would have been a stretch for Miramax, but the indie company's recent sale to the Walt Disney Corporation filled their coffers and gave them relative autonomy. Miramax matched the $900,000 TriStar fee and agreed to a budget of $8.5 million.

Tarantino was well aware that he was taking on a much bigger responsibility (and risk) with a budget that was roughly eight times that of his first film. But it was also a very different movie than *Reservoir Dogs*, which was small and intimate, set almost entirely on a single location. *Pulp Fiction* was vast. "This is supposed to be an epic," he said. "An epic in structure, an epic in scope, in intention. An epic in everything but budget." But he was determined to get bang for his buck: "I always wanna make sure I put the money on the screen." This time, that would mean a ten-week shoot (instead of *Dogs*' five) and a larger cast with bigger names.

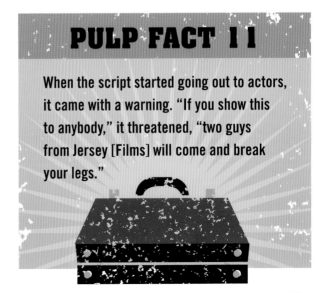

PULP FACT 11

When the script started going out to actors, it came with a warning. "If you show this to anybody," it threatened, "two guys from Jersey [Films] will come and break your legs."

One of those names was an early sticking point. Before official negotiations with Miramax began, Mike Simpson, Tarantino's agent, rustled up a counteroffer from a French production company, which gave him leverage when taking his client's term sheet to Miramax. Tarantino had four demands: a running time of up to 165 minutes, a back-end from first dollar of the gross, approval of the final edit, and the ability to cast, in his leading role, a name that hadn't even crossed Weinstein's mind.

Weinstein grumbled about each of the terms, complaining but accepting. He had a harder time backing down on the last one, though, insisting that he wasn't about to greenlight the film without a bigger name. He finally offered a compromise, telling Tarantino he would "consider" the actor, but refusing to lock him in.

The director wouldn't budge. He was prepared to walk, and when Weinstein realized that's what they'd come to, he gave in. But he didn't understand why Tarantino was being so dramatic about it. Why on Earth was he so worked up about a has-been like John Travolta?

"Let's Get into Character": Casting

Initially, Tarantino wasn't thinking of Travolta at all for the role of Vincent Vega. He had written it for Michael Madsen, who played Vic Vega (aka Mr. Blonde) in *Reservoir Dogs*; Vincent was presumably his brother. The meeting with Travolta was to discuss the role of Seth Gecko in Tarantino's old *From Dusk Till Dawn* script, which he was setting up for his festival circuit buddy, *El Mariachi* director Robert Rodriguez. But discussion of that potential project was also a pretense for Tarantino to meet one of his favorite actors.

There was a weird serendipity about the evening, which began before the men even met. As Travolta arrived at Tarantino's building, he realized that the director was living in the very same apartment where he had taken up residence upon his initial arrival in Los Angeles nearly twenty years earlier. The two hit it off immediately. At dinner, Tarantino casually mentioned that he collected pop culture artifacts, including the long-forgotten board games for Travolta's breakthrough TV show *Welcome Back, Kotter* and his movie *Grease*. Sounding less like Hollywood's hottest director and more like the kid in front of Connie's TV, Tarantino asked if Travolta wanted to play a game or two. "I was so touched by his infatuation with my career," the actor recalled, "that I went with it." Back at his apartment, Tarantino let Travolta take *Kotter*'s Vinnie Barbarino game piece, even though that was who he usually played.

But mostly they talked, until the small hours of the morning. Tarantino, never one to mince words, came at Travolta hard for his recent career choices, which included the talking-baby-turned-talking-dog franchise *Look Who's Talking* and troubled-teen fare like *Shout* and *Chains of Gold*. "Don't you remember what Pauline Kael said about you?" Tarantino charged. "Don't you know what you mean to the American cinema? John, what did you *do*?"

At first, Travolta was hurt. But then he realized what his longtime fan was driving at. "He's saying, 'I see what you are, and what you can be, and what you will be,'" Travolta realized, and he was so touched by the filmmaker's concern

Jackson in *Jungle Fever,* with Ruby Dee. *Mary Evans / Universal Pictures / Ronald Grant / Everett Collection*

that he wished he were more enthusiastic about *From Dusk Till Dawn.* "I'm just not into vampires," Travolta admitted. Tarantino didn't take it personally. "Well, we'll find something, someday." Over the course of that long night, he told Travolta about *Pulp Fiction,* but made it clear that he'd promised the role of Vincent to another actor. Travolta was disappointed but understood. Six months later, the *Pulp* script showed up at the actor's door. There was a handwritten note from Tarantino inside. "Look at Vincent," it read.

According to Eric Stoltz, this kind of extended casting courtship was par for the course in putting together *Pulp Fiction.* "It's really the best way to cast a film," he explained. "You want a cast and crew that you're gonna want to hang out with, and the only way to determine that is to hang out with them." Producer Lawrence Bender concurred: "What we were trying to do was find the group that really made the most sense because it's an ensemble piece. It's gotta be right because John is with Sam and John is with Uma and then John is with Eric, who's with Rosanna. There is a lot of interplay."

It was also important that the cast and director get along because, well, they certainly weren't getting rich on this one. All agreed to cut their fees in order to make the movie, to the same rate of $20,000 per week, with the larger roles making more simply by working more weeks. "Travolta, I think he worked seven weeks, so he made $140,000," Bender confirmed. "John used to laugh that by the time he rented his place at the Four Seasons Hotel he basically paid to be in the movie."

"Everybody made the same grade," Samuel L. Jackson confirmed. "At least, that's what they told me." To cushion the blow, Miramax offered each actor one point on the film's net profits, which they didn't think would amount to all that much.

Now that he had his Vincent, Tarantino needed a Jules. Luckily, he had one in mind when he wrote the script. Jackson had read for the role of Haldaway, Mr. Orange's undercover contact, when Tarantino and Bender took that Keitel-funded trip to New York while casting *Reservoir Dogs.* Jackson didn't land that part (he later said he didn't realize the bad actors he was reading with were the director and producer), but he did have a small yet memorable role, as Big Don, whom Gary Oldman's Drexl blows away early in *True Romance.* And he'd electrified audiences with his portrayal of cracked-out Gator in Spike Lee's *Jungle Fever* in 1991. The next time they ran into each other, Tarantino told Jackson he'd written something for him, and a copy of *Pulp Fiction* followed. Jackson read it cover to cover and then read it again, to make sure it was as good as he thought. It was.

But there was a hiccup. Tarantino and Bender had Jackson come in for what he thought was a casual reading, just to hear how

Contemplating the IFs

The *Pulp Fiction* ensemble has become so firmly entrenched in our moviegoing consciousness that it's hard to imagine anyone else playing those roles. But just for fun, let's try! Here are a few of the actors who got close to joining Tarantino's ensemble:

Vincent Vega: As mentioned, Tarantino wrote the role of Vincent Vega for Michael Madsen, who played Mr. Blonde in *Reservoir Dogs*. But Madsen ultimately passed, having already committed to appear in *Wyatt Earp* for director Lawrence Kasdan. (He would later reunite with Tarantino for *Kill Bill*.) Tarantino briefly flirted with the idea of moving Tim Roth into the role, casting Roth's pal Gary Oldman as Jules, and rewriting it as "two English guys," but his heart was set on Roth playing Pumpkin. Harvey Weinstein suggested Daniel Day-Lewis (who had won his first Oscar for the Miramax-distributed *My Left Foot*), and the actor wanted the role badly, but by then Tarantino had decided no one could play Vincent but John Travolta—not even Bruce Willis, who (according to Tarantino's agent, Mike Simpson) was initially incredulous about playing a supporting role: "Of course, Bruce is, 'What? I'm not going to play the lead? I'm going to be bound up by some hillbilly in a pawnshop so that *John Travolta* can be the lead?'"

Jules: Calderón's brush with the role of Jules has been well documented. Less known is Calderón's claim about Tarantino's *real* first choice for the role: "I took the material home, and the rhythms were similar to Laurence Fishburne, and Tarantino told me later Fishburne, whether it's true or not, turned it down."

Butch Coolidge: At the urging of Avary, Tarantino initially offered the role of Butch to Matt Dillon, who had launched a successful comeback as an indie leading man in Gus Van Sant's 1989 sleeper *Drugstore Cowboy*. But Dillon didn't accept immediately, asking for a day to think about it. Unluckily for him, that was the very same day that Tarantino met Willis at Keitel's barbecue.

Mia Wallace: Tarantino's first choice for the most hotly contested role in the movie was, believe it or not, *Red Sonja* star and Stallone ex-wife Brigitte Nielsen. This was back in 1991, when Tarantino was an unknown, *Pulp Fiction* was still an abstract, and Mia Wallace had not yet been written. Tarantino's friend Catalaine Knell (who had introduced him to Tony Scott, pre–*True Romance*) was friends with Nielsen, and Tarantino though her involvement could help get the low-budget short made. That never came to pass. (Knell's distinctive bob hairstyle, however, became part of the character, as it had in Scott's *Beverly Hills Cop II*, in which Nielsen wore a bob wig as part of a disguise.) Come 1993, the role could have gone to Michelle Pfeiffer or Meg Ryan (whose agents pitched them), Holly Hunter or Meg Tilly or Alfre Woodard (whom Tarantino considered), or Rosanna Arquette (who tested). But he went with Thurman and offered Arquette the role of Jody as a consolation prize.

Pulp Fiction was the start of a long collaboration between "Q and U." *Andrea Blanch / Getty Images*

Marsellus Wallace: Tarantino had toyed with the idea of casting Max Julien, who played the iconic role of Goldie in the blaxploitation classic *The Mack* (Drexl Spivey's background movie during Clarence's visit in *True Romance*), as the crime boss. But according to Jackson, the pawnshop rape was a sticking point. "Max Julien wasn't going to do that," Jackson told *Vanity Fair*. "He's the Mack. He's Goldie. He's like, 'No, I don't think my fans want to see that.'"

Jody: Ellen DeGeneres, who was trying at the time to transition from sitcom to film acting, came in and read for the role. So did Tarantino's idol Pam Grier, whom he almost cast in the role before deciding that no one would believe Stoltz could (or would) yell at her.

PULP FACT 12

Some interesting actors turn up in that first Ezekiel scene. Frank Whaley, who plays Brett, had a tiny role in *Natural Born Killers* as a cop tearing up at the memory of his Knox-slain partner. Burr Steers, who plays Roger (aka Flock of Seagulls), did voice-over work on *Reservoir Dogs* and would later become known as a filmmaker in his

own right, helming the 2002 film *Igby Goes Down* and the Zac Efron vehicles *17 Again* and *Charlie St. Cloud*. And the man in the bathroom, Alexis Arquette, is the sibling of *True Romance*'s Patricia and *Fiction*'s Rosanna Arquette.

The real Flock of Seagulls. *Ron Wolfson / WireImage / Getty Images*

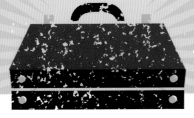

it sounded. Because he already had the role, Jackson didn't think much of it, reading the lines without much pizazz, then heading back to New York to shoot *Fresh* (also for Bender and Miramax). But when Paul Calderón came in to audition for a small role, he asked to read Jules. "All of a sudden Sam's job was not so damned secure," Tarantino explained. He and Bender decided to cast Calderón instead. When word got to Jackson, he hit the roof. "Nobody told me

I had to *audition*," he later explained. He went back loaded for bear, with full-tilt performances of both the initial "Ezekiel 25:17" speech and the closing scene. He got the role, again. "It was one of those Hollywood lessons," he reflected, "that you always have to do the things you do." Calderón was cast in the bit role of English Bob (aka Paul, as in "My name's Paul, and this shit's between y'all.").

Casting the role of Mia was nearly as complicated. It was a juicy female lead, and agents all over Hollywood were pitching their clients. One of those agents was Jay Moloney, who represented Uma Thurman, but Tarantino thought she wasn't right for it. Moloney went around him and set up a meeting anyway, via Tarantino's manager, and by the time Tarantino realized what had happened, it was too late to cancel. Tarantino kept the meeting—and the pair hit it off immediately. "Our first dinner together was like a dinner of two close friends," Thurman recalled. "He met me and thought he had met Mia." But

PULP FACT 13

A peculiar footnote about the casting of his lead couple: at Jackrabbit Slim's, they refer to each other as "cowboy" and "cowgirl." Travolta's last pre–*Look Who's Talking* hit had been *Urban Cowboy*; Thurman had just starred in Gus Van Sant's film version of *Even Cowgirls Get the Blues*.

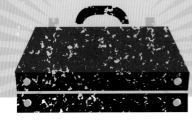

now Thurman wasn't so sure. She turned down the role; now she was convinced that she wasn't right for it. Tarantino wouldn't waver—he kept asking until she said yes.

Other actors fell into place more easily. By now it was assumed that there would be a role for Uncle Harvey Keitel, and Tarantino had him in mind when he wrote Mob fixer Winston Wolf. Around the same time as *Reservoir Dogs*, Keitel had made the Alan Rudolph thriller *Mortal Thoughts* with Bruce Willis and Demi Moore and had remained friends with them after. (Their kids played together.) When Tarantino was casting *Fiction*, Keitel invited him to a barbecue and introduced him to Willis, who was a huge

Reservoir Dogs fan. The actor had also gotten hold of the *Pulp* script and let Tarantino know he was available. "I didn't ask for any particular role," Willis said. "I left it up to him. I said whatever you want me to do, I'll do. I didn't flex. How much I was paid wasn't a consideration." That was an understatement—the entire budget for the film was smaller than Willis' paycheck for *Die Hard 2*.

Tarantino was excited to have him on board. "For me," he explained, "he's the only star of today who evokes the actors of the fifties, guys like Aldo Ray, Ralph Meeker, Cameron Mitchell, Brian Keith. . . . I told him that and he liked it, he understood the register he was going

Henry and June, 1990. Maria de Medeiros played Anaïs Nin; Thurman was the wife of Nin's lover Henry Miller. *Etienne George / RDS / Getty Images*

Signatures:
The Foot Fetish

One can't help but wonder if, at some point in the casting process, Tarantino had to take a look at Thurman's feet—just to be safe, since he would be showcasing them so prominently in the film. It would not be the last time a leading lady's tootsies would meet with the gaze of Tarantino's lens; in his first, unfinished film *My Best Friend's Birthday*, Tarantino himself admitted "I have a foot fetish," and his filmography backs up that claim impressively.

Pulp Fiction: Extensive discussion of Mia Wallace's feet in the post-title sequence is followed by close-ups of said bare feet when she makes her entrance. She also dances barefoot. Esmerelda Villalobos drives barefoot, information imparted courtesy of a close-up of her foot hitting the gas.

Four Rooms: Angela (Jennifer Beals) spends the entirety of Tarantino's segment lounging around his penthouse suite barefoot in a bathrobe.

From Dusk Till Dawn: As Tarantino's Richie Gecko lusts for hostage Kate Fuller (Juliette Lewis), we see close-ups of her bare feet. Later, exotic dancer Santanico Pandemonium (Salma Hayek) makes Richie (played by Tarantino—remember, he wrote this!) suck on her toes as part of her performance. She then pours tequila down her leg and into his mouth via her feet.

Jackie Brown: Bridget Fonda's "little surfer gal" Melanie is introduced with lingering close-ups on her toe-ringed bare feet. She later wears open-toe sandals while doing the money pickup in the department store dressing room.

Kill Bill, Volume 1: In the back seat of Bud's "Pussy Wagon," The Bride forces her lower body to come out of its four years of atrophy by commanding herself to "Wiggle your big toe"—a struggle illustrated with slow, loving close-ups. In the House of Blue Leaves sequence, there is a quick, appreciative cutaway of the bare feet of the female house band, the 5.6.7.8's.

Kill Bill, Volume 2: The Bride wears open-toe sandals in the flashback to her "wedding dress rehearsal." She loses her boots during her extraction from an early grave and battles Ellie Driver shoeless, squashing Driver's plucked eye between her toes.

Death Proof: The only film to date that Tarantino has photographed himself—and, rather unsurprisingly, his most foot-crazy as well. The opening credits intercut the bare feet of Arlene (Vanessa Ferlito) on Shanna's dashboard with Jungle Julia (Sydney Tamila Poitier) padding around her apartment barefoot; the latter's bare feet hang out the passenger window when Stuntman Mike (Kurt Russell) smashes into them. Later, Mike stops to ogle the bare feet of Abernathy (Rosario Dawson), who is sleeping in the back seat of a parked car. In a subsequent dialogue scene, while listing the limited sexual activity granted to a would-be paramour, Abernathy notes, "I've let him give me a foot massage."

Inglourious Basterds: "Put your foot in my lap," commands Colonel Hans Landa (Christoph Waltz) to Bridget von Hammersmark (Diane Kruger), so that he may try on, Cinderella-style, a discarded shoe. She complies, as we see in loving mediums and close-ups.

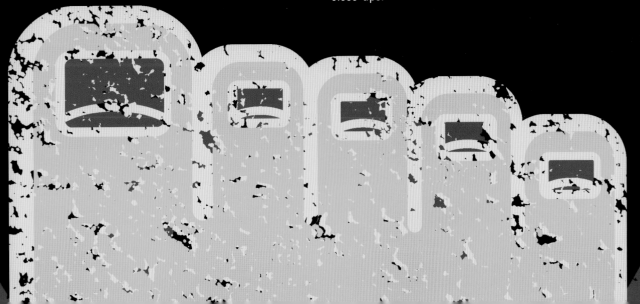

to act in." The boys at Miramax couldn't have been happier; because of Willis' involvement, they sold foreign rights for $11 million against the picture's $8.5 million budget, meaning it had gone into profit before the cameras even rolled.

Keitel's fellow *Reservoir Dog* Tim Roth was also lined up—again in a role Tarantino created especially for him—as was Roth's pal Amanda Plummer. Both came on board after hanging out with Tarantino at the premiere of Plummer's film *The Fisher King.* "It was a director's moment," Tarantino said. "I've got to put these two together in a movie." Roth agreed, but with a condition: "I want to work with Amanda in one of your movies, but she has to have a really, really big gun." Tarantino, needless to say, was happy to oblige.

Like Jackson, Ving Rhames (who had appeared in Tarantino's beloved *Casualties of War*) auditioned for the role of Haldaway in *Reservoir Dogs,* and like Jackson, he didn't get it. But he too was rewarded with a custom-made role in *Pulp Fiction.* "I'd written it with Ving in mind," he said of crime boss Marsellus Wallace. "I'd always heard his voice saying that dialogue.

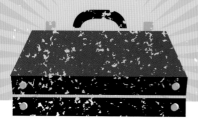
The words trickle off Ving's tongue because I wrote it for his cadence."

Tarantino met Maria de Medeiros (who'd costarred with Thurman in the 1990 drama *Henry and June,* the first movie rated NC-17) while in New York for the East Coast premiere of *Reservoir Dogs,* and after two more encounters on the European festival tour, he decided to rewrite "the girl" in the middle section for her. At another festival, he saw a short film called *Curdled,* in which Angela Jones plays a woman obsessed with death and the logistics of cleaning up after it. That short inspired Jones' character of Esmerelda Villalobos—and, to some extent, "The Bonnie Situation"—in *Fiction.* (Quentin would repay the debt by executive-producing a 1996 feature film version of *Curdled.*)

Christopher Walken's single scene in *True Romance* had been that film's highlight, so he was a no-brainer for the one-scene monologue role of Captain Koons. "He's just so good at doing monologues, about the best guy there is

>>>> *Frame of Reference* <<<<

[The Groundlings]

The Groundlings are a Los Angeles-based improv and sketch comedy troupe/school that served as training ground for a remarkable number of comic stars, including Will Ferrell, Phil Hartman, Kristen Wiig, Laraine Newman, Lisa Kudrow, Paul Reubens, Jon Lovitz, Maya Rudolph, Tim Matheson, and Melissa McCarthy.

© David Crausby / Alamy

© David Crausby / Alamy

at it," Tarantino explained, "and that's why he did the movie, because he doesn't get the chance to do three-page monologues in movies knowing it's not gonna be cut."

Tarantino met Stoltz at Sundance '92, via an introduction from Roth, who was working with Stoltz on the film *Bodies, Rest and Motion*. Over a year later, they ran into each other on New York's Upper West Side. The director dragged Stoltz to a phone booth and put him on the horn with Roger Avary, who wanted Stoltz to play the lead in his film *Killing Zoe*. After the call, the actor made a deal with Tarantino: he'd do *Zoe* if Tarantino would do a cameo in *Sleep with Me*, an indie rom-com he was producing and starring in. Tarantino worked Stoltz doing a small role in *Pulp Fiction* into the bargain, and they shook on it.

He had Stoltz in mind for one of the bathrobe roles: either Vincent's drug dealer buddy, Lance, or Jules' domesticated pal Jimmie, whichever one Tarantino decided not to play. Ultimately, he had Stoltz take Lance, because he wanted to be able to focus behind the camera during the

shooting of the adrenaline shot sequence, and cast himself as Jimmie. ("Did you sleep with the director?" asked Jon Stewart a few months later. "I gave him a hand job," Tarantino replied, "every night!")

Smaller roles fell into place. Tarantino's friend, *Saturday Night Live* cast member Julia Sweeney, had him do a one-week, $100,000 rewrite of the script to her ill-fated spinoff film *It's Pat* during *Pulp* preproduction. In turn, she took the role of Raquel, heir to the Monster Joe's Truck and Tow dynasty. Her then-husband, fellow Groundlings alum Stephen Hibbert, played the Gimp, with the Groundlings also yielding Phil LaMarr (Marvin) and Kathy Griffin (traffic accident onlooker). Steve Buscemi had to turn down a large role due to other commitments, but he did

PULP FACT 15

Laura is the sister of Grace Lovelace, Tarantino's longtime on-again, off-again girlfriend. He named Zed's chopper after Grace, though some choose to read its name as an abstract idea rather than an actual moniker.

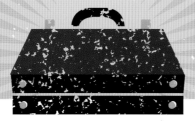

a day of work as a Buddy Holly–inspired waiter at Jackrabbit Slim's. Video Archives coworker Linda Kaye, who appeared in *My Best Friend's Birthday* (as "Ex-Girlfriend") and *Reservoir Dogs* (as the "Shocked Woman" pulled from her car by Mr. Pink), was here cast as the "Shot Woman"—plugged in the aftermath of Butch and Marsellus' car wreck. Another former coworker and previous bit player, Rich Turner, voiced one of the radio sportscasters; the other was voiced by Richard Ruth, the "shot cop" from *Reservoir Dogs* who also played *Pulp Fiction*'s coffee shop manager. Producer Bender took two small roles, as a bystander in the coffee shop and as a waiter (in a Zorro costume) at Jackrabbit Slim's. And music consultant Laura Lovelace played the coffee shop waitress whom Pumpkin erroneously calls "Garçon"—which, as we all know, means "boy."

His cast was in place. Now it was time to go to work.

Pulp Production

Before the cameras rolled in the fall of 1993 on Quentin Tarantino's second film, he wanted to try something that was quite out of the ordinary for Hollywood: a rehearsal period. While most directors don't get the opportunity to work their scenes until they're on the set, Tarantino

PULP FACT 16

One of the props came directly from Tarantino's script: Vincent's toilet reading, *Modesty Blaise*, the first in a series of pulp books adapted from the British comic strip. The title character wasn't far removed from Mia's *Fox Force Five* character, or The Bride—Modesty was a resourceful and occasionally deadly young woman with a sketchy past. After *Pulp*'s success, Miramax bought the film rights to the series, hoping it would be a franchise for Tarantino and Thurman. They never made the films, but Tarantino's old friend Scott Spiegel—responsible for his crucial introduction to Bender—made a direct-to-DVD 2003 adaptation called *My Name is Modesty*, for which Tarantino was executive producer.

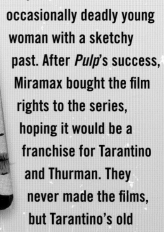

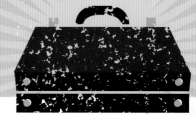

managed to lock in his cast for ten days of pre-shoot, late-summer rehearsal. "We spent several days in that room at Jersey Films," recalled Thurman, "a studio like a huge garage, we sat there at a card table in the middle of the room and worked and worked and loved it."

She and Tarantino blocked out her Tasmanian devil–style resurrection from the adrenaline shot. She and Travolta met with Tarantino's old acting school buddy Craig Hamann, whom he'd brought in as an informal "drug adviser," walking Thurman through her overdose and showing Travolta how to shoot up convincingly. Travolta convinced his director to modify Marvin's death from an accidental shot to the throat and mercy shot to the head to just an accidental head shot. He also suggested a slight alteration to Vincent's reaction: "I changed the line from 'Oh, I shot him,' to 'Oh, I just shot Marvin in the face,' which made it funny. Using the

Marsellus. From the series *Does he look like a bitch?,* by Jessica Gonzalez. Digital painting, 2012. *Courtesy of the artist. www. jessicaspitsfire.com*

Tarantino directs on the streets of Los Angeles, autumn 1993. Producer Lawrence Bender (left) looks on. *Courtesy of Miramax*

Opposite: Tarantino works out blocking with Amanda Plummer at the shoot's first location, the Hawthorne Grill in West L.A. *Courtesy of Miramax*

word 'face' and using his name, Marvin, made it personal, like I had just stepped on his toe."

Tarantino had his director of photography, Andrzej Sekula, sit in on the rehearsals as well, since, according to Roth, "While he's watching rehearsals, he's picking his shots." Extras were cast, with the August 25 *Hollywood Reporter* carrying a call for fifties icon look-alikes. And Tarantino again went to the KNB EFX group, which had given him his first writing job, to provide practical effects: a corpse for Marvin, blood and guts for the pawnshop rape scene, a phony syringe for Travolta to shoot up with, and a fake chest piece to go over Thurman for the adrenaline shot scene. Props were assembled, with special attention given to the drug paraphernalia; according to Thurman, they used sugar for cocaine, brown sugar for heroin, and Campbell's mushroom soup for the spittle that comes out of her mouth when Vincent finds her on the living room floor.

Costume designer Betsy Heimann found costumes for Mia and Vincent at the clothing chain Agnès B., while Jules' suit came from Perry Ellis. One costume proved harder to come by: the leather bondage suit for the Gimp. Heimann ultimately had to pick one of those up at a West Hollywood sex store called the Pleasure Chest. Tarantino brought Heimann the "Orby" T-shirt he wanted to wear under his bathrobe; Orby was the mascot of the Detroit alt-weekly *Orbit*, and the T-shirt had been given to him by *Orbit* contributor Paul Zimmerman. Tarantino had promised him it would show up in his next movie.

For more cosmetic concerns, there were hair and piercings to consider. For the latter, Travolta and Arquette went the clip-on route, while Rhames used the piercing he already had in his left ear. (They decided to cover the scar on the back of his neck with a Band-Aid, a decision that would have some ramifications once the film entered its hyperanalyzed phase.) Vincent's hair extensions were Travolta's idea—a "Euro haircut," he explained, "which is sometimes Eurotrash and sometimes elegant"—while Thurman was given a wig that properly echoed the looks of Louise Brooks in *Pandora's Box*, Anna

Karina in *A Woman Is a Woman*, and Melanie Griffith in *Something Wild*.

There was a fortuitous mistake when it came to Jules. Jackson always wore his hair shaved or clipper-short, but Tarantino wanted Jules to have an Afro. "I've always liked Afros," he explained. Jackson was down, but destiny intervened. "The makeup woman went out to get some Afro wigs," Tarantino recalled, "but because she didn't know the difference she also showed up with the Jheri curl wig. Sam put it on, and it was great, it was Jules." Jackson liked the look—he felt that it bridged the gap between the classic movie gangster of the black suit and the more modern California gangsta style personified by rap groups like N.W.A., who all wore Jheri curls.

Finally, at the end of the rehearsal period, Tarantino and his cast went out for a big kickoff dinner, taking over the back room of a Hollywood restaurant for upwards of five hours, hanging out, drinking, joking, and getting ready for the ten weeks ahead of them. Quentin was ready. It was the movie he'd been working towards his whole life.

>>>> *Frame of Reference* <<<<

[Video Playback]

Video playback is a line that runs from the camera to a video monitor, allowing the director to see what the camera sees, often from a tent or bank of monitors dubbed "video village." This technique was developed in the 1960s by Jerry Lewis, so he could better judge his own performances when directing his comedies.

Principal photography of *Pulp Fiction* commenced on September 20, 1993, with much of Tarantino's *Reservoir Dogs* crew intact. The first scene shot was the first scene in the film (a fairly unusual occurrence): the prologue with Pumpkin and Honey Bunny plotting to rob the diner/coffee shop, shot at the Hawthorne Grill in west Los Angeles.

By all accounts, it was a smooth, energetic, and happy production—for everyone but cinematographer Sekula, who shattered his leg in a car accident halfway through the shoot and had to work the back half of the show in a wheelchair. Tarantino would recall spending the time on "a creative and imaginative high. I was just living my dream." During the shoot, he charmed a visiting reporter with his habit of eschewing the traditional "Cut" for more enthusiastic responses ("We're loving it!"), and of making his encyclopedic film knowledge part of his direct interaction with actors ("The camera's right on you. You're Robert Mitchum in *Thunder Road*").

Tarantino went without the industry standard video playback monitor—he didn't want anything getting between him and his cast. His excitement was a major factor of the high-spirited set, according to Jackson: "Quentin has an energy about him that's very wild and open, that just has a way of transferring to everyone else. He's so excited about seeing his words come to life, it's contagious. It turns out to be a real productive energy."

Much of the work was done in a giant warehouse in Culver City, which housed not only the production offices, but also the sets for the pawnshop basement, the boxers' dressing rooms, Butch and Fabienne's motel room, and Brett's

Red Line 7000, the 1965 Howard Hawks film that influenced Jackrabbit Slim's décor and vibe. *Everett Collection*

apartment. (The high ceilings of the warehouse help explain the echoed quality of some of the dialogue, particularly Jackson and Willis' angriest, top-volume lines.) That giant warehouse also gave them plenty of room to build the film's most famous set, Jackrabbit Slim's restaurant.

The restaurant's exteriors were shot at a re-dressed, out-of-business bowling alley, but nothing on this Earth remotely resembled the ultimate fifties diner in Tarantino's head. The set devised by production designer David Wasco and set decorator Sandy Reynolds-Wasco took up 25,000 square feet of the warehouse (and a significant portion of the picture's budget). Tarantino suggested an automotive theme and had movies for them to watch: the late period Howard Hawks film *Red Line 7000* and the Elvis Presley vehicle *Speedway,* which both had elements that were worked into the set.

There was a lot happening on the Jackrabbit Slim's set, from the countless look-alikes (Sullivan and Nelson, Martin and Lewis,

PULP FACT 17

While they were shooting Mia's description of her ill-fated TV series *Fox Force Five,* Tarantino got the idea of another vehicle for Thurman, an action film centered on a similar group of deadly women. He wrote the first thirty pages, then put it away for several years. But one day they would return to that project, which he dubbed *Kill Bill.*

I Want That Trophy, by George Ioannou. Acrylic on canvas, 2006. "I went to the cinema with a conventional attitude and left with my eyes wide open to new possibilities. *Pulp Fiction* had ripped up the rulebooks of structure and given me a whole new thought process. It dared to be bold and in your face without apologizing for its violent subject matter that was rendered with clever dialogue and slick characters. I decided that my art was going to be no different." —Ioannou. *Courtesy of the artist and Art Rebellion*

and, as Vincent points out, both Mamie Van Doren and Marilyn Monroe) to the B-movie posters (painstakingly selected by Quentin himself) to the raised stage, which was shaped and painted like an automobile tachometer. There was Buscemi, once the tip-resistant Mr. Pink, now on the other side of the transaction as a waiter ("I think Quentin should do a cutaway to show that I don't get a tip," he joked). And there was the shooting of what would become an iconic sequence: the twist of Vincent Vega and Marsellus Wallace's wife.

Though the scene was written before Travolta was cast, both he and his director

were well aware of the cultural baggage the *Saturday Night Fever* star brought to the scene. "There must be something with me and that form that communicates, you know, it's just a kick," Travolta shrugged.

"I had a very specific, severe twist in mind," Tarantino recalled. He showed Travolta what he wanted, which tickled the actor to no end—"It was like watching a twelve-year-old at his first dance," Travolta laughed. Travolta had some ideas of his own for the scene. "I said, 'Well, Little Johnny Travolta won the twist contest when I was eight years old, so I know every version. But you may add other novelty dances that were very special in the day.' He said, 'What do you mean?' I said, 'There was the Batman, the Hitchhiker, the Swim, as well as the twist.' And I showed them to him, and he loved them. I said, 'I'll teach Uma the steps, and when you want to see a different step, call it out.'"

But his costar was getting a case of cold feet. She was worried about looking silly next to a legendary hoofer like Travolta. Unsurprisingly, Tarantino was able to calm her nerves with a movie clip: the dance scene from his dear *Bande à Part*, which was less about technical dancing skill than freedom and enjoyment. It put Uma at ease—as did her director's willingness to cut a rug first. At the end of the day of shooting, Tarantino applauded his stars. "For thirteen hours," he told them, "you have completely captivated us."

Travolta wasn't the only legend on the *Pulp* set. While promoting *Reservoir Dogs* in Japan, Quentin had finally met his idol Sonny Chiba (whom he name-checked in *True Romance*) and invited Chiba to visit the *Pulp* set if he found himself in Los Angeles. He did—and significantly enough, he stopped in on the day that Jackson was shooting his "Ezekiel 25:17" monologue in Brett's apartment, a scene directly inspired by Chiba's work. "And it was like so cool," Quentin recalled, "because Sam is always real cool, nothing affects him or anything like that. He was *affected* by seeing Sonny Chiba."

Night shoots are always a bit of trip for film crews, something of a vampire existence, up while the world is asleep, which only made the shooting of the "adrenaline shot" sequence all the more surreal. "The crew always gets tired,"

A long and fruitful collaboration: Writer/director Quentin Tarantino and producer Lawrence Bender, on the Jack Rabbit Slim's set. *Courtesy of Miramax*

noted Stoltz, "but I always feel like we're a bunch of criminals doing vaguely illegal things, so I'm wide awake." Tarantino, ever the board game enthusiast, tucked two wittily appropriate ones (Life and Operation) into Lance and Jody's living room, while giving a shout-out to his production designer with the brand name of the adrenaline shot (WascoMed).

Travolta drove Quentin's own Malibu—the one he'd bought with his *Natural Born Killers* money—and the scene was framed so that it wouldn't be wrecked: one Malibu drives by Lance's front door, but another was preset in the crash position outside the house. (If you look closely, you can see tire tracks in the grass where the action car swerves around the pre-set one.) When the time came to shoot the administration of the adrenaline shot, Tarantino decided to dispense with the false chest and go low-tech: they did the action in reverse, with Travolta pulling his hand away from Thurman's chest, and then ran the film backwards.

Christopher Walken's scene was shot on the last day of production, November 30, 1993. "We started shooting at about eight in the morning," Walken recalled. "Everybody had gone home. It was just a small crew in a house out somewhere, with me, the little boy, and his mother."

"It felt like we made three different movies," Tarantino said, "and then made this little short film on the last day." The Oscar-winning actor "knew the monologue word for word, perfectly," according to the filmmaker, but crew members noticed his peculiar choice of tasty beverage: between scenes, he was drinking Tabasco sauce. It wasn't Method madness,

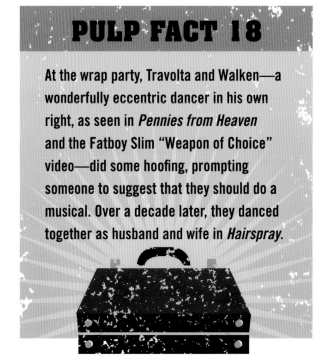

PULP FACT 18

At the wrap party, Travolta and Walken—a wonderfully eccentric dancer in his own right, as seen in *Pennies from Heaven* and the Fatboy Slim "Weapon of Choice" video—did some hoofing, prompting someone to suggest that they should do a musical. Over a decade later, they danced together as husband and wife in *Hairspray*.

or Walken weirdness. Because his director was letting him do the two-page monologue straight through, drinking the Tabasco helped him keep his mouth lubricated during the long speech.

By the end of the day, Walken recalled, "The little boy was getting sleepy, and I just did the rest into the lens." They did about fourteen takes, changing the shot size and intention slightly from take to take, and that was a wrap on *Pulp Fiction*. The cast and crew held the wrap party at the best dive in town: the set of Jackrabbit Slim's.

"It was so much fun," Stoltz recalls. "It's exactly what you wish your work experience would be like, every time." His onscreen wife, Arquette, agrees. "It's the way movies should be made."

Quentin's longtime editor, Sally Menke, finished the rough cut by Christmas. It ran three and a half hours. They still had some work to do.

L.A. Privileges: Los Angeles As City and Character

Though born in Knoxville, Tennessee, Tarantino is an L.A. guy. His mother took him to California when he was two and a half, and he didn't leave for decades. The story goes that when he went to Utah in January of 1992 for the Sundance premiere of *Reservoir Dogs*, he had never seen snow. A LIVE Entertainment executive, perturbed by the sight of her filmmaker wandering through the snowy Park City streets in a T-shirt, finally bought him a parka.

The Californian would make up for years of lost travel time and cultural education by seeing the world while working the festival circuit with *Reservoir Dogs* (and later, promoting its international release). The insights and observations of this Los Angelino abroad worked their way into the *Pulp Fiction* screenplay, mostly for comic effect, but they don't feel like the kind of disconnected chat-for-chat's-sake dialogue that Tarantino's imitators would create; they're all of a piece with the film, which is in many ways a valentine to the City of Angels.

(continued on page 104)

The City of Angels (more specifically, Beverly Hills, where Marcellus and Mia Wallace live).
© *ZUMA Wire Service / Alamy*

JULIA SWEENEY | Raquel

PULP CREDITS

When you think of funny closing credits, you usually think of films like *Airplane!* ("Author of *A Tale of Two Cities*: Charles Dickens") or *Hot Shots!* (which includes two recipes and a list of "things to do after the movie"). But *Pulp Fiction* has some pretty wacky credits— you just have to look closely for them.

KATHY GRIFFIN

In the screenplay, her two-line character is listed as "Gawker #2." But the end credits read "Kathy Griffin: Herself"—an amusing credit, considering that Griffin was still an unknown when the film was released (her breakthrough role on *Suddenly Susan* was two years away) and not yet the self-proclaimed "D-Lister" that would get such a listing.

"LONG HAIR YUPPY SCUM"

Producer Bender, an extra in the coffee shop scene who is accosted by Pumpkin, is credited as "long-hair yuppy scum." The credit stuck—he played the same "role" in his cameos in *Fresh* (1994) and *Four Rooms* (1995).

AN ACTOR PLAYING A COFFEE SHOP

Robert Ruth plays the role of the coffee shop manager. But when he explains that he is just that (and not a hero), he is cut off by Roth; thus, he says "I'm just a coffee shop—" and finishes the line after a beat. But the credits take him for his words; Ruth is credited as "Coffee Shop."

EMIL SITKA

The great character actor and foil is seen on a television at Lance's house, where his scene in the Three Stooges short "A Brideless Groom" (one of their most widely seen, since it's one of four that fell into the public domain) is playing as the phone rings. He's seen saying "Hold hands, you lovebirds," so that's how he's credited in the final roll: Not as himself (like Griffin), or "Actor on Television," but as "Hold Hands You Lovebirds."

A TARANTINO FAN

Here's one way to keep getting work. One of the drivers, Earl Thielen, was a *Reservoir Dogs* aficionado and asked to be credited as Earl "Mr. Blonde" Thielen. Tarantino was apparently tickled; Thielen worked in the transportation departments of *From Dusk Till Dawn* and *Jackie Brown* as well, and took the same credit in those films.

Production Manager | PAUL HELLERMAN

TARANTINO'S L.A.

BEVERLY HILLS:

1 Marcellus and Mia Wallace's house, *Pulp Fiction*.
1541 Summitridge Dr.

BURBANK:

2 Karina's Jewelry Store, *Reservoir Dogs*.
2612 W. Burbank Blvd.

3 Safari Inn, Clarence and Alabama's hotel, *True Romance*.
1911 West Olive Ave.

CANOGA PARK:

4 Maynard's Pawn Shop, *Pulp Fiction*.
Crown Pawn Shop, 20933 Roscoe Blvd.

CARSON (south of Los Angeles):

5 Cherry Bail Bonds, *Jackie Brown*.
Carson Bail Bonds, 724 E. Carson St.

COMPTON:

6 Where Ordell has both Simone (off Florence Blvd.) and
Sharonda "set up," *Jackie Brown*.

EAGLE ROCK (northeast of downtown Los Angeles):

7 The pre-heist diner, *Reservoir Dogs*.
Pat and Lorraine's, 4720 Eagle Rock Blvd.

GLENDALE:

8 Butch and Fabienne's motel, *Pulp Fiction*.
River Glen Motel (now demolished), 2934 Riverside Dr.

9 Jackrabbit Slim's exterior, *Pulp Fiction*.
Re-dressed Grand Central Bowl, 1435 Flower St.

HAWTHORNE:

10 Diner in opening and closing scenes, *Pulp Fiction*.
Hawthorne Grill (now demolished), 13763 S. Hawthorne Blvd.

11 Cockatoo Inn, *Jackie Brown*. Jackie's favorite hangout, two
minutes from her home, ten minutes from Los Angeles
International Airport (LAX), at 4334 West Imperial Hwy. at
Hawthorne Blvd.

HERMOSA BEACH:

12 Melanie's apartment, *Jackie Brown*.

HOLLYWOOD:

13 Vista Theatre, home of the Sonny Chiba triple feature,
True Romance.
Scene is set in Detroit, but shot at 4473 Sunset Dr.

14 Brett's apartment building, *Pulp Fiction*.
Now demolished, the building stood at Van Ness Ave. and
Harold Way, just north of Sunset Blvd.

15 Lance's house, *Pulp Fiction*.
3519 La Clede Ave, Atwater Village.

16 Hotel Mon Signor, *Four Rooms*. Exteriors shot at the famed
Chateau Marmont, 8821 Sunset Blvd.

INGLEWOOD:

17 Where Jules lays his head, according to dialogue.
"The sticks," according to the Wolf.

LANCASTER:

18 Two Pines Wedding Chapel, *Kill Bill Volume 2*.
Scene is set in El Paso, Texas, but shot at the Calvary
Baptist Church, 198th Street East and East Avenue G.

LOS ANGELES:

19 The rendezvous warehouse, *Reservoir Dogs*.
Mr. Orange's apartment was also shot at this now-destroyed
building, 5860 Figueroa Blvd.

20 Mr. Orange and Haldaway's meeting place, *Reservoir Dogs*.
Johnie's Coffee Shop, 6101 Wilshire Blvd.

21 Mr. Brown crashes, Mr. White shoots cops, *Reservoir Dogs*.
Alley at 5522 Marmion Way.

22 Mr. Pink makes his getaway, *Reservoir Dogs*.
York Blvd and N. Ave. 51.

23 Mr. Orange and Haldaway rehearse, *Reservoir Dogs*.
Junction of Beverly Blvd., Second St., and Toluca St.

24 Clarence nurses Alabama's wounds, *True Romance*.
Construction site near LAX, 1 World Way

25 Lee Donowitz' suite, The Beverly Ambassador, *True Romance*.
Ambassador Hotel (now demolished), 3400 Wilshire Blvd.

26 Butch hits Marcellus with Fabienne's Honda, *Pulp Fiction*.
Corner of Atwater and Fletcher Dr.

27 Ordell's alibi strip bar, *Jackie Brown*.
Sam's Hofbrau, 1751 East Olympic Blvd. (also used for the
interiors of the "My Oh My Club" in *Kill Bill Volume 2*)

28 Los Angeles International Airport, *Jackie Brown*.
Where Jackie works, and is busted by the ATF (in the parking
garage). 1 World Way.

PASADENA:

29 Boxing arena, *Pulp Fiction*. Shot in front of the
now-destroyed Raymond Theater, 129 N. Raymond Ave.

30 Vernita's house, *Kill Bill Volume 1*. 5506 Atlas St.

31 The Bride's hospital, *Kill Bill Volume 1*.
St. Luke's Medical Center (now closed and used exclusively
for film shoots), 2632 E. Washington Blvd.

REDONDO BEACH:

32 Where Vincent makes his home, according to dialogue.
"The sticks," according to the Wolf.

SANTA MONICA:

33 Rae's Coffee Shop, where Clarence and Alabama go for pie,
True Romance. Scene is set in Detroit, but shot at 2901 Pico Blvd.

TOLUCA LAKE:

34 Jimmy's House, *Pulp Fiction*.
Shot at 4149 Kraft Ave., Studio City.

TORRANCE:

35 Del Amo Fashion Center, *Jackie Brown*.
3535 W. Carson St.

VALENCIA:

36 Clarence, Alabama, Dick, and Elliot's roller coaster ride,
True Romance.
Six Flags Magic Mountain, Magic Mountain Pkwy. (off I-5).

(continued from page 100)

It is, make no mistake, a blood-soaked valentine, a far cry from Woody Allen's *Manhattan* or Jean-Pierre Jeunet's *Amelie*. But Tarantino loves the quirks of the city, the cross-section of characters it offers, dreamers and druggies and criminals and would-be actresses. And most admirably (considering the remarkable number of films shot in L.A. that can't even get their basic geography right), he writes with a native's knowledge of the ins and outs of the landscape. As someone who spent his formative years on the outer edges of the sprawling metropolis, living in Harbor Beach or Manhattan Beach or Torrance, he understands the little nuances that give those suburbs their identity—and he writes with that specificity.

So there are unambiguous choices in the settings of his films, which are often identified explicitly either in dialogue or by formal onscreen titles. There is a reason that *Jackie Brown*'s Max Cherry runs his bail bond business out of the working class "City of Carson," rather than, say, "The City of Pasadena," the more upscale enclave where *Kill Bill*'s Vernita Green makes her home. It's not just a matter of knowing that Ordell Robbie's female runners in *Jackie Brown*, Sharonda and Simone, would live in Compton—any screenwriter with an N.W.A. record could guess that—but that Vincent Vega would live in the beach-bum haven of Redondo.

One gets the feeling that the precise suburbs, the neighborhoods and surroundings of each character, are as carefully considered by Tarantino as any of his dialogue.

When promoting *Pulp Fiction* in 1994, Tarantino emphasized that it "takes place in Hollywood—not the industry, but the town." The difference is subtle. *Pulp Fiction* does not take place in Hollywood the way that, say, *The Player* or *Get Shorty* do, but it is a city that is defined by that industry, often to the chagrin of its residents. Tarantino deals with this intersection most convincingly when it comes to the matter of *Fox Force Five*. *Pulp Fiction* may not be *about* Hollywood per se, but it is about a Hollywood where a gangster's moll was also a supporting player on a *Charlie's Angels* rip-off. And beyond that, it's about a city where even a pistol-packing enforcer can, when necessary, delicately and clearly explain the ins and outs of the intricate pilot-and-pickup process by which television programs are created and aired. It is, in other words, a city that may not be defined by film and television, but they are constantly embedded within it, and living there sanely depends to a great extent on one's ability to see everything that happens through that particular prism.

Which, of course, makes it a perfect setting for a Quentin Tarantino movie.

Signatures:
Diners and Coffee Shops

"Everything in Los Angeles revolves around restaurants," Tarantino told *New York Times* film writer Manohla Dargis. "You get together with your friends at restaurants, you have dates at restaurants, business meetings at restaurants. In many other cities you have to be of a certain wealth to go to restaurants, but in Los Angeles we have coffee shops that are open all night long. So you can not have a pot to piss in and still afford to go to a coffee shop and hang out. My friends and I would go to coffee shops late at night and be there for hours, like our version of hanging out in a Parisian café and discussing existentialism, except we were talking about New World Pictures and whether we were ever going to be with a woman."

The importance of coffee shop/diner culture in Tarantino's life is reflected in most of his films, where he uses those locations for key scenes—both for sequences of narrative importance and ones that merely establish characters and relationships via hanging out and talking (and talking, and talking).

Reservoir Dogs: Before they "go to work," the dogs enjoy breakfast, coffee, and conversation at a small diner ("Uncle Bob's Pancake House," according to the screenplay). Later, Mr. Orange meets up with his undercover contact Haldaway at an all-night diner (the script specifies Denny's, though it was shot at Johnie's—a local spot later used by the Coen Brothers for the "I can get you a toe" scene in *The Big Lebowski*).

True Romance: After Clarence and Alabama meet at the movies, they go out for coffee and pie. "After I see a movie," Alabama explains, "I like to go get a piece of pie and talk about it. It's sort of a little tradition I have." (It sounds like a tradition Tarantino probably has too.)

Natural Born Killers: Both Tarantino's original screenplay and Oliver Stone's eventual film version open with a lazy-lunch-turned-bloodbath in a roadside New Mexico coffee shop, where Mickey decides to give key lime pie "a day in court."

Pulp Fiction: Pie is a hot topic again—this time for Fabienne, who plans to have a slice of blueberry pie with her pancake breakfast, because "any time of day is a good time for pie." We don't see her trip to the diner, but we do spend considerable time at the Hawthorne Grill, where Vincent and Jules discuss pigs and miracles and Pumpkin and Honey Bunny reassess their criminal strategies, before the four characters memorably intersect.

From Dusk Till Dawn: The Fuller family—Jacob, Kate, and Scott—pull their RV over for a meal at Emma's Eats, where they strategize the rest of their road trip, and Jacob and Kate discuss faith.

Kill Bill Volume 2: After emerging from her premature burial, The Bride stops for a much-needed glass of water at a small roadside diner.

Death Proof: After picking up Zoe at the airport, Abernathy, Kim, and Lee take her for coffee, a bite, and a chat at a coffee shop. As a way of bringing this (the last of Tarantino's contemporary films, to date) full circle with his debut, the scene is shot in a style reminiscent of *Reservoir Dogs'* opener.

Soundtrack: The Perfect "Quentin Tape"

"Directing is actually like making a mix tape of music," Tarantino has said, "because you're taking all these people's talents and adding an aesthetic of your own, depending on what you've selected and how well you arrange what you've selected." He also found the creation of the mix tape (those personal assemblies of taped songs that went the way of the dinosaur when mp3s and CD-burning came into play) an apt comparison for creating *Pulp Fiction*'s soundtrack. "I make tapes for friends, you know, and this could easily be a Quentin tape," he said, explaining how he'd sit on the floor with his albums, selecting the order and setting the mood, quick hits from comedy albums serving the same purpose as the dialogue bits culled from the film. "And then you get your pen and write all the songs down on the sleeve of your little cassette, and give it to your friend. . . . Believe me, if you've ever heard any of my tapes and then you heard the *Pulp Fiction* soundtrack—well, that's like a really well-produced version of one of Quentin's handwritten tapes."

Growing up, Quentin was surrounded by an eclectic mix of music. This was thanks to his mother, who thrilled her son not only with albums by Elvis (obviously) or Fats Domino, but oddities like the *Dr. Doolittle* soundtrack or the work of comedian José Mendez, whose comedy album little Quentin knew by heart, and would recite at any opportunity.

As a filmmaker, he uses his wide variety of musical influences to find the voice and style of his stories. According to Tarantino, "One of the hooks that I use when I'm trying to find the personality of a movie, even if it's a story I might do three years from now, is to find a song that could be a good representation of the movie. I might not end up using that song, but it really helps me find the personality of it." The result is an organic use of music quite rare in the world of film, where music choices are usually limited to either (a) the lazy deployment of an easily identifiable song to directly telegraph time and place, and to shoplift its cultural currency, or (b) the gathering of hot, charting artists, whether the songs fit the film or not, in order to generate a profitable soundtrack album.

PULP FICTION

SOUNDTRACK

ABOUT THE FILM: *Pulp Fiction* was written and directed by Quentin Tarantino (Reservoir Dogs) and stars John Travolta, Samuel L. Jackson and Uma Thurman, with special appearances by Christopher Walken, Eric Stolz, Bruce Willis, Harvey Kietel, Rosanna Arquette, Peter Green, Amanda Plummer, Tim Roth, Duane Whitaker, Jerome Patrick Houban and Maria de Medeiros. The film will be released October 14.

FEATURED TRACK: The first single from the *Pulp Fiction* soundtrack is Urge Overkill's cover of the Neil Diamond chestnut "Girl, You'll Be a Woman Soon."

RELEASE DATE: September 27, 1994

OTHER TRACKS: "Misirlou," by Dick Dale & His Del-Tones
"Jungle Boogie," by Kool & the Gang
"Let's Stay Together," by Al Green
"Bustin' Surfboards," by the Tornadoes
"Lonesome Town," by Ricky Nelson
"Son of a Preacher Man," by Dusty Springfield
"Bullwinkle Part II," by the Centurians
"You Never Can Tell," by Chuck Berry
"If Love Is a Red Dress (Hang Me in Rags)," by Maria McKee
"Comanche," by the Revels
"Flowers on the Wall," by the Statler Brothers
"Surf Rider," by the Lively Ones
plus several snippets of dialog from the film.

FILM FACT: *Pulp Fiction* won the Palme d'Or award at the 1994 Cannes Film Festival.

CONTACT: Angee Jenkins/(818) 777-8907
Caroline Prutzman/(212) 841-8050

The press kit description of the soundtrack, 1994.

[Diegetic]

The concept of diegesis is a broad classification of storytelling and fictional style, but in film terms, it is most often used to define music and its source. Diegetic music is music that is an organic element of a scene that can be heard by the characters in it: Max Cherry listening to the Delfonics in his car, Mr. Blonde dancing and slicing to "Stuck in the Middle with You" on K-BILLY, Vincent and Mia twisting to "You Never Can Tell" at Jackrabbit Slim's. Nondiegetic music underscores the action for the viewer but is not heard by the characters: your standard motion picture score music, for example, or "Bullwinkle Part II," which we hear as Vincent shoots up and heads over to Mia's.

Pages 108–109: Shooting the twist contest. Tarantino and Travolta taught Thurman the various dances at the beginning of the day; Quentin yelled them out during the take. *Courtesy of Miramax*

The music in Tarantino's films, on the other hand, is a vital component of his overall aesthetic. As Spence wrote in *Quentin Tarantino and Philosophy*, "Tarantino uses music in his films (and this is especially true of *Pulp Fiction*) to provide the tonal core around which the entire film is constructed. It is as if on some deep level the images are dictated by and added to the music, rather than the reverse."

Pulp Fiction also marked a divergence in musical attitudes from his first film, where music was mostly used for ironic counterpoint, grisly violence underscored by light seventies pop. He would explain why he used those bubblegum records: "One, because some people are annoyed by it and two, because I grew up with it. The sugariness of it, the catchiness of it,

really lightens up a rude, rough movie." He also decided that all of the music in that film would be diegetic—source music, originating from a radio somewhere in the scene.

For *Fiction*, Tarantino decided to use a more conventional "score," albeit in a less-than-conventional way. He did not commission a composer to create music that complemented, and was timed to, the action onscreen. Instead, he tracked down existing music cues, most of them from the sixties rock-and-roll subgenre known as surf rock.

Of that label, Quentin mused, "I always really dug surf music, but I never quite understood what the hell it had to do with surfing. To me, it sounded like rock 'n' roll spaghetti Western music. Which made it perfect for this movie, because this movie is kind of like a rock 'n' roll spaghetti Western." The most memorable of those songs was Dick Dale's 1962 instrumental "Misirlou," which plays over the opening credits. "It sounds like the beginning of *The Good, the Bad, and the Ugly* with those trumpets, that almost Spanish sound," Quentin explained. "Having 'Misirlou' as your opening credits, it just says, 'You're watching an epic, you're watching this big old movie, just sit back.' It's so loud and blaring that it throws down a gauntlet that the movie has to live up to."

Midway through the credits, though, it seems that we might still be in the radio-listening world of *Reservoir Dogs*. The song is abruptly interrupted by the static of stations changing, the dial landing on Kool & the Gang's "Jungle Boogie," already in progress. When the "Royale with Cheese" scene begins after the credits, "Jungle Boogie" becomes source music,

Wild and Peaceful (1973), Kool & the Gang's sixth album, included "Jungle Boogie" (which was sampled two years before *Fiction*'s release by a favorite Tarantino dialogue subject: Madonna). © *EyeBrowz* / Alamy

emanating from Jules' radio. So the opening credits changeup was the sound of Jules channel surfing. According to Tarantino, this wasn't solely an artistic choice: "'Misirlou' is actually a very short song, so it played perfectly when it came to going through all the actors. But then when it came to the technical credits, we'd have to keep repeating it." At home, giving "Jungle Boogie" a spin, Tarantino realized that it represented "the other personality that's in the movie. There's a spaghetti Western kind of thing in there, and there's also this black exploitation kind of thing." So he put them both in to encompass the full scope of the picture's style.

Elsewhere in the film, Tarantino seems to build entire scenes around songs. This is particularly true with the music we hear at Mia's house, in two scenes that are less about plot and more about a building and sustaining of mood. When Vincent arrives to pick up Mia, Dusty Springfield's 1968 hit "Son of a Preacher Man" fills the home, Springfield's voice tenderly underlining the tension of the night ahead (and of the viewer's eagerness to get a look at the notorious Mrs. Wallace). "That whole sequence, I had in my head for six or seven years," Quentin explained. "And it was always scored to 'Son of a Preacher Man.' That was the key to that

sequence. I can't even imagine it without 'Son of a Preacher Man.' I probably would have cut it out if I couldn't get 'Son of a Preacher Man.'"

When Vincent and Mia return from their date, Vincent excuses himself while Mia cues up Urge Overkill's cover of Neil Diamond's "Girl, You'll Be a Woman Soon," a track whose wild vacillations between somber cool and manic energy heighten the choices the pair are about to make. That song, too, had been on Quentin's radar for a while; during his fall 1992 trip to London to open *Reservoir Dogs*, he discovered it on an EP in a Soho record store. It got into his head and stayed there.

In those cases, Tarantino lucked out and was able to get the music he'd set his heart on. But he wasn't always so fortunate. He'd learned one lesson on *Reservoir Dogs*: "Never write the song title in the script. I want to write the song that I want to use in the script so people reading the script will get the full flavor, but then they've got a gun to your head"—"they" being the people in charge of licensing music for movies. "They

know that you have every intention of using their song," Tarantino despaired, so to keep them off the scent, he not only didn't put song titles into the *Pulp* screenplay, but he put dummy songs in that he had no intention of using. According to the script, the post–Jackrabbit Slim's scene is to be accompanied by a CD of k.d. lang; the pawnshop basement rape is scored with "The Judds, singing in harmony."

Quentin's *real* first choice for the rape scene didn't work out, however. He had eyes for The Knack's kitschy 1979 track "My Sharona," but the makers of another Jersey Films production, Ben Stiller's *Reality Bites*, wanted it for a cheery scene of convenience store dancing. "The licensing people had to decide between us and *Reality Bites*," Tarantino recalled, granting, "They ultimately made the good choice." Tarantino went with The Revels' 1961 track "Comanche" instead.

That song and the others on the *Pulp* soundtrack were not only given new exposure and cultural weight by their presence in the film; they were forever attached to it, tied in

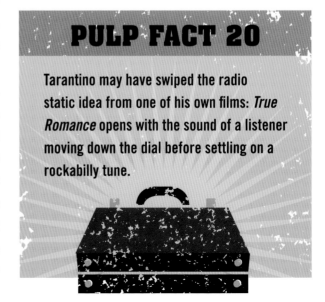

perpetuity to the visuals and attitudes Tarantino had married to them. "When you do it right and you hit it right," he would later say, "then you can never really hear that song again without thinking about that image from the movie." The songs in his movies are throwbacks, as are the devices for their consumption—Mia Wallace has a designer CD player, but she'd never do anything as gauche as listen to music on it, going instead for the purist formats of vinyl and reel-to-reel tape.

When Vincent calls Lance from his car, we notice that Lance has a reel-to-reel as well. It's an awfully exotic format for so many people within such a small sampling to enjoy, but that's Tarantino's world: one of connoisseurs and collectors, seeking out and sharing obscurities, just like the man who created them.

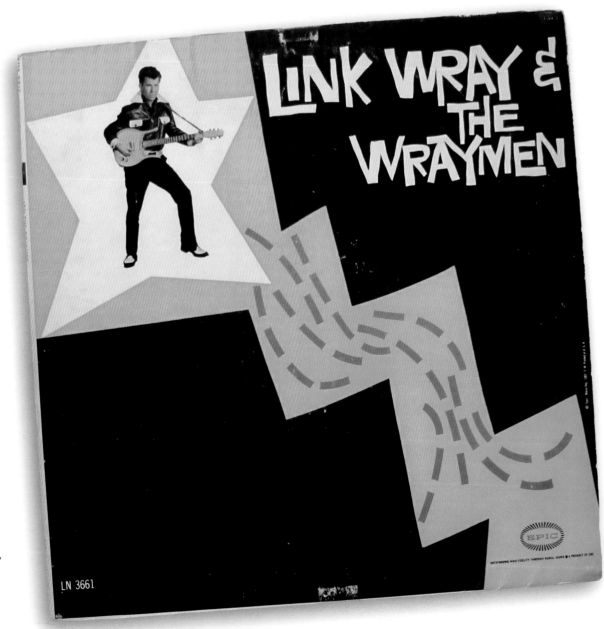

Guitar legend Link Wray's songs "Rumble" and "Ace of Spades" were featured in the film. *Voyageur Archive*

LN 3661

PULP MUSIC

By Gary Graff

Pulp Fiction may be decidedly urban, but its music starts on the surf—specifically with "Misirlou," a fiery blast of biting, industrial-gauge guitar played at hyperspeed, a clarion call of action, adventure, danger, and damn good fun. Everything, in other words, that Pulp Fiction brings during the subsequent two and a half hours.

And rest assured that "Misirlou" was no random choice to be the movie's musical starting point. "I'm always trying to find, like, what the right opening credit . . . should be early on, when I'm just even thinking about the story," Tarantino explained in an interview included in a 2002 collector's edition of the soundtrack album. "I find that it really kind of triggers me in to what the personality of this piece should be, what the rhythm of this piece should be . . . the rhythm and more or less the personality you're trying to inject into the film.

"Having 'Misirlou' as your opening credit, it's just so intense. It just says you're watching an epic, you're watching this big, ol' movie, just sit back. 'Cause it's so loud and blaring at you. . . . It throws down a gauntlet that the movie now has to live up to. It's just saying, 'We're big!'"

Pulp Fiction was indeed a big musical piece, as carefully crafted as Tarantino's script, with songs chosen using the same exacting discretion he applied to casting actors. The result was a seamless relationship between movie and music that made the two inseparable. Just as we'll never think of Stealer's Wheel's "Stuck in the Middle with You" the same way again after watching Mr. Blonde sever Marvin Nash's right ear in Reservoir Dogs, Pulp Fiction recast familiar songs in bold new cinematic settings—Thurman's Mia Wallace dancing to Urge Overkill's rendition of Neil Diamond's "Girl, You'll Be a Woman Soon," Thurman and Travolta cutting a rug to Chuck Berry's "You Never Can Tell"—that are now inextricably part of the tunes' legacies.

Dick Dale, the king of surf rock.
Voyageur Archive

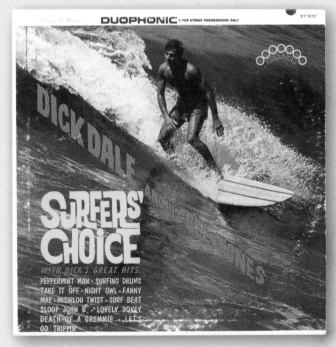

The music plan for *Pulp Fiction* was altogether different than anything in previous Tarantino films (though, because he did not direct them, he may not have had much of a say in the soundtracks for *Natural Born Killers* or *True Romance*). *Reservoir Dogs*' songs, for instance, were woven into the story as source material—"Stuck in the Middle with You" was a random song playing on the radio for the scene, though deliberately chosen for that role by Tarantino. In *Pulp Fiction*, however, he wove his choices together to serve a more traditional score function. "In a lot of movies," he said, "they just turn up the soundtrack to create a false energy or . . . to create a sense of period that they're investing in the picture—'Okay, it's the sixties. We'll play a lot of sixties songs and that will create the period.' To me that's cheap and annoying and like listening to the radio and watching a movie at the same time. They don't really go together, and it just seems cheap to me.

"I try to avoid that. I really want the songs that I'm using in the movie—like in the case of Maria McKee ('If Love Is a Red Dress (Hang Me in Rags)') and Al Green ('Let's Stay Together') or in the case of anything—to work in the crux of the scene. . . . We're really trying to make it, like, fun and neat and not just a collection of songs."

Song selection is key, according to Tarantino, who was assisted on *Pulp Fiction* by musician Boyd Blake Rice, a member of California's UNPOP Art Movement; friend and fellow film director Allison Anders, and others. "You are such a poseur and such a lame-o for using a song another movie has already christened," Tarantino contended. "They've used 'Stand by Me' so many times, but to me the one that used

'Stand by Me' the [best] was in *The Wanderers*. They're playing 'Stand by Me' as the lead character realizes JFK's been shot, and it's perfect. Even *Stand by Me* are poseurs by that [standard]. You can't use 'Stand by Me' after *The Wanderers*. And when *Dirty Dancing* used 'Be My Baby,' that is the opening theme to *Mean Streets*. Excuse me? How can you use 'Be My Baby?'"

Pulp Fiction was defined by the breadth of Tarantino's soundtrack choices, from obscurities to classics, from funk and soul to rock 'n' roll, with the bookends of "Misirlou" and the Lively Ones' "Surf Rider" and the Centurions' "Bullwinkle, Part II" in the middle. "The movie's all over the map," Tarantino acknowledges. "The movie uses a bunch of different styles in order to kind of tell three stories . . . constantly switching gear. It has an overdrive gear, it has a cruise control, and it has a first and second and third all the way through the movie . . . I want it to move like a bullet when it's supposed to, the other times I want it just kind of like, 'Okay, let's hang out for awhile.'"

Tarantino still considers "Misirlou"—suggested by Anders—to be one of his crowning movie music moments "for just sheer, rock-charge visceral . . . I was going for this rock 'n' roll/spaghetti Western/blaxploitation vibe. It screamed, 'We're an epic!' It had profound feeling." It also had a profound impact on Dick Dale, the surf-guitar hero who had largely faded from view but came back storming after *Pulp Fiction*, landing a new album deal and reclaiming the legacy he'd established with other early sixties singles such as "Let's Go Trippin'" and "Jungle Fever."

"A lot of movies in the sixties used to use surf music songs, but [*Pulp Fiction*] really brought me back," Dale said during the mid-nineties.

"I was still out there working. I hadn't stopped. But it's a whole different game now." Producer Bob Keane's Del-Fi records, which originally released "Surf Rider" and "Bullwinkle, Part II," capitalized on *Pulp Fiction* by releasing a CD compilation called *Pulp Surfin'* in 1995, while surf music began popping up in commercials, TV shows, and other movies. A decade later the Black Eyed Peas sampled "Misirlou" for their 2005 hit "Pump It"—at which time group leader will.i.am referred to it as "that *Pulp Fiction* song."

Diamond's "Girl, You'll Be a Woman Soon" also enjoyed a second life thanks to *Pulp Fiction*. A top-ten hit in 1967, the tune had been recorded by Urge Overkill for its 1992 extended-play recording "Stull," which Tarantino found in a Dutch record store. "We just loved the song—we love Neil Diamond, really, although it's maybe not cool to say that," said the group's Nash Kato. "We kind of felt like we could really heavy it up and make it sound like one of our songs. We had a lot of fun doing it." Tarantino even considered using the Diamond version, but felt that Urge Overkill's version "is even better." After hearing it, the director described how "All of a sudden (I knew) this is it. Beyond the shadow of a doubt, this is the song Mia has to dance to by herself. I played it to Uma. Uma flipped; 'Yes, you're right. You're right. This is great! This is fantastic!' It was one of those things where I was in love with about four or five songs; I could've used any one of them, and I kept flip-flopping. Then I found my true love."

Diamond, meanwhile, wasn't sure he loved the idea at first. "I heard Quentin Tarantino and thought, 'My song is going to be playing and there's going to be blood splattering everywhere,'" Diamond noted with a laugh. "But I have to say that I really liked what [Urge Overkill] did with the song, and how [Tarantino] used it. It really brought people back to that song, my version of it, too." Urge Overkill's version even charted, hitting number fifty-nine on *Billboard*'s Hot 100 chart and number eleven on *Billboard*'s Hot Modern Rock Tracks chart.

Pulp Fiction was, at the time, accepted as an original musical project as well as a film companion; it reached number twenty-one on the Billboard 200 chart and earned rave reviews. The album has sold more than 3.6 million copies since its release, and Tarantino continued to set high standards for soundtrack concept in film such as *Jackie Brown*, both parts of *Kill Bill*, *Grindhouse,* and *Django Unchained*.

Gary Graff is the coauthor of Rock 'n' Roll Myths **and** Neil Young **and founding editor of the MusicHound Essential Album Guide series.**

Eddie "King" Roeser of Urge Overkill, during a 1993 concert in New York City. *Photo by Steve Eicher / WireImage / Getty Images*

The Tarantino Style

In interviews, Tarantino will sometimes minimize the difficulty of film directing, or the complexity of his technique, by focusing on minor technical concerns. Talking with *Film Comment* on the eve of *Pulp Fiction*'s release, he insisted, "Far and away, forget what anyone else says, the biggest problem with making movies is that fucking axis line." Such bravado is a cover, as is the at-first-glance assumption that his directorial style is simple and straightforward. It is anything but, as a close examination of his film reveals.

Pulp Fiction illustration by Tim Scoggins. Originally published in *Copley Los Angeles Newspapers*. Courtesy of the artist

Even on first viewing, a savvy viewer will note Tarantino's use of long, unbroken, traveling Steadicam shots, a signature visual device of his longtime hero Brian De Palma. Let us consider the second Steadicam shot first. At the eighty-eight-minute mark, Tarantino spends nearly a full minute following Butch from his car to his apartment building, past another building (and an open window, through which we hear an ad for Jackrabbit Slim's on the radio—maybe it's tuned to K-BILLY?), employing a series of back routes and fence holes to reach his destination. On a surface level, it reiterates the danger of Butch's situation; that is, *look at all the trouble he's taking to avoid the main entrance.* But its real-time element also recalls Mr. Blonde's stroll out to the car in the midst of "Stuck in the Middle with You" in *Reservoir Dogs*; it gives us time to fully consider what he's doing, what he might be walking into. And it heightens the suspense of what will happen once he gets there.

The first Steadicam shot comes early on, with Jules and Vincent's walk through the halls of Brett's apartment building as they discuss the implications of Tony Rocky Horror's foot massage. The scene runs just over two and a half minutes without interruption, and its absence of cuts, along with the constant access it allows to both Vincent and Jules, gives us the opportunity to observe their relationship—the way they interact with each other, the chemistry they've developed as (we gather) longtime friends and coworkers.

Beyond that, the scene establishes Tarantino's camera as an active, rather than passive, observer. Note that when the two men step away from Brett's door, hanging back until the predetermined time of morning is reached, the camera does not follow them. It pivots but remains at the transom, almost impatiently, anxious to find out what's on the other side of that door.

It's a move echoed by another of the film's other uninterrupted takes, as Lance searches for the medical book that will provide guidance for Mia's adrenaline shot. Though the shot runs over a minute without a cut, and in almost constant motion, this time Tarantino adopts a documentary-style handheld approach to emphasize the chaos of the situation. Yet when Lance disappears into the cluttered second bedroom to find the book, the camera remains in the living room, where the action is, where Mia may be drawing her last breath, reminding us of the matter at hand.

Compositionally, Tarantino and cinematographer Sekula tend to favor either loose medium-wide shots or tight, claustrophobic close-ups. They're not much interested in what's in between. Some scenes, like Jody and Vincent's conversation about her piercings, are shot only in close-ups, with no establishing shots to give viewers their bearings. But this isn't always Tarantino's play. In the screenplay, the Jackrabbit Slim's scene begins with Mia and Vincent already at their table/car, and "Vincent

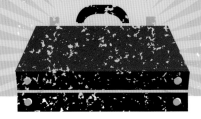
takes a look at the place" (presumably in a series of medium or wide shots) after Buddy takes their order. But Tarantino changed that for the film, both to show off his expensive set and to satisfy the audience's curiosity immediately. The tracking shot that follows Vincent through the restaurant was done "so he could discover the restaurant at the same time we did; then he sits down and talks to Mia for twenty minutes," Tarantino explained. "The subject of the film is not Jackrabbit Slim's, but what happens between these characters. That's why, during their conversation, there are no shots of the set."

Other sequences use the contrast of wide shots and close-ups to disorient and discomfort the viewer. The genial, humorous "foot massage" conversation outside Brett's apartment plays out in one long, shambling shot, but once

>>>> *Frame of Reference* <<<<

[Axis Line]

Axis line is a tricky compositional concept on film sets that establishes where characters are in relation to each other and where the camera must be placed to keep their spatial relationships clear.

they enter the apartment and get "into character," the visual approach is more businesslike as well. Jules' intimidation of Brett and his associates is played primarily in big, full close-ups and short, clipped shots; we can relax in the earlier scene, but this one is shot and chopped to put us on edge. The scene comes to a climax of tent-revival shouting, guns blasting, and blood shedding, before fading—first to blood red, then to black. The calm music of Al Green fills the soundtrack, soon joined by the dulcet tones of Rhames, and another long shot, this time of Willis listening. Tarantino's understanding of tempo is masterful; he knows when to change speeds, and how. Later, the hominess and intimacy of Butch and Fabienne's relationship is similarly emphasized by the change in mood and speed—especially in the their long dialogue scenes, seen mostly in two-shots with very little intercutting.

Likewise, Jules and Vincent are often seen in two-shots (particularly early on), placed together in the same frame to emphasize their closeness. But after they split on the meaning of their near-death experience in Brett's apartment, the frame splits as well: they are seen separately, the way they will live their lives from here on out (only briefly, for Vincent). When they talk about bacon and dogs, joking and getting along like the old days, they are again in the same frame together, but once the conversation turns to Jules' "moment of clarity," they are again seen apart.

In that scene, their inability to connect is dramatized by one of Tarantino's favorite visual cues: the close-up in profile. Throughout the film, characters shot in complementary profile are battling a psychological distance larger than their physical one: the first few, awkward minutes of Vincent and Mia's date; Jules and Vincent's discussion of Jules leaving the life; Jules and Ringo negotiating once the guns have been drawn. But if those bridges are built, we see the characters in cozier and more accommodating direct close-ups, shot either over the other character's shoulder or straight on, almost from the opposite character's perspective. As they chat, Vincent and Mia's scene switches to these more direct compositions; likewise, Jules and Pumpkin/Ringo eventually communicate directly and honestly, and the camera pivots to place itself between them, rather than next to them. (As Jules and Ringo's conversation grows more urgent, the wide frame of each man's close-up is half-filled by the back of the other's head, a darkness that shutters off complementary halves of the screen, creating something akin to an individually considered split screen.)

Directorial Influences

DIRECTOR	Q.T. QUOTE	Q.T. INFLUENCE
Brian De Palma (*Blow Out, Carrie, Casualties of War, Scarface*)	"De Palma was probably the first working director of his generation that I got into. It's exciting when you love someone who's currently making movies and you're waiting for their new one."	Long, unbroken, showy Steadicam shots (most memorably in *Pulp* and *Kill Bill*); ingenious use of the split screen for counterpoint (see *Jackie Brown* and *Kill Bill*).
Abel Ferrara (*Bad Lieutenant, King of New York, Ms. 45, The Funeral*)	"As far as I'm concerned, *King of New York* is better than *GoodFellas*. That is about as pure a vision as you're going to imagine. . . . It has the polish and the artistry of a pure vision, and at the same time, it's just *full on out* action."	Frequent use of Ferrara regulars Walken and Keitel; full ensembles with rich supporting characters. **Walken in *King of New York*.** © *Photos 12 / Alamy*
Jean-Luc Godard (*Breathless, Contempt, Weekend, Bande à part*)	"To me, Godard did to movies what Bob Dylan did to music: they both revolutionized their forms."	Acknowledgment and subversion of American crime movie archetypes and iconography; "musical sequences" in nonmusical movies (like the Jackrabbit Slim's twist contest).
Howard Hawks (*His Girl Friday, Rio Bravo, Red River, Bringing Up Baby*)	"He's just too damned enjoyable."	Fascination with group dynamics, particularly among male characters; love of rapid-fire, overlapping dialogue.
Walter Hill (*48 HRS., The Driver, The Warriors, Southern Comfort*)	"The difference between what I'm doing and what Hill did is that he plays his tough-guy existentialism straight, and I don't have the guts to go all the way."	The black-and-white buddy action/comedy mix of *48 HRS.*, manifest in Jules and Vincent's byplay; contemplation of masculinity, honor, and machismo (particularly in *Reservoir Dogs* and "The Gold Watch" section of *Pulp Fiction*).
Sergio Leone (*A Fistful of Dollars, For a Few Dollars More, Once Upon a Time in the West, The Good, the Bad, and the Ugly*)	"My favorite director is Sergio Leone. Hands down, he's the one who's influenced me most. . . . I can't imagine doing something as perfect as the closing sequence in *The Good, the Bad, and the Ugly*. I will always try to reach that, but I don't think I will ever get there. It is just so cinematically perfect."	Frequent use of the so-called Mexican standoff; musical and visual cues from Leone's famed spaghetti Westerns in *Kill Bill Volume 2* and *Django Unchained*.
Jean-Pierre Melville (*Bob le flambeur, Le Doulos, Le Samurai, Army of Shadows*) *Everett Collection*	"He made, like, the coolest gangster films ever. They're fantastic. He took the Bogart, Cagney, the Warner Brothers gangster films . . . and just gave them a different style, a different coolness. They had this French Gallic thing going through it, yet they were still trying to be like their American counterparts, but they had a different rhythm all their own."	Similar subversion of traditional crime film style, but by seeing it through an American low-culture prism; self-aware characters, cognizant of their own coolness.
Martin Scorsese (*Mean Streets, Taxi Driver, Raging Bull, GoodFellas*)	"Like him, I like mixing fast-cutting scenes and more deliberate ones, and I'm very particular with the frame. But he's almost a stone around young filmmakers' necks. So many new films are aping Scorsese. I don't want to be a poor man's Scorsese."	Aside from the similarities Tarantino mentioned: preoccupation with criminal activities; frequent use of Keitel; free and frequent use of profanity; unexpected intermingling of violence and dark humor.

[Shot Size]

Marsellus Wallace, from the series *Movie's Eyes*, by Ricardo Ribeiro. *Courtesy of the artist.* *www.flickr.com/photos/riczribeiro*

Close-up: Some close-ups are closer than others (hence modifiers like *tight* close-up or *extreme* close-up), but it's safe to bet that a shot that frames its subject's face and little else is a close-up.

Medium shot: A partial view of a subject, wider than a close-up but closer than a wide shot—a view from the waist up, for example. Sometimes also called a mid-shot. A medium close-up or MCU is somewhere between a medium and close.

Medium-wide: Somewhere between a medium and wide (or long) shot, showing a person or persons and their surroundings. Tarantino favors medium-wides for shots of two actors. (Some call this a full shot or figure shot.)

Wide shot: Also called a long shot. A shot wide enough to establish an environment—a room, a building, maybe even a city.

Jules does not bring Vincent over to his point of view, so that ocular shift is never achieved.

The director adopts a similarly precise visual strategy for Captain Koons' monologue to the young Butch. They shot the scene straight through with several interpretations, giving Tarantino multiple options in the editing room.

"I chose from among these shots," he explained, "according to the three stages of the story: the great grandfather's, the grandfather's, and the father's. And for each section there was a different connotation which corresponded to the various interpretations offered by Walken." The first, in which the great-grandfather makes it home from World War I, is a lighthearted opening, done in a medium close-up. He cuts away to young Butch listening during the transition to World War II, and when he returns, the shot is much tighter, Walken's tone more appropriately somber, as Dane Coolidge did not survive Wake Island. Cut back to Butch, and then back to the same close-up, but from a take that was, according to Tarantino, "more matter-of-fact and informative." The length of Walken's monologue is quite unusual for a film (particularly one usually classified in the action genre); Tarantino realized it was vital to change the visual and emotional cadence in order to keep an audience's interest.

A condition of his deal with Miramax, "a make-or-break point," according to Tarantino, was that "I would not allow cards or focus groups or questionnaires. Basically, when I showed the movie to them, it was like, 'This is how it is.'" There were test screenings to gauge reaction, and to fine-tune the editing, but in many ways the film he shot was the film they got, partly because it was shot in a way that was impeccably worked out in advance. That his direction was so accomplished and so confident on only his second effort speaks volumes to what he'd learned from those many years of studying the filmmakers he admired—and it speaks to a natural talent for communicating his ideas visually as well as aurally.

Signatures:
The Trunk Shot

The trunk shot is one of the few specific visual cues that appear in all of Tarantino's contemporary films. In it, the camera is placed inside a trunk that the characters open, creating an image shot from the perspective of either the trunk, or the poor soul inside it.

- *Reservoir Dogs:* (37:26) Mr. Blonde opens his trunk for Mr. White and Mr. Pink, to show them the uniformed cop that he's kidnapped and hidden inside it.

Shooting the *Reservoir Dogs* trunk shot.
© *Miramax / Courtesy Everett Collection*

- *Pulp Fiction:* (8:00) Jules and Vincent retrieve their handguns from the trunk, discuss the uncertain number of people inside the apartment, and agree that they should have shotguns for this kind of deal.

- *From Dusk Till Dawn:* (12:41) Though Tarantino handed directorial duties over to Robert Rodriguez, Rodriguez aped his pal's signature shot by showing Seth and Richie Gecko opening their trunk and taking out the bank teller whom they're holding hostage.

- *Jackie Brown:* (19:13) Ordell opens his trunk to show poor Beaumont where he'd like him to hide—and, ultimately, die. (1:43:30) Jackie opens up her hatchback to switch the money around before going into the mall for the drop.

- *Kill Bill Volume 1:* (1:38:38) The Bride opens her trunk, where she's holding Sofie Fatale, to extract information and explain why she's leaving her alive, if mutilated.

The trunk shot was modified slightly for Tarantino's next two films:

- *Kill Bill Volume 2:* (31:46) The Bride is taken to her early grave in the bed of Budd's truck, so we get a shot from her point of view of Budd peering over the back gate and opening it up to drag her out.

- *Death Proof:* (1:19:41) Tarantino moves the shot to the front of the car, shooting from under the front hood as Kim and Zoe check out the engine of Jasper's 1970 Dodge Challenger.

The Righteous Man, by George Ioannou. Acrylic on canvas, 2006. *Courtesy of the artist and Art Rebellion*

PART IV

"Let's Get Down to Brass Tacks, Gentlemen"

Sampling Cinema: The Director As DJ

In the summer of 1989, the Beastie Boys released *Paul's Boutique*, the long-awaited follow-up to their multiplatinum 1986 smash *License to Ill*, and a marked departure from it—they had abandoned the jokey, simple style of their debut for an extravagant, textured, musical mosaic. That multilayered sound was provided by the Dust Brothers, Los Angeles–based producers/DJs and specialists of sampling. Sampling—extrapolating pieces of previously existing musical works into new compositions—had been a cornerstone of hip-hop from its humble beginnings, the turntable transforming from an electronic appliance into an instrument for would-be musicians who couldn't play, or afford, more entrenched instruments. But on *Paul's Boutique*, the Dust Brothers (like the Bomb Squad on Public Enemy's *It Takes a Nation of Millions to Hold Us Back* and Prince Paul on De La Soul's *3 Feet High and Rising*) transformed sampling from a necessity to an art form. They sampled from over one hundred songs on the album's fifteen tracks, exponentially grafting elements of the old to create something vibrantly new.

Tarantino was listening. In those early screenplays, he couldn't help but write in the language of the films he'd seen and loved, and as a result, they were filled with references and homages, a line here, a scene there, a character in this script, a situation in that one. It may have been a choice; it was more likely just the way he saw the world. Tarantino biographer Aaron Barlow calls him "perhaps the first director to speak 'film' natively and fluently in his discussions of the world. He negotiates reality through film."

Over the years, his critics have contended that Tarantino is less a creator than a repository, less an artist than a recycler of ideas and dialogue from Hollywood's past. It's a charge that's haunted him since the controversy over *Reservoir Dogs*' debt to the 1987 Ringo Lam film *City on Fire*, and it's revisited anew whenever a Tarantino film arrives, with online articles and chat rooms dissecting the genealogy of his latest work. Don Murphy, *Natural Born Killers* producer and long-time Tarantino nemesis, voiced his opinion on

Opposite:
Furious Anger, by Serge Gay Jr. Giclée print. *Courtesy of the artist. sergegayjr.com*

the matter bluntly: "Quentin doesn't have a single bone of originality in his body."

But Tarantino doesn't see Murphy's notions of originality and his own considerable film savvy as mutually exclusive. "I steal from every movie," he said, unashamedly, at Cannes in 1994. "I steal from every single movie made, all right? I love it. If my work has anything it's because I'm taking from this and from that, piecing them together. If people don't like it, tough titty, don't go see it." In other words, he is—like the Dust Brothers and the Bomb Squad and DJ Shadow and DJ Premier—collecting bits and pieces, both popular and forgotten, and sculpting them into a transformative work.

Like the Dust Brothers, he casts a wide net for inspiration. The samples of *Paul's Boutique* range from the expected hip-hop standbys of funk (Sly and the Family Stone), disco (Rose Royce), and R & B (James Brown) to more far-flung sources: the Beatles, Pink Floyd, Loggins & Messina, the Ramones, Black Oak Arkansas, jazz drummer Alphonse Mouzon, folk guitarist David Bromberg, German Italo disco singer Fancy, even John Williams' *Jaws* theme. The obscurity of the cuts is a badge of honor for DJs, as is the skill with which they intermingle such seemingly incompatible sounds. Tarantino has likewise ingeniously mixed and matched throughout his career, most notably in *Kill Bill* (kung fu, anime, Western, drama), *Death Proof* (horror, action, grindhouse homage), and *Django Unchained* (spaghetti Western, blaxpoitation, comedy).

"I don't consider myself just as a director," he explained, "but as a movie man who has the whole treasure of the movies to choose from and can take whatever gems I like, twist them around,

give them new form, bring things together that have never been matched up before."

There is a history of this kind of thing. The Film Society of Lincoln Center's longtime programming director Richard Peña has dubbed Quentin a "second generation movie brat," after the movie-crazy kids of the seventies (Spielberg, Scorsese, Lucas, Coppola) who became that era's cinematic superstars. In 1993, Graham Fuller went a step further, calling Tarantino "not so much a postmodern auteur as a *post*-postmodern one, for he is feverishly interested in pop-cultural artifacts and ideas . . . that themselves spring from earlier incarnations or have already been mediated or predigested." For example, he notes, *True Romance* is inspired by *Badlands*, but *Badlands* was inspired by earlier films like *Gun Crazy, They Drive by Night*, and *You Only Live Once*, creating a "double frame of reference."

The question becomes: to what degree are audiences aware of those frames? David Bordwell contends that Tarantino deliberately signals his sources to his audience, "in order to tease pop connoisseurs into a new level of engagement," while Aaron C. Anderson writes that by using framing markers and calculatingly phony distancing devices (like, for example, the black-and-white process shots in *Pulp Fiction*), "Tarantino draws attention to his film's status *as a film*, as a constructed work of fiction, and as a 'simulation.'" As mentioned in the earlier discussion of *Pulp Fiction*'s archetypes, Tarantino's works are self-aware texts, and even the casual viewer who may be unfamiliar with specific references is certainly cognizant that Tarantino is dealing in "cinematic" situations, for which there are forerunners and precursors. He uses our knowledge of them, and the baggage they bring, to both flesh out his stories and to confound our own expectations.

In his book *The Sundance Kids*, James Mottram puts it another way. The key to understanding Tarantino's reappropriation, he says, is to see contemporary cinema as "a constantly evolving organism; just as genres could be recycled, so could plot lines and dialogue, with Tarantino acting as curator. The ultimate fan appropriating his favorite clips and assimilating them into something new, he never desecrates but merely redecorates." Sometimes the shout-outs are inconspicuous—you might not remember that, say, Butch's boxing opponent shares the last name of the fighter to whom Marlon Brando's Terry Malloy took a dive, just as you might not fully hear all nine of the songs whose components make up the Beastie Boys' "Hey Ladies." But they're all there, part of the tapestry, a piece of the song's (or film's) world.

But, Anderson asks, "to what extent do these references actually throw back to their originals and to what extent do they simply exist as references (that reference nothing)?" That crucial distinction—between references for the sake of reference and references that define the storyteller's universe, and propel it—is what separates Tarantino from the scores of imitators who sprung up in the wake of *Pulp Fiction*'s astonishing success. It is not enough to have an encyclopedic knowledge of film and to toss in smirky, elbow-in-the-ribs quotations. One must not bypass the basic work of engaging an audience by telling a story. "Part of the fun of making movies is that you're on ground that's been covered before," Tarantino explained in 1994, "and you can use that as a jumping-off point for all the weird places you want to go. I'm trying to make a combination of a 'movie movie' and a real movie. I want to make 'movie movies' with real consequences."

Pulp Fiction Retro Vibe for Crazy4Cult 5, by Bobby O'Herlihy. Digital art, 2011. *Courtesy of the artist. cynicwithapencil.blogspot.com*

(continued on page 128)

Pieces of PULP:

FILM	DIRECTOR, YEAR	*PULP* INFLUENCE
American Boy: A Profile of Steven Prince	Martin Scorsese, 1978	Rock roadie, actor, and raconteur Steven Prince thrills Scorsese with his story of rescuing a woman from a heroin overdose with a medical book, a magic marker, and a shot of adrenaline administered with "a stabbing motion."
Assault on Precinct 13	John Carpenter, 1976	Like Butch, Napoleon Wilson's (Darwin Joston's) moral code prevents him from escaping a dangerous situation and leaving behind a man who is, by all definitions, his enemy. *Assault on Precinct 13*, with Austin Stoker and Laurie Zimmer. *Everett Collection*
Bande à parte	Jean-Luc Godard, 1964	The high-spirited café dance inspired the twist at Jackrabbit Slim's. "It's so infectious, so friendly," Tarantino explained.
The Bodyguard (aka Karate Kiba)	Ryuichi Takamori and Simon Nuchtern, 1976	Tarantino was introduced to the (creatively rewritten) Ezekiel 25:17 passage through the scrolling text prologue of this Sonny Chiba movie.
Body and Soul	Robert Rossen, 1947	A tough boxer gets in too deep with a crime boss in this noir classic.
Breathless	Jean-Luc Godard, 1960	Butch and Fabienne's motel scenes recall the extended section of Jean-Paul Belmondo and Jean Seberg hanging out in her apartment.
Breathless	Jim McBride, 1983	Black-and-white rear projection in driving scenes; post-shower frolicking with a French girlfriend.
Charley Varrick	Don Siegel, 1973	Marsellus' most chilling threat echoes that of Mob money man Maynard Boyle (John Vernon), who tells a bank manager: "They're gonna strip you naked and go to work on you with a pair of pliers and a blowtorch."
Coffy	Jack Hill, 1973	Tarantino's favorite blaxploitation movie features future Jackie Brown star Pam Grier as "Coffy" Coffin, who works as a night nurse (just like Bonnie).
Deliverance	John Boorman, 1972	The granddaddy of all "hillbilly rapist" movies.
The Deer Hunter	Michael Cimino, 1978	Christopher Walken won an Oscar for his portrayal of an American prisoner of war in Vietnam—an experience shared by Captain Koons.
The Doll Squad	Ted V. Mikels, 1973	This pre–*Charlie's Angels* film concerns a squad of six sexy but deadly women with specialized skills, like Fox Force Five.
The Godfather	Francis Ford Coppola, 1972	The Wolf is a dead ringer for Brando's Don Corleone in the opening section of *The Godfather*—from the tux to the slicked-back hair and pencil-thin mustache.
Hi Diddle Diddle	Andrew L. Stone, 1943	One of Tarantino's favorite movies includes a set piece in a private gambling club, similar to where we first see the Wolf.
Jaws	Steven Spielberg, 1975	Tarantino recreates the famed reverse zoom shot (in which a person seems to go forward and backward at the same time) on Roy Scheider with his shot of Mia Wallace after she snorts Vincent's heroin.
Jules and Jim	Francois Truffaut, 1962	Though Tarantino says he prefers Godard to Truffaut, he may well have named his character of Jimmie after the buddy of moviedom's other famous Jules.
The Killers	Don Siegel, 1964	Opening sequence follows a pair of cool-as-cucumber hit men as they carry out a mysterious assignment.

An Incomplete Index of Homages and References

FILM	DIRECTOR, YEAR	*PULP* INFLUENCE
Kiss Me Deadly	Robert Aldrich, 1955	Centers on a mysterious briefcase that glows when finally opened (before setting off a nuclear explosion); Tarantino has also said that Ralph Meeker's characterization of Mike Hammer inspired Butch's hard edge.
Kung Fu	TV series, 1972–å1975	Jules longs to "walk the earth," like this show's main character Caine (played by future *Kill Bill* star David Carradine).
La Femme Nikita	Luc Besson, 1990	Keitel's cleaner character of the Wolf was inspired by Vincent (Jean Reno), the cleaner in Besson's film—as well as by Victor, the cleaner played by Keitel himself in the American remake *Point of No Return* (1993).
Man Hunt (aka *The Italian Connection*)	Fernando Di Leo, 1972	Two hit men—one black, one white—are on assignment in Italy; European culture shock ensues.

The Italian Connection, with Woody Strode and Henry Silva as Jules and Vincent predecessors.
Michael Ochs Archives / Getty Images

FILM	DIRECTOR, YEAR	*PULP* INFLUENCE
The Night of the Hunter	Charles Laughton, 1955	Like Jules Winnfield, Harry Powell (Robert Mitchum) is prone to preaching to his victims before killing them.
Once Upon a Time in America	Sergio Leone, 1984	Tarantino's lighting of Vincent's face as he enjoys his heroin high echoes that of Robert De Niro taking in his opium in the final shot of Leone's epic.
On the Waterfront	Elia Kazan, 1954	Brando's Terry Malloy takes a dive for the Mob when facing a boxer named Wilson—the same surname as Butch Coolidge's opponent.
The Panic in Needle Park	Jerry Schatzberg, 1971	The scene at Lance's with the overdosing Mia recalls the OD of Bobby (Al Pacino) in this heroin drama.
Psycho	Alfred Hitchcock, 1960	The framing of Butch and Marcellus' unexpected encounter at a crosswalk echoes Marion Crane seeing her boss on her way out of town.
Red Line 7000	Howard Hawks, 1965	Tarantino told production designer David Wasco to watch this late Hawks film for its racecar-inspired club scene, which influenced the look of Jackrabbit Slim's.
Repo Man	Alex Cox, 1984	Like the briefcase, the object of this film's attention is a glowing McGuffin—this time the trunk of a Chevy Malibu (the same car driven by Vincent Vega).
The Set-Up	Robert Wise, 1949	Robert Ryan plays a tough, aging boxer who will not take a dive.
Shadow Warriors	TV series, 1980–1985	Tarantino and his pals never missed an episode of this Sonny Chiba TV show. Each episode ended with Hattori Honzo (Chiba, a role he reprised in *Kill Bill*) delivering a speech on good and evil. "The guy who listened to this speech was sure to die in the end!" Tarantino said.
Speedway	Norman Taurog, 1968	Another inspiration for Jackrabbit Slim's—specifically the combination car/dining tables.
They All Laughed	Peter Bogdanovich, 1981	Another of Tarantino's oft-mentioned faves, this forgotten screwball comedy features a pretty, sharp-tongued female cabbie.
Unforgiven	Clint Eastwood, 1991	Both *Unforgiven* and *Fiction* have characters named "English Bob," though in the former, the character is actually English.
The Wild Bunch	Sam Peckinpah, 1969	The freeze-frame at the end of *Pulp*'s prologue recalls the unexpected freezes in Peckinpah's opening—particularly the last one, with the line "If they move, kill 'em!"

(continued from page 125)

In another interview, he noted that quotation and sampling "should never become referential to the point of stopping the movement of the film. My first concern is to tell a story that will be dramatically captivating." Peña concurs: "His films are playful in a way that invites the audience to come along and play." And the argument can be made that the origins are less important than the outcome—or, as Mottram puts it, "Call it plagiarism, call it intertextuality, but Tarantino has the ability to make anything sound his own."

Jackson approaches it on simpler terms: "He loves film. He loves storytelling. There aren't a lot of people who do this job who have the kind of genuine adoration for what the cinema is, or what cinematic history is, or what made us fall in love with movies in the first place. And he's one of the people who gives his soul to those particular things when he goes to work."

And there's a chance that those of us who nose through the work playing spot-the-homage are missing the point anyway. As *Entertainment Weekly*'s Owen Gleiberman wrote when *Pulp* archaeology was reaching a fever pitch, "In the two and a half hours of *Pulp Fiction* there are plenty of scenes that recall other movies, but the bulk of the movie does not. The whole idea is that we watch these movies in a kind of postmodern way, ticking off the references. Anyone who watches a Tarantino movie like that is phony; he is not admitting the true narrative drive that Tarantino creates."

Or, as the grinning director once told an interviewer, "The fact of the matter is, the shots I actually did rip off no one has caught yet."

Pulp Fiction in Its Time: Narrative As Hyperlink

On August 6, 1991, as Tarantino was shooting *Reservoir Dogs*, the World Wide Web went online. On that day, the first website was published by a thirty-six-year-old Swiss physicist named Tim Berners-Lee, who had led the development of a system to share information and navigate the Internet via hypertext. Thus, personal computer users could simply point their mouse at words of interest and click, the words on their screen linking them to further information on other web pages. The Internet, a global system of computer networks, had existed in various forms since the 1960s, but with the World Wide Web service, it was penetrable for the first time by the average citizen.

Not that Quentin was likely aware of any of this, or that he was using the nascent information superhighway while penning *Pulp Fiction* in that Amsterdam apartment. This, after all, was the man who wrote his scripts in longhand, a near-Luddite who insisted, "You can't write poetry on a computer." So why does the construction of *Pulp Fiction* dovetail so neatly with the rise of this new way of gathering information?

The answer may have less to do with how *Pulp Fiction* was made than how it was received—after all, Tarantino had been writing this way for years, and was inspired as a writer by that lowest of technologies, the novel. And in spite of its digital formatting, it's an aggressively analog movie, from Lance and Mia's reel-to-reels and Mia's vinyl to Lance's Fruit Brute cereal (an item missing from grocery shelves since 1983) to heroin, Vincent's hardware-heavy bebop drug of choice.

But it was Tarantino's good luck that his structurally off-kilter picture arrived as dial-up home Internet services like Prodigy and America Online were making younger audiences more receptive to fresh methods of navigating content. By the time *Pulp Fiction* premiered in October 1994, the number of hosts and domains online had nearly doubled from October of the previous year. Upon its release, it would become the first new film whose fans embraced the Web as a method for its deconstruction. They used their AOL website generators to create tributes to Tarantino and his film; they gathered in chat rooms and forums to share their theories and tell its secrets.

Breakfast of drug dealers.

Pulp Fiction lent itself to the Web. It spoke to the Internet generation, in their language, and smart movies of the ensuing two decades followed suit. *Film Comment's* Alissa Quart called them "hyperlink films," coining the term in a review of Don Roos' *Happy Endings*, which "toggles back and forth between its ending and beginning. . . . When we're given information about a character's fate, the action then clicks back to fill in the missing pieces."

There is an element of interactivity that separates the Web user's experience from that of the moviegoer (a separation best left separate, if misfires like 1995's "interactive movie" *Mr. Payback* are any indication). Web surfing, as M. Keith Booker wrote in *Postmodern Hollywood,* "gives users much more control over where they go, even if they are likely to encounter unexpected information along the way."

But it's that "unexpected information" that Tarantino provides—gleefully—throughout his film. "Part of the fun of *Pulp*," he explained, "like in the middle story with Willis, is that if you're hip to movies, you're watching the boxing movie *Body and Soul* and then suddenly the characters turn a corner and they're in the middle of *Deliverance*. And you're like, 'What? How did I get into *Deliverance*? I was in *Body and Soul*, what's going on here? I turn a corner and I'm in the middle of *Deliverance*—*Deliverance* already in progress. How did that happen?'"

It happened the way it always happens: you click that link, you follow that thread, you Google that name, you end up somewhere totally unexpected, vaguely connected, and you find yourself either entirely fascinated or totally repulsed. Or sometimes, both.

Buttons, Links, and Connections

Big man's wife: We can probably all agree that the primary motivation for skipping from Jules and Vincent's morning hit to Vincent and Mia's date (and thus saving "The Bonnie Situation" for later) is to end the film on the strong note of the redemption of Jules (and Pumpkin and Honey Bunny). But here's another reason: after Jules and Vincent's comprehensive discussion of Mia Wallace—her aborted acting career, her femme fatale nature, and (most pressingly) her feet—it simply wouldn't do to veer off and spend the next forty minutes on other matters. We, as an audience, are as fascinated and intrigued by Mia Wallace as Vincent is, so it only makes sense to click ahead and meet her for ourselves.

Marsellus' sexual preferences: The point when we return to Jules and Vincent's morning hit (at the beginning of "The Bonnie Situation") connects not only to the beginning of the film, but to the sequence that has just ended. In "The Gold Watch," Marsellus Wallace is bound and raped by Zed and Maynard. He is rendered "pretty fuckin' far from okay" by this turn of events, so he shoots Zed in the crotch and promises his attacker a shortened life spent "in agonizing pain." When we return to Jules, he is concluding his interrogation of Brett with the assurance that "Marsellus Wallace don't like to be fucked by anybody except Mrs. Wallace"—a fact that we, in the audience, have just seen ably demonstrated.

Pits of hell: In explaining his experience with Butch's father in that "Hanoi pit of hell," Captain Koons tells young Butch that men in that situation "take on certain responsibilities of the other." Later, Butch finds himself in a "pit of hell" with Marsellus (in a the basement of a pawnshop in Canoga Park—an area not exactly known for its basements), and realizes he must take on certain responsibilities himself.

The lighting link: As previously noted, at the beginning of "The Gold Watch," young Butch is connected to older Butch (whom we haven't seen since clear back at the beginning of "Vincent Vega and Marsellus Wallace's Wife") by the lighting design of his listening close-up—strong and bright on one side of his face, dark and shadowed on the other.

On the count of three: Tarantino loves the dramatic count to three. In *From Dusk Till Dawn*, Seth and Big Emilio argue over who gets to count to three first; later, Jacob only gives his son till the count of three to agree to kill him once he turns into one of the undead. In *Inglourious Basterds*, the manner in which Archie Hicox displays a count of three is a major plot point. *Pulp Fiction* features two dramatic counts to three: the countdown to Mia's injection, and Pumpkin's count for Jules to show him the briefcase.

Wake in fright: *Pulp Fiction* is a film where the number three is a guiding principle. In addition to the three stories at its center, there are three scenes where characters awaken with a scream: Mia from her overdose, Butch from his prefight nap (remembering the visit from Captain Koons), and Butch the morning after his fight. The end of that night's sleep is connected by the same sound it began with: Fabienne brushing her teeth.

Three deals: Three deals are made in the film: Butch and Marsellus' agreement that Butch will throw the fight (which he breaks), Vincent and Mia swearing the events of their evening to secrecy (which, based on their interaction at the fight, they keep), and Butch and Marsellus' final deal, in which Butch lives in exchange for his secrecy and exit from L.A. (which he keeps).

Three home invasions: Vincent drags Mia in to Lance and Jody's, Jules and Vincent enter the home of Brett and his crew, and Jules and Vincent crash Jimmie's place. None are home invasions in the strictest sense, but none are particularly welcome either. The homeowners are, in two out of three cases, clad in bathrobes; in one of them, the now-reluctant host had earlier promised "mi casa es su casa," a courtesy he presumably comes to regret.

Genre-Jumping with the "Gun Guy"

"The entire time I was writing Pulp Fiction *I was thinking: This will be my Get-It-Out-of-Your-System movie. This will be the movie where I say goodbye to the gangster genre for a while, because I don't want to be the next Don Siegel—not that I'm as good. I don't want to just be the gun guy. There's other genres that I'd like to do: comedies, Westerns, war films."*
—Quentin Tarantino, *Film Comment,* 1994

There's a bit of bravado in that statement, which Tarantino made on the *Pulp Fiction* press tour—not that it's inaccurate, just incomplete. In many ways, *Pulp Fiction* does feel like a Get-It-Out-of-Your-System movie, and Tarantino is a filmmaker who has often stressed his disinterest in being confined to the crime genre. "What I would like to do is be like Howard Hawks and work in a whole load of different genres," he said, around the same time. "I'd like to do a Western, I'd like to do a war film. . . ."

And he would, in due time. But when he was writing *Pulp Fiction,* there were no guarantees. *Reservoir Dogs* was a critical success, but not a commercial one. If *Pulp Fiction* didn't turn a profit, it might well be his last time at bat; he could have easily been another Matty Rich or Charles Lane, indie filmmakers whose sophomore studio pictures sunk without a trace, and took them down, too. (Rich's breakthrough had been *Straight out of Brooklyn* [1991], made when he was just 19; Lane's was the black-and-white, nearly silent film *Sidewalk Stories* [1989].)

Jules, by Spacebar + 77.
Courtesy of the artists. www.spacebar77.com

These days, Tarantino can pretty much make any movie he'd like (or can choose not to make movies at all, as he's indicated recently). But he didn't know what the future held in 1994, so he seized on his unique opportunity and infused *Pulp Fiction* with touches and flourishes from a variety of crisscrossing genres—just in case the gravy train came to an end, and he never got the chance to make his romantic comedy, or his buddy movie, or his Western. By doing so, Gavin Smith wrote in *Film Comment,* "Tarantino achieves the remarkable feat of remaining a genre purist even as his films critique, embarrass, and crossbreed genre." Or, as the director himself explained, "I love it when someone just starting out in the movies reinvents an entire genre from inside out."

But what genre *is* it, exactly? Judging by synopsis alone, it's a crime movie, which

ostensibly puts it in the action genre: men with guns, brutal deaths, stolen briefcases. But the character arc of Jules, his last scene with Pumpkin—that's serious dramatic stuff. So is *Pulp Fiction* a drama? Tarantino won't hear of it. A video store clerk to his soul, he spent a good portion of a 1995 dual interview with *Forrest Gump* director Robert Zemeckis (his competitor for the Best Director Oscar) discussing what sections their movies should be filed in. "For any video store owners out there," he announced, "when *Pulp Fiction* comes out, I want it in the comedy section! If I come in and *Pulp Fiction* is in the drama section, that'll be the last time I go into *your* closed-minded video store!"

He's right. Throughout the Tarantino filmography, easy categorization is thwarted by the simple fact that his films are wildly funny—while confounding traditional comic definition. "All my movies, I definitely stop short of calling them comedies, because there's stuff in them you're not supposed to laugh at," he told *The Observer*. "But *Pulp*, more than any, has an overtly comic spirit, pretty much from the beginning to the end." Ultimately, it's a testament to Tarantino's sheer ambition as a filmmaker and storyteller, as an artist who's not satisfied by taking the easy route to an easy payoff. When you go to see *Pulp Fiction*, he explained, "You saw a *movie*. You've had a night at the movies; you've gone this way and that way and up and down. And it wasn't just one little tone that we're working to get right."

"I love playing with my viewer's expectations and, in the end, crossing him up." That's Tarantino's MO, throughout his body of work but particularly in *Pulp Fiction*, which changes

Pumpkin (Tim Roth) and Honey Bunny (Amanda Plummer), another of Tarantino's beloved criminal couples.
Courtesy of Miramax

channels as sharply and unexpectedly as that car radio in the opening credits. "I know I won't live long enough to do all the movies I wanna do," he said at the time, so "with every movie the goal is to wipe out as many as I can. But *Pulp Fiction* is maybe even more of a kitchen sink movie than I'll probably ever make again. It really is three movies for the price of one."

Tarantino is being modest. If you take each section individually, it's actually *five* movies for the price of one.

"Prologue" As Caper

In considering how *Pulp Fiction* played upon first viewing (and outside of our frame of analysis), it's useful to remember what we did and did not know in 1994. *Pulp Fiction*'s pre-title sequence runs four and a quarter minutes and features only two important characters: the lovers and partners in crime, affectionately self-branded as Pumpkin and Honey Bunny, played by Roth and Plummer. At the time of *Pulp Fiction*'s release, Tarantino's most recent works (as a writer but not director) were *Natural Born Killers* and *True Romance*, both of which centered on young criminal couples. By spending the first five minutes of his new film with yet another pair of smooching lawbreakers, he's toying with our expectations of what exactly his new film is going to be: is he strolling down that garden path *again*?

Hardly. But remember, we didn't know that the first time we saw it—indeed, by the time the duo reappear two-plus hours later, we may very well have forgotten they were even in the movie. No, Tarantino instead uses their one scene to

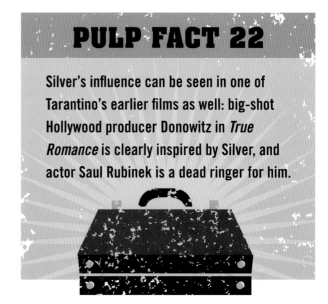

PULP FACT 22

Silver's influence can be seen in one of Tarantino's earlier films as well: big-shot Hollywood producer Donowitz in *True Romance* is clearly inspired by Silver, and actor Saul Rubinek is a dead ringer for him.

flirt with an expectation suggested by his *other* previous credit: that he's following up *Reservoir Dogs* with another caper movie.

In the prologue of *Pulp Fiction*, Tarantino presents an entire heist movie in miniature, with the boilerplate expositional beats intact: the old pro lured out of semiretirement for one more job (Pumpkin, who has sworn off liquor store jobs as too dangerous), the introduction of the plan ("This place? A coffee shop?"), and the discussion of the particulars (with Roth echoing the explanation of pushover managers and crowd control imparted to him by Keitel in *Reservoir Dogs*).

The difference, though, is in the timing: whereas a typical heist picture gives us a job that is intricately planned days or weeks in advance, Pumpkin and Honey Bunny are robbing the coffee shop "right here, right now." "Let's go," Honey Bunny says, impatiently—and that immediacy, that forward momentum, is not just that of the character, but of the man putting words into her mouth. Keep going, pushing forward. Caper movie: done, check, moving on.

"The Morning Hit" As Buddy Movie

Pulp Fiction's screenplay, Tarantino noted in 1994, "works in a series of couples—everybody's a couple all the fucking way through. It starts off with Tim Roth and Amanda Plummer, then it goes to Sam Jackson and John Travolta, then John Travolta and Uma Thurman, then it goes to Bruce Willis and the cab driver . . ." and so on and so on. But none of those couples is as significantly realized as Jackson and Travolta, aka Jules and Vincent, who dominate the film's second section, the untitled early morning hit at Brett's apartment that occupies the time between the opening credits and the first proper, titled sequence, "Vincent Vega and Marsellus Wallace's Wife."

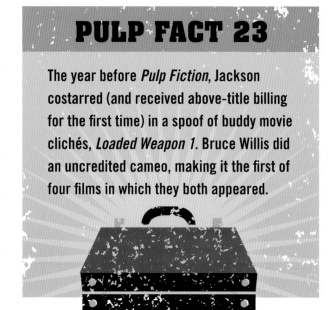

PULP FACT 23

The year before *Pulp Fiction*, Jackson costarred (and received above-title billing for the first time) in a spoof of buddy movie clichés, *Loaded Weapon 1*. Bruce Willis did an uncredited cameo, making it the first of four films in which they both appeared.

Tarantino explained Jules and Vincent's dominance over the film with another example of his preoccupation with showing what other films skip. This early sequence is "more or less the opening three minutes of *Action Jackson, Commando*, every other Joel Silver movie—two hit men show up and blow somebody away. Then they cut to 'Warner Bros. Presents' and you have the credit sequence, and then they cut to the hero three hundred miles away." The idea for "The Bonnie Situation" was to *not* cut away, to return to those hit men and see how they spend the rest of their day. But in this opening, we see Tarantino taking a stab at the genre through which superproducer Silver made his name: the buddy action/comedy.

Silver's first big hit was the 1982 Walter Hill film *48 HRS.*, in which dour tough-guy police detective Nick Nolte was paired with fast-talking street criminal Eddie Murphy. They were opposites in every way: white and black, cop and crook, gruff and slick, serious and funny. And audiences ate it up. The film raked in $78 million

Tasty Burger,
by Jenn Gaylord.
Digital print, 2013.
Courtesy of the artist.
www.etsy.com/shop/
TheSilverSpider

and prompted a glut of movie odd couples cracking wise over a cacophony of shattered glass and gunfire. The next dozen years paired a wiseass Chicago cop with a visiting by-the-book Russian (*Red Heat*); a veteran cop with a certifiably crazy one (*Loose Cannons*); an old pro with a young Turk (*The Rookie*, co-penned by Quentin's pal Scott Spiegel); a bounty hunter and a Mob accountant (*Midnight Run*); a slick cop and a sloppy one (*Tango and Cash*); and a private eye and a disgraced football player (*The Last Boy Scout*). That last one was another Silver production, and he was also responsible for the most lucrative buddy franchise of them all, the cop series that paired a wild, semi-suicidal white widower with a safety-first black family man: *Lethal Weapon*.

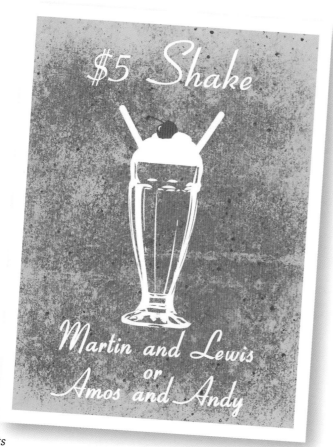

Pulp Fiction:
$5 Shake poster, by Freddy Clark and Lisa Sullivan, aka Fox & Dragon Emporium.
Courtesy of the artists

By the end of that film (and thus for all of the sequels), and in other buddy movies like *Running Scared* and *Bad Boys*, the initial resistance and differences have been shed—our two heroes have become both pals and partners. Jules and Vincent fit firmly within this tradition. On the drive to Brett's, their chemistry and familiarity (in spite of Vincent's recent sojourn to Amsterdam) are apparent. They're comfortable with each other, and throughout this long sequence, they have the timing of a great comedy team, reacting to each other with ease, sparking off each other's energy.

They're so good together, and their back-and-forth is so funny, that we don't realize until later exactly how much intelligence we're receiving in this scene: we get the details of Vincent's trip, vague but pertinent information about their destination, and full descriptions of not only Mia Wallace's background, but the danger of getting too close to her. But it's not just exposition. By witnessing their byplay, the crafty manner of their interaction, the way they not only talk to each other but *listen* to each other (and deftly deflect each one's words back to the other), we understand both the characters and the world they inhabit.

"Vincent Vega and Marsellus Wallace's
Wife" As Romantic Comedy

There's a place where lovers go," croons Ricky Nelson as Vincent strolls through Jackrabbit Slim's early in his evening with Mia Wallace—an evening which, he insists, is "*not* a date." That it turns out to be that very thing (until Mrs. Wallace's taste for white powder nearly gets her killed) allows us the rare opportunity to get a look at a Tarantino-style rom-com.

After the rat-a-tat-tat prologue and the jokes-and-bullets Jules-and-Vincent morning hit sequence, the Jackrabbit Slim's scene is one of the first during which the audience is allowed to settle in and get comfortable. As both screenwriter and director, Tarantino takes his time with this sequence (luxuriates in it, really), giving the characters and the actors room to first get to know, and then to like, each other.

As a result, the date scene plays in something akin to real time. It is in this simple choice that *Pulp Fiction* departs most sharply from what we think of as romantic comedy onscreen. More often than not, the creators of rom-coms aren't willing to do the hard onscreen work of showing a couple making a connection; instead, they either set them up as antagonists, sniping at each other on the outside and crushing on the inside,

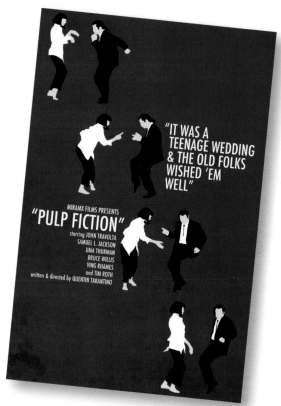

The Dance, by Michael Sapienza. Digital print, 2011. *Courtesy of the artist*

or queue up their record collection and let the couple fall for each other over a cutesy music montage sequence. We take their attraction to each other as an act of faith, a presumption of

Mia and Vincent's dance, enshrined in wax at the Hollywood Wax Museum, 1998. *Photo by Gilles Mingasson / Getty Images*

Signatures:
Genre-Bending

Pulp Fiction wasn't Tarantino's first time mixing up cinematic styles—and it was far from his last. Here's a quick roundup of the genres sampled in each of his films:

Reservoir Dogs
Heist/caper, action, drama, comedy (opening sequence), horror (ear scene), buddy movie (Mr. Orange/Mr. White scenes)

True Romance
Action, romance, drama, comedy (any scene with Brad Pitt), gangster (Walken)

Natural Born Killers
Action, romance, drama, anime, black comedy ("I Love Mallory"), drugs (snakebite sequence, surrealistic cut-ins)

Jackie Brown
Heist/caper, romance, drama, blaxpoitation, hip-hop comedy (any scene with Chris Tucker)

Kill Bill Volume 1
Martial arts, action, drama, grindhouse, anime, gangster (subgenre: Yakuza)

Kill Bill Volume 2
Martial arts, action, family drama, romance, grindhouse, Western (spaghetti), comedy, animals running amok

Death Proof
Grindhouse, horror, car chase/hillbilly exploitation, showbiz satire

Inglourious Basterds
War, action, comedy, drama, "guys on a mission" movie, history (alternate)

Django Unchained
Blaxpoitation, comedy, buddy movie, action, Western (domestic), Western (spaghetti)

The genre-bending
Kill Bill Volume 1.
© Photos 12 / Alamy

the genre rather than a conclusion based on the evidence the film has presented, which is less dialogue of connection than convenience—or, as Mia puts it, "the usual mindless, boring, getting-to-know-you chitchat."

Quentin will have none of that. He lives in the conversational dead-ends, the offhand exchanges, and the uncomfortable silences. "The idea behind this scene," editor Sally Menke said, "was that basically Quentin wanted it to be as drawn out as possible, as it would be if you were meeting someone for the first time, and you're a little bit awkward, because you don't have anything to talk about." In its initial version (seen in the published screenplay and in the DVD and Blu-ray's deleted scenes), it ran even longer, with "a lot of dialogue that's been taken out of the scene," Menke said, noting that she "lobbied hard to take out even more dialogue."

Pulp Fiction: The Captain, by Michael Grey. *Courtesy of the artist. Grey Matter Prints. Greymatter.me*

Eenie, Meany, Miney, Moe . . . , by Tamsin Hazlewood-Harmer. Digital art, 2010. *Courtesy of the artist. Tamify-Hazlewood. artistwebsites.com*

But the director wouldn't budge. "I don't find it boring it all," he explained, deftly grasping the importance of a varied tempo. The easygoing vibe of the date scene—a lull, almost—makes the action after it (the overdose, the frantic ride to Lance's house, the lead-up to the injection) seem that much faster, considerably more frenzied and out of control. But beyond that, the filmmaker explained, "I like the fact that you actually hang out with them, that you get to know Mia, and you get to know Vincent via Mia, through the course of the time that they're together." Tarantino's patience with the scene is exemplary. The two mismatched souls, paired on a date of convenience, slowly shed their veneers of cool detachment through the delicately constructed dialogue. And then, when Mia enters them in the twist contest, they shed their inhibitions. Look closely at the way Vincent grins after she reads him the riot act about dancing with her; he knows the kind of dancer that he is, and what she's in for. "Oh, it's on," that grin says, and the scene that follows backs it up: as the camera moves in from a wide shot to mediums, the dance morphs from a lark to downright foreplay, their eye contact growing more intense and loaded. In the fifteen minutes he spends at Jackrabbit Slim's, Tarantino builds and conveys an attraction more electric than in the entire running time of countless so-called "romances."

"The Gold Watch" As Western

It would be a cinch to view "The Gold Watch" as Tarantino's mini-riff on the war movie. It's an easy leap to make, from the initial appearance of Captain Koons and the war stories he tells to Butch's immersion in his own "war" (explicitly stated in the original screenplay: "This is my World War Two. That apartment in North Hollywood, that's my Wake Island") to the capture of Butch and Marsellus, who become POWs in Maynard and Zed's basement. But it's more interesting—and more enlightening, in understanding the filmmaker—to frame the section as his first stab at the Western form.

Throughout the first half of "The Gold Watch," Butch is the gunslinging outlaw, the cold-blooded killer who has done wrong by his Western town's most powerful man. He hides out from him as long as he can, but when they finally come face to face, the iconography is striking: their standoff at the crosswalk may quote Hitchcock's *Psycho*, but it also calls up every Western showdown ever filmed. They squint, they glare, and then Butch does the closest thing to drawing that he can come up with on short notice: he hits the gas.

The showdown continues once both men come to, with Marsellus drawing his pistol across the deserted intersection, shooting a bystander and proceeding to chase Butch through what has become a ghost town. But once they arrive at the pawnshop and are taken hostage by Maynard and Zed, a shift in the power dynamic occurs (as mentioned, placing the two men on equal footing), mirrored by an adjustment of allegiances. (In explaining how the spirit of *Pulp Fiction* is

embodied by "a series of couples," Tarantino described the outcome of "The Gold Watch" sequence almost as a matter of fate, predetermined by the pairings inherent to the film: "For a moment after [Butch] leaves [Fabienne], he's the only character in the movie who's viewed completely alone. Then he makes a bond with this other character and they become a team. It's only when they become a team that they can do anything. Circumstances make them a couple.")

The classic Westerns are filled with unlikely alliances, former enemies who band together to fight a common enemy whose crimes against them outweigh their grievances against each other. The most appropriate example of this is *Rio Bravo*, in which young hotshot Colorado (Ricky Nelson) at first refuses to join Chance (John Wayne) and Dude (Dean Martin) in fighting the Burdettes. He only throws in when his boss becomes one of their victims. The themes of honor, duty, and loyalty aren't all *Rio Bravo* and "The Gold Watch" share; Butch's taunt to Zed ("Go ahead and pick it up . . . I want you to pick it up") is a thinly rewritten riff on Chance's own dare ("You want that gun, pick it up. I wish you would"). Eighteen years later, Tarantino would finally get to make a full-on Western (*Django Unchained*), but in "The Gold Watch," his interest in taking on the genre was already clear.

"The Bonnie Situation" As Sitcom

There's a slapstick vibe to Jules and Vincent's adventures disposing of Marvin's body, but not in the traditional sense (the closest we get to physical comedy is the visualization of Bonnie's possible return home, brief and barely fleshed out). It's more a matter of spirit, as the knockabout shenanigans of our suited heroes play less like anything that has come before them in *Pulp Fiction*, and more like the darkest Laurel and Hardy short ever made. Brains on the upholstery: another nice mess you've gotten me into.

But those Laurel and Hardy shorts—and those of their comic contemporaries—were less slapstick farces than they were early forerunners of sitcoms, with laughs generated by the

By Aled Lewis.
Courtesy of the artist

"You ready to blow?"

For Nurse Bonnie, there is only one taste that *truly*

Satisfies.

Red Apple

PERDIDO HILLS HOSPITAL
BONNIE

You'll quickly discover why it seems as though everyone is smoking RED APPLE. Nothing matches the blend of costly tobaccos for that distinctive crisp and sweet flavor! Toasted for no irritation. IT'S EASY ON THE THROAT!

"An Apple a day keeps the Doctor away!"

Red Apple ™

CIGARETTES

appearance of set comic types in a specific, far-out situation. Here, two tough criminal types are placed in a scenario beyond their control, and in the process, they reveal their true colors. They suddenly appear to be not hardened killers, but a bickering old couple ("I can feel your look!").

In the scenes that follow, Tarantino examines these characters through the preoccupation of so many sitcoms, both the aforementioned early cinematic forays and their less reputable television permutations (which were, after all, a steady course in the viewing diet of Tarantino's youth): the peril of gender roles. In what Tarantino analyst Edward Gallafent calls "a triumphant escapade in domestic comedy," we meet Jules' buddy Jimmie, a stay-at-home husband who doesn't fear a headless body, his gun-wielding friend, or the connected guy who joins them. His only concern is upsetting his wife. "They're not worried about cops," Tarantino laughed, "they're worried about this guy's wife coming home."

In their home, Bonnie is the breadwinner, while Jimmie attends to the domestic duties, from preparing the gourmet coffee to fretting over the wedding linens provided by the late Uncle Conrad and Aunt Ginny. In order to keep from upsetting the fearsome Bonnie, the characters of Jules and Vincent—traditionally masculine types, clad in suits and ties, wielding phallic pistols—are "feminized," charged with the cleaning of blood (complete with menstrual overtones, in the form of Jules' reprimand about leaving Jimmie's washcloth looking "like a fucking maxi pad").

Within that broad frame, there's plenty of room for the comedy of minutiae (like the

obsession with Jimmie's tasty coffee, down to the Wolf's perfectly-timed "Mmm!") and for broad visual gags (such as the Wolf's lightning-fast trip to Jimmie's, his nine-minute-and-thirty-seven-second arrival time illustrated in a mirthful font straight out of *It's a Mad Mad Mad Mad World*). By having a hearty laugh at Vincent's clumsiness and Jules' pettiness, Tarantino manages to defang these men, to infantilize them. "They're afraid of mom coming home," Tarantino said of the men. "You spilled shit on the carpet—clean up the mess you made from screwing around before your mom gets home." It gets a laugh, certainly. But it also makes these cold-blooded killers sweeter, less threatening, and more vulnerable—an important emotional beat for the filmmaker to hit before coming to Jules' redemption at the Hawthorne Grill.

If *Pulp Fiction* is a stew of so many different styles, why does the picture feel so cohesive? Less attuned filmmakers who tried to emulate it—and there were plenty of them—found their own attempts at mixing comic, dramatic, and action beats far less fluid. Not everyone can loop the loop like Tarantino can, and an amateur was likely to give an audience whiplash.

So how does Tarantino get away with it? His own thoughts on genre, conveyed to the *New York Times* in 2012, may hold the key: "I think every movie is a genre movie. A John Cassavetes movie is a John Cassavetes movie. Eric Rohmer movies are their own genre." And so, then, is *Pulp Fiction* more than a crime movie, a caper, a romantic comedy, a Western, a sitcom, or a drama; it is a Quentin Tarantino movie. That genre encompasses all of the above and more.

PULP FICTION

Many words come to mind when I think of *Pulp Fiction*. Tarantino. Thurman. Zed. Royale with Cheese. The Wolf. The Gimp.

Fuck.

I would say *Pulp Fiction* is a smorgasbord of the f-word, but that doesn't quite cover it. I didn't care enough to count myself, but according to a list on *Slash Film*, *fuck* appears 264 times, ranking it just below *Reservoir Dogs* and above *The Big Lebowski* in total f-bombs.

In the spirit of a movie that begins with a definition—of *pulp*—here's an English lesson on *fuck*, with examples from *Pulp Fiction* and history from the *Oxford English Dictionary* (OED) and Jesse Sheidlower's *The F-Word*: the largest, most comprehensive histories of English and *fuck*, respectively. I hope this will be more entertaining than fuckin' English class.

fucking as an intensifier—the equivalent of *goddamned*

When Winston Wolf says "Pretty please, with sugar on top, clean the fuckin' car" to a petulant Vincent Vegas, he's using *fucking* to add volume and intensity to his thoughts. Like most of the uses in *Pulp*, this sense of *fucking* has nothing to do with making sweet love down by the fire. One of the earliest known uses of this sense is from *The Stag Party,* an 1888 collection of American dirty stories: "Now this gives us another fucking scene, leastways it is not exactly a fucking scene, though it came near being one."

fuck: a somewhat vague noun roughly equivalent to *damn*

In the opening scene at the diner, Roth's character Pumpkin/Ringo explains why bank workers aren't supposed to interfere with a robbery, wondering: "Why should they give a fuck?" As the OED says, this meaning expresses "annoyance, hostility, urgency, exasperation, etc." Some popular variations are used by Mia ("That's when you know you've found somebody really special. When you can just shut the fuck up for a minute and comfortably share silence.") and the Wolf ("That gives us forty minutes to get the fuck out of Dodge.")

fuck it: the hell with it, screw it, forget it

Also in the opening scene, Pumpkin says, "Fuck it, forget it" when trying to talk Honey Bunny (and himself) out of future liquor-store robberies. The OED defines this sense as "expressing dismissal, exasperation, resignation, or impetuousness." It was used in censored form in E. E. Cummings' *The Enormous Room,* back in 1922: "I said, 'F— it, I don't want it.'" This is a close relative of *fuck you,* which Jules says twice during the foot-massage discussion.

motherfucker: a bad person, a badass person, or just a person

AND THE F-WORD

By Mark Peters

This memorable rant from Jules is like a symphony of profanity, with three uses and two meanings of *motherfucker*: "Now look, just 'cause I wouldn't give no man a foot massage don't make it right for Marsellus to throw Antoine off a building into a glass motherfuckin' house, fuckin' up the way a nigger talks. That shit ain't right. Motherfucker do that shit to me, he'd better paralyze my ass, 'cause I'll kill the motherfucker, you understand?"

Who's Bad!?!, by Andrew Spear. Pen, ink, and markers on board. *Courtesy of the artist*

The second and third uses seem to have the oldest and most traditional meaning, which Sheidlower defines as "A despicable or contemptible person." The second use is as an intensifier, and it's pretty close to an infix: *glass motherfuckin' house.*

The infix is the sibling of the prefix and suffix. While a prefix is attached to the front of a word (like *non* in *nonfat*), and a suffix is attached to the back (like *free* in *sugar-free*), an infix is sandwiched in the middle, like *fucking* in *absofuckinglutely* or *fanfuckingtastic*. *Glass motherfuckin' house* is similar, as is *Jesus fucking Christ*, which Vincent shouts after discovering Mia has overdosed on the drugs she found in his jacket pocket. A 1967 use quoted from the OED would fit right into *Pulp Fiction*: "Yeah! Emanci-motherfuckin'-pator of the slaves."

f-word: fuck

When Mia is quizzing Vincent about the rumors he's heard about her and Antoine, she asks, "Did it involve the f-word?" *F-word* is almost as popular as the f-word itself. It's the title of Sheidlower's book about *fuck,* and it's probably the most common euphemism for it. A 1973 use in a *New York Times* review shows it can be used almost as diversely as the word it replaces: "I ain't got time to be outraged about these books. I dismiss them. The kids use the expression 'f-word', the 'f-word', when they want to talk about it without saying it. Well, I say, 'f-word' them books, and 'f-word' the pretentious writers who write them."

to fuck up: to hurt someone, get wasted, or screw something up

When Jules says "Marsellus fucked him (Antoine) up good."—of the alleged balcony-throwing—he's using a sense of *fuck up* that implies you were brutalized but not snuffed out, as in this 1987 OED use: "I don't want anyone to die in the riot. . . . Some will definitely get fucked up, but as of now, no one will be killed." This is closely related to another sense of *fucked up* used by Lance the drug dealer, who does not initially put down a welcome mat for Vince and an OD-ing Mia: "You are not bringing this fucked-up bitch into my house!"

fucking A: an R-rated version of *right on!*

When describing a bank robbery involving a phone instead of a gun, Honey Bunny asks, "Did it work?" Pumpkin replies, "Fucking A, it worked." This can have a few meanings, but it usually means something like "right on" or "damn straight." Back in 1948, it was euphemized by Norman Mailer in *The Naked and the Dead* as *fuggin ay. Fucking A* was originally used by the military, and Sheidlower suggests it might have evolved from *you're fucking A-number-one right!*

Holy fuck, that's a lot of *fuck*s. However, despite its reputation, *Pulp Fiction* does not showcase a wide variety of uses. It sticks with the most common ones, which makes the characters sound profane yet naturalistic. There are no *clusterfuck*s, *starfuck*s, *mercy fuck*s, *ratfuck*s, *fuckwad*s, or phrases like *hunched over like a monkey fucking a football* and *I been to three county fairs and a goat-fuckin' and I ain't never seen the like of* that. (Thank you, Sheidlower, for recording those.) The dialogue is among the wittiest ever written, but the *fuck*s aren't a main ingredient of that wit. They merely add flavor to a rich meal.

Mark Peters (@wordlust) is a language columnist and humorist living in Chicago.

Toilet Drama

Vincent Vega would have come out of *Pulp Fiction* smelling
a lot better if he'd steered clear of the bathroom. Trouble lurks there
from the chronological beginning of the story, when it hides the fourth man
with the "hand cannon" who nearly takes out our heroes. Later, when Vincent
excuses himself to Mia Wallace's commode—ostensibly to "take a piss," but in fact
to talk himself out of a looming sexual encounter with her—he's gone long enough
for her to mistake his heroin for cocaine and nearly kill herself.

A trip to the Hawthorne Grille toilet, both to use the facilities and brush off a few
pages of *Modesty Blaise*, is unfortunately timed precisely to Pumpkin and Honey Bunny's
holdup. And, finally, when Vincent uses Butch's toilet (again, both to move his bowels
and move through *Modesty*), he emerges to find his target holding Marsellus' gun,
which is the end of Mr. Vega.

Bathroom scenes occur in almost all of Tarantino's films, and frequently with dire
consequences to the bathroom user. In the fake-story-within-the-story in *Reservoir Dogs*,
Mr. Orange very nearly gets himself busted by stumbling into a gathering of deputies
in a bus station bathroom. In *True Romance*, Clarence goes to Lee Donowitz'
bathroom to urinate and receive counsel from his Elvislike "Alter Ego,"
emerging (like Vincent) to find a Mexican standoff in progress.
And in *Kill Bill Volume 1*, Sofie Fatale leaves herself vulnerable
to The Bride by using the facilities at the House
of Blue Leaves.

If there's a consistent message in Tarantino's work,
it's a simple one: just hold it
until you get home.

Secrets, Facts, and *Fiction*

The Briefcase

By Patricia Póvoa.
Courtesy of the artist

Late in *Pulp Fiction*, during Pumpkin and Honey Bunny's robbery of the coffee shop, Jules is forced to open the mysterious briefcase he and Vincent retrieved earlier that morning. As the light within shines onto Pumpkin's face, he mutters, "Is that what I think it is?" Honey Bunny, nearby, asks eagerly: "What *is* it?"

Her question is one that moviegoers have been asking unceasingly since October of 1994. The question of the briefcase's contents is one that has haunted Tarantino, Avary, and their actors, as the combination of the film's cult status and the obsessive inclinations of its fans have transformed a simple MacGuffin into one of modern cinema's greatest mysteries.

The reason it has become such a preoccupation, of course, is because Tarantino refused to explain what was in the briefcase and has held firm on that conviction. His natural inclination as a filmmaker is to leave things open, to let audiences interpret things as they wish. "I always hope," he has said, "that if one million people see my movie, they see one million different movies." This approach wasn't new to his second film; at the Toronto Film Festival press conference for *Reservoir Dogs*, he shrugged off a reporter's inquiry about that film's title. "I don't answer that question," he said, "because I really believe in what the audience brings. With movies as an art form, I think twenty percent of that art form is supplied by what the audience brings to the movie. People come up to me and tell me what they think it means and I am constantly astounded by their creativity and ingenuity. As far as

>>>> *Frame of Reference 19* <<<<

[MacGuffin]

Director's lingo for an object that the characters are pursuing—the thing that a movie is about, so that it can be about *something*. Examples include Rosebud in *Citizen Kane*, the statue in *The Maltese Falcon*, the uranium in *Notorious*, and the briefcase in *Pulp Fiction*. (Ebert reports a discussion where the golden glow inside and the early morning timeframe of the movie led one person to guess that it contains "an Egg MacGuffin.") The

phrase was coined by Alfred Hitchcock, who explained it thus: "It might be a Scottish name, taken from a story about two men in a train. One man says, 'What's that package up there in the baggage rack?' And the other answers, 'Oh that's a MacGuffin.' The first one asks 'What's a MacGuffin?' 'Well' the other man says, 'It's an apparatus for trapping lions in the Scottish Highlands.'

An early MacGuffin:
the Maltese Falcon.
© Photos 12 / Alamy

The first man says, 'But there are no lions in the Scottish Highlands,' and the other one answers 'Well, then that's no MacGuffin!' So you see, a MacGuffin is nothing at all!"

I'm concerned, what they come up with is right, they're one hundred percent right."

Left to their own devices, fans have come up with some fairly wild explanations. Some

Could the King's suit be in Marsellus Wallace's briefcase?

seize on the amber light emanating from the case and claim it's carrying gold bars. Nuttier theories place stolen Oscars in the briefcase (maybe Tarantino swiping the Best Director and Best Picture statues from Zemeckis and *Forrest Gump*?) or a gold lamé Elvis suit (like the King wore on the cover of *50,000,000 Elvis Fans Can't Be Wrong*—and Val Kilmer wore in *True Romance*). And then there is the king mother of wacky Internet briefcase theories: that it contains Marsellus Wallace's soul.

As the story goes, Marsellus sold his soul to the devil, which was removed from his body via the back of his head (as souls are, supposedly). The wound from its removal is still fresh—hence the prominently displayed Band-Aid on his neck. But Marsellus decided to buy his soul back from the devil, and sent Vincent and Jules to complete the purchase. Brett and his boys were the devil's helpers, turning over his soul in the briefcase (locked with the devil's favorite three-number combination, 666). And when one of those helpers tried to shoot Jules and Vincent

Briefcase,
by Michael Sapienza.
Digital print, 2010.
Courtesy of the artist

dead, "God came down and stopped the bullets," an act of divine intervention in the service of saving a soul.

It's a fun theory, but a silly one. Tellers of this theory, for example, will insist that this soul-from-the-back-of-the-head business is common knowledge, though it comes from absolutely nowhere, biblical or otherwise. The Band-Aid on Rhames' neck, as previously mentioned, had less to do with a satanic backstory than it did with covering up a preexisting scar.

The real story, according to the closest source that *would* talk—cowriter Avary—is that the briefcase held boring old diamonds. But since a case of diamonds had been the

MacGuffin for *Reservoir Dogs*, he and Tarantino decided to leave the contents a mystery and let people figure it out themselves. In a 2003 interview, Tarantino held firm: "Stuff that's open for interpretation, I want your interpretation. The minute I tell you what I think, you'll throw away whatever you've come up with in your head. You can't help it. I would too. You'd feel like a fool.

"So you tell me what's in the briefcase. If you think it's Marsellus' soul and he's bought it back from the devil, which is one guess I've heard, well, you are right: It's his soul. That I actually did a movie that can inspire such wildly imaginative readings makes me proud."

What we *can* take from the events onscreen is that the briefcase functions as a Pandora's Box. It is, after all, Vincent who looks inside—and who later dies. So do Brett and his boys, devil's helpers or not. But Jules, who walks away from his life of crime (a decision confirmed by the appearance of English Bob/Paul as Vincent's new partner in "The Gold Watch"), does not gaze upon its beauty, and he lives to tell the tale. Does Pumpkin? We can only guess.

But for the ultimate, final, end-all explanation of what was in the briefcase, we turn to Samuel L. Jackson. Interviewed in the April 1995

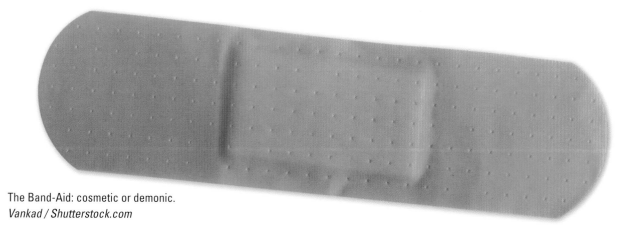

The Band-Aid: cosmetic or demonic.
Vankad / Shutterstock.com

Cowriter Avary explained the briefcase's contents, and his objections to the eventual presentation of it, to Ebert: "All you were supposed to know was that it was 'so beautiful.' No prop master can come up with something better than each individual's imagination. At least that was the original idea. Then somebody had the bright idea (which I think was a mistake) of putting an orange light bulb in there. Suddenly what could have been anything became anything supernatural. Didn't need to push the effect. People would have debated it for years anyway, and it would have been much more subtle. I can't believe I'm actually talking about being subtle."

characters and weaving it in, that's what ended up coming out, because that's what I really believe in." It would be easy to surmise that Tarantino backed into the spiritual aspect of *Pulp Fiction* by accident—maybe he, like Jules, wanted to use the modified Ezekiel 25:17 quote from the Sonny Chiba movie because he thought "it was some cold-blooded shit to say," but then, like his protagonist, he began to consider the implications of the speech.

Or it could just be that, as Quentin says, the film's subtle but heartfelt message about redemption and forgiveness is his own deeply held conviction. By his reckoning, *Pulp Fiction* "ends up being quite a moralistic film. You could even make the case that *Dogs* ultimately ended up being very moralistic. I never intended it to be this way but in some ways my films go by the old Hays Code. You can do anything you want in the first eighty-eight minutes as long as in the last two minutes there's some retribution for what the characters have done."

issue of *Playboy*, Jackson offered up the last word on the issue: "I assumed it was something that, when people looked at it, seemed like the most beautiful thing they had ever seen or their greatest desire. When I looked inside, between scenes, I saw two lights and some batteries."

"God Got Involved": Spirituality

I never said, 'I'm gonna write a redemption story,'" Tarantino told the *Los Angeles Times* in 1995. "But if I'm writing this big passel of

The Path of the Righteous Man, by John Pennisi. Computer graphic, 2011. *Courtesy of the artist.* www.monsterplanetdesign.etsy.com

[Hays Code]

The term *Hays Code* is shorthand for the Motion Picture Production Code (abbreviated to reference Will Hays, Hollywood's chief censor), which regulated onscreen content from roughly 1930 until 1968, when it was supplanted by the MPAA's ratings system. Among its many rules was the insistence that any criminal behavior be duly punished by the picture's conclusion.

Pulp Fiction's three-story structure allows Tarantino to do better than that: each of its episodes concludes with a salvation (or two, if you count the person doing the saving). Vincent Vega saves Mia Wallace from death by overdose—and in doing so, saves himself from the certain death of responsibility for her passing.

PULP FACT 25

Even *True Romance* considers consequences of faith: in the original screenplay (but, tellingly, not in Tony Scott's film), Clarence returns to their motel room to find Alabama "absent-mindedly saying the prayer of Saint Francis of Assisi" after killing the hired goon Virgil (played in the film by James Gandolfini).

Butch saves Marsellus from his brutal sexual assault (and perhaps subsequent murder) at the hands of Maynard and Zed—and thus cleans his own slate with his former employer, quite possibly saving his own life (and that of his beloved Fabienne) down the line. Both of those salvations are sealed with an agreement that the events will remain solely between the parties involved, but because the third redemption—in which Jules chooses not to take the lives of Pumpkin and Honey Bunny, and determines to save his own—is done publicly, it carries more weight.

Strangely, as it follows three films (*Reservoir Dogs, True Romance,* and *Natural Born Killers*) filled with important police characters, the world of *Pulp Fiction* is a nearly lawless one. (Zed the "rent-a-cop" is the closest thing to law enforcement, and he may be the film's most reprehensible character.) These people, it is made clear, are on their own. Jules may pinpoint Pumpkin as "the weak" in "the valley of the shadow of darkness," but then so are Mia, and Butch, and Marsellus, and Vincent . The latter, by ignoring the sign (be it a miracle, a freak occurrence, or divine intervention) that sends Jules on his righteous path, remains weak, the blind man, and pays the ultimate price. But we hold out hope for the other three, and for Pumpkin and Honey Bunny as well, and certainly for Jules.

Which brings us to Ezekiel 25:17. The verse is the film's moral backbone, even if the form it appears in here bears only a passing resemblance to the real thing. "I rewrote it a little bit," Quentin shrugged, as (presumably) did the writers and translators of *The Bodyguard*, the Sonny Chiba film that suggested the quotation. What we can be certain of is that, as Jules says,

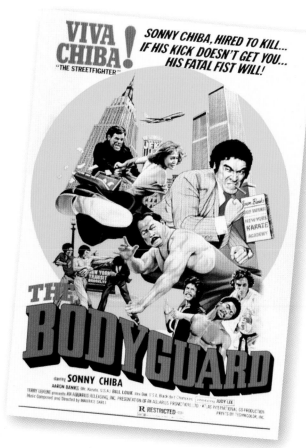

The Bodyguard (1976) opens with the text of Ezekiel 25:17 scrolling across the screen. (Like Jules' version, there are more than a few discrepancies between the Bible text and the screen version.) *Everett Collection*

the speech/verse/sermon/rave-up is merely a text, recited for effect, until the epiphany that follows his near-death experience.

He clearly makes a choice to read that experience as a fated event rather than the random, "freak occurrence" of Vincent's interpretation—a notion lent further credence by Marvin's shooting immediately thereafter (one intended murder fails, one accidental murder succeeds; it's all willy-nilly, the luck of the draw, how the cards fall). Jules holds firm: "Naw, naw, naw. That shit wasn't luck." And to that end, the discussion of whether it was a miracle or freak occurrence becomes moot—Jules *believes* it was a miracle and changes his behavior (and his life) accordingly.

The opportunity presents itself rather quickly, as these things sometimes do. But his actions at the coffee shop are carefully considered. He does not, first of all, choose the simplest method of saving himself, his fellow diners,

and the fifteen hundred dollars tucked away in his "bad motherfucker" wallet: pulling his handgun and plugging Pumpkin and Honey Bunny.

PULP FACT 26

Here is Ezekiel 25:17 as it appears in the King James Bible: "And I will execute great vengeance upon them with furious rebukes; and they shall know that I *am* the LORD, when I shall lay my vengeance upon them." That's it—no brothers, no shepherds, no valley of darkness, though the latter two phrases appear in similar form in Psalms 23. The opening crawl/voice-over of *The Bodyguard*, though attributed as Ezekiel 25:17, is much closer to Jules' speech: "The path of the righteous man and defender is beset on all sides by the iniquities of the selfish and the tyranny of evil men. Blessed is he, who in the name of charity and goodwill, shepherds the weak through the valley of darkness, for he is truly his brother's keeper, and the father of lost children. And I will execute great vengeance upon them with furious anger, who poison and destroy my brothers; and they shall know that I am CHIBA the BODYGUARD when I shall lay my vengeance upon them." It seems that Jules—like Tarantino—learned the verse from the Sonny Chiba movie, and not from the King James Bible.

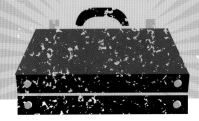

He could do it, certainly—both of them are pre-occupied with the logistics of the robbery, and aren't expecting that kind of behavior from a diner patron (see their earlier comments about cutting down on the hero factor in a place like this).

But that's not good enough for Jules. It might have been, a few scant hours earlier, but not now. He must not only save himself and his fellow diners, but the two lost souls (the weak) God has placed in front of him, as surely as He diverted the bullets coming at Jules earlier that morning. Jules, as Gavin Smith noted in *Film Comment*, "survives death through 'divine intervention,' is blessed and cleansed by Keitel's debonair angel, and discovers mercy."

That mercy is the "something" he's buying for his money, and in the closing scene of *Pulp*

"It's the one that says 'bad motherfucker'."

Fiction, we are given a taste of what Jules will do, and what he will (scratch that—already *has*) become. These two common thieves aren't just saved but tamed, sent out the door in each other's arms, and though Jules must first wield his pistol, it is not his gun but his words that reach them. He saves them not with force but with

Jules with his wallet.
Courtesy of Miramax

honesty and vulnerability, not by preaching at them, as he usually does when reciting Ezekiel 25:17, but by speaking *to* them.

"Jules couldn't say this religious epiphany in the same way as he'd said it before," Tarantino explained, and he not only changes the tone, but the words themselves (the impersonal "my name is" and "thee" are transformed into the more intimate "I am" and "you"). "After using it for ten years, for the first time he realizes what it really means. And that's the end of the film." The experiences of this morning have not just changed Jules. They have made him into an agent of change. What could be more fundamentally spiritual than that? If such a man as Jules Winnfield can find a new path and a new place for himself in the world, who among us can't?

Violence and Tap-Dancing

I make violent movies," Tarantino announced in 2012. "I like violent movies. I'm on record about how I feel there is no correlation between art and life in that way." It's a question he had been answering, at that point, for twenty years (and would answer many more times that fall, often testily, as his ultraviolent *Django Unchained* opened shortly after the bloody school shooting in Newtown, Connecticut). His impatience with it is understandable. On one hand, he is an artist whose films traffic in—perhaps even revel in—intense, graphic violence. On the other, he is but one of hundreds of filmmakers who paint with those images, and most of his fellow travelers do so with far less artistry than he. So why does Tarantino always seem to be wearing a bull's-eye?

Whatever the reason, he has been consistent on the subject. Clear back in 1992, he had this to say: "I love violence in movies, and if you don't, it's like you don't like tap-dancing, or slapstick, but that doesn't mean it shouldn't be shown. My mom doesn't like Abbott and Costello or Laurel and Hardy, but that doesn't mean they shouldn't have been making movies." The same year, he told *Variety*'s Todd McCarthy, "I'm not going to be handcuffed by what some crazy fuck might do who sees my movie. The minute you put handcuffs on artists because of stuff like that, it's not an art form anymore."

The cause for all of this discussion was *Reservoir Dogs*—specifically, the infamous scene where Mr. Blonde tortures uniformed cop Marvin Nash to the strains of Steeler's Wheel's "Stuck in the Middle with You." It prompted a discussion of both the morality and the aesthetics of onscreen violence that has followed the director throughout his career, with much wringing of hands from even his friendliest critics. "What's transgressive in *Reservoir Dogs*," wrote Amy Taubin in *Sight and Sound*, "is not the level of violence or the terrifying realism of bodies that bleed and bleed, but the way Tarantino lays bare the sadomasochistic dynamic between the film and the spectator." Tarantino told McCarthy, "The cinema isn't intruding in that scene. You are stuck there, and the cinema isn't going to help you out. Every minute for that cop is a minute for you." But McCarthy demurred: "He's wrong; the cinema is intruding. That scene is pure set piece; it may even be pure art. That's what scares me."

In retrospect, it seems that what frightened these critics was not a filmmaker who dramatized violence, but one who took it seriously. There was nothing "scary" or "transgressive" about the *Friday the 13th* films or Charles Bronson's revenge thrillers. But here was a director who understood what he was doing and was willing to grapple with the implications of it. "There are two kinds of violence," he explained while promoting *Reservoir Dogs*. "First, there's cartoon violence like *Lethal Weapon*. There's nothing wrong with that. I'm not ragging on that. But my kind of violence is tougher, rougher, more disturbing. It gets under your skin. Go to a video store, to the horror section or the action-adventure section, nine out of ten of the films you get there are going to be more graphically violent than my movie, but I'm *trying* to be disturbing. What's going on is happening to real human beings. There are ramifications to it."

An Australian Tarantino-inspired dance.
© *Angus Gough / Alamy*

Forcing his audience to deal with those ramifications can lead to overreaction and hyperbole, and it's amusing to read reviews and profiles in esteemed periodicals like the *Los Angeles Times* reporting breathlessly that *Reservoir Dogs* contains a "ten-minute torture sequence," when

a **Quentin Tarantino** film

PULP FICTION

JOHN TRAVOLTA   UMA THURMAN
BRUCE WILLIS   SAMUEL L. JACKSON

MIRAMAX FILMS PRESENT A BAND APART AND JERSEY FILMS PRODUCTION A FILM BY QUENTIN TARANTINO PULP FICTION MUSIC SUPERVISOR KARIN RACHMAN
COSTUME DESIGNER BETSY HEIMANN PRODUCTION DESIGNER DAVID WASCO EDITOR SALLY MENKE DIRECTOR OF PHOTOGRAPHY ANDRZEJ SEKULA
STACEY SHER STORIES BY QUENTIN TARANTINO & ROGER AVARY PRODUCER BY LAWRENCE BENDER WRITTEN AND DIRECTED BY QUENTIN TARANTINO

By Danna Podstudensek. Photo retouching digital art, 2012. *Courtesy of the artist, © 2012 Danna Podstudensek. www. behance.com/ph_ danna_podstu*

the scene itself runs barely half that time (for the record: four minutes and forty seconds elapse between the time Mr. Blonde pulls out his razor and when he is shot dead by Mr. Orange). What no one mentions is the way that Tarantino holds on Roth's face as he witnesses the violence his trusted friend Mr. White inflicts upon his fellow officers, or as he realizes that he has just shot a woman in cold blood.

Now consider *Pulp Fiction*, which favors intensity over explicit gore and often either places violence outside the frame or shoots it in an oblique way. When Butch takes out Maynard with the samurai sword, the camera is at first between him and his victim, so we only see Maynard's back; after he turns and Butch steps into close-up, the second slash is below the frame line. "Flock of Seagulls" is dispatched in a long shot, his shooting a surprise, but accompanied by no gore. When Jules and Vincent kill Brett and the fourth man in the bathroom, the camera stays on the killers, not their victims. Even the messy shooting of Marvin is seen from outside Jules' car, the explosion of blood softened by our view of it through the back window.

"As I saw it a second and third time," Roger Ebert wrote in 1995, "I realized it wasn't as violent as I thought—certainly not by the standards of modern action movies. It *seems* more violent because it often delays a payoff with humorous dialogue, toying with us." Ebert also noted that, in a rather sly bit of gun control commentary, the weapons in the film are seldom used by the person, or on the victim, for which they were intended: Marsellus' gun kills Vincent instead of Butch, Maynard's gun maims Zed, the fourth man's gun doesn't kill Vincent and Jules, Vincent's gun accidentally kills Marvin, and Jules' gun prevents, rather than causes, violence in the coffee shop.

Writer Edward Gallafant points out another interesting moment, one that is not "narratively necessary" (and one that is curiously absent from the screenplay): the brief exchange between Vincent, Jules, and Marvin after Brett's shooting. Marvin seems panicked and upset by what he's seen, and Vincent advises Jules that Marvin should either quiet down or leave.

Gallafant suggests that it "underlines the massive difference in sensibility here between the hit men, who have no reaction to the situation beyond a calculation of who is dead and who is not, and Marvin, to whom the violence is present as something awful and immediate happening to the body of another." It's the kind of moment all too uncommon in mainstream cinema—one in which a character is allowed not only to consider violence, but also to be affected by it. What's particularly crafty about that beat is that Tarantino places it at the moment in his screenplay when his two cold, calculating killers are about to approach something like those feelings themselves (by the oncoming miracle/freak occurrence).

"I get a kick out of violence in movies," Tarantino has said, while emphasizing, "I don't get a kick out of *badly done* violence or action scenes in movies. It's like, 'How far is too far?' Well, if they do it well, there shouldn't be, 'How far is too far?'" Besides, he points out, everyone's tolerance is his or her own. "What I find offensive," he was fond of saying during the *Dogs* publicity tour, "is that Merchant-Ivory shit."

>>>> *Frame of Reference* <<<<

[Merchant-Ivory Productions]

Producer-director team of Ismail Merchant and James Ivory purveyed British films of impeccable taste and high intellect—the kind of thing art houses were full of in the pre-Tarantino era. Best-known works include *A Room with a View*, *Maurice*, *Howard's End*, and *The Remains of the Day*, all released between 1985 and 1993. During *Pulp*'s test screenings, Tarantino was fond of asking audiences if they'd liked *Reservoir Dogs*, *True Romance*, and *The Remains of the Day*. He'd beam proudly at those who'd seen the first two, while thundering at those who answered affirmative to the latter, "Get the fuck outta here!"

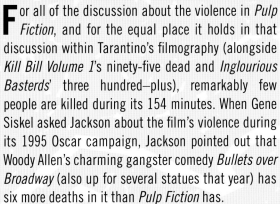

Body Count

For all of the discussion about the violence in *Pulp Fiction*, and for the equal place it holds in that discussion within Tarantino's filmography (alongside *Kill Bill Volume 1*'s ninety-five dead and *Inglourious Basterds*' three hundred–plus), remarkably few people are killed during its 154 minutes. When Gene Siskel asked Jackson about the film's violence during its 1995 Oscar campaign, Jackson pointed out that Woody Allen's charming gangster comedy *Bullets over Broadway* (also up for several statues that year) has six more deaths in it than *Pulp Fiction* has.

How many people, exactly, get bumped off in this superviolent movie? Nine—only six of them onscreen.

- Three men in the apartment: Brett, "Flock of Seagulls," and the "fourth man" in the bathroom.

- Marvin, accidentally shot in the face by Vincent in the car.

- Vincent Vega, killed by Butch in his apartment.

- Butch's opponent, Floyd Wilson—killed offscreen, but seen dead in his dressing room.

- Maynard, disemboweled by Butch.

- Presumptive pawnshop deaths: Zed, only maimed onscreen, but certain to live "the rest of his short-ass life in agonizing pain"; and "the Gimp," punched out and seemingly hung by Butch.

- Not counted: the brunette woman who catches Marsellus' stray bullet (it hits her in the leg, and does not appear to be a life-threatening injury).

Split Personality

"My only obligation is to my characters," Tarantino says, "and they came from where I have been." The question of how much a writer's characters reflect themselves is asked of every distinctive wordsmith, particularly someone like Tarantino, whose creations tend to speak in his same language of tough-guy patter and pop culture references. But each has his or her own unique variation on that voice, and each comes from a different archetypal tradition (as discussed earlier).

That said, the two most interesting characters to trace back to their creator are Jules and Vincent. One of them is an "Elvis man." The other is a blaxpoitation-era badass. Combined, they are the man Tarantino would like to be and has styled himself as. They are the two halves of his imagined, idealized personality.

The scene in which Vincent Vega identifies himself as an "Elvis man" was left on the cutting room floor (see "Deleted Scenes," page 182), but even without it, Mia's identification of him as such isn't much of a leap. With his black suit, bolo tie, and throwback style, he is the quintessential rockabilly cool cat, and his personality matches. In a portion cut from the opening monologue of *True Romance* (which features an Elvis figure dispensing fatherly advice to its hero), Clarence hones in on Elvis' attitude, discussing a scene in *Jailhouse Rock*: "I love that scene where after he's made it big, he's thrown a big cocktail party, and all these highbrows are there, and he's singing, 'Baby You're So Square . . . Baby I Don't Care.' Now, they got him dressed like a dick. He's wearing these stupid-lookin' pants, this horrible sweater. Elvis ain't no sweater boy. I even think they got him wearin' penny loafers. Despite all that shit, all the highbrows at the party, big house, the stupid clothes, he's still a rude-lookin' motherfucker."

In spite of his idiosyncratic and sometimes goofy personality, friends of Tarantino during the Video Archive years say he was a tough and somewhat imposing figure, less for his physical prowess than his refusal to back down. "I used to live and walk around in some of the most fucked-up areas you could ever imagine," he recalled. "I went out of my way to go to those areas, you know. I never once gave, like, two thoughts about it. I used to have the biggest balls in the world. I'd see a guy coming towards me. I'd look like a badass and dare him to say something."

That youthful sense of machismo (which Tarantino was careful to point out he'd outgrown—"Being the baddest guy in the world isn't the most important thing anymore") doesn't just manifest itself in *Reservoir Dogs'* tough guys, waving their guns and sticking out their chins ("I'll bet you're a big Lee Marvin fan"). It's there in the way Vincent Vega deals with the world around him, in demanding the kind of "respect" that his hero Elvis did. "A please would be nice," he tells the Wolf, though he is also careful to note that "I don't mean no disrespect. I respect you and all." The last half of that statement is, almost verbatim, what Jules tells Vincent in Jimmie's bathroom, as a method of calming him down. It's inherent in their crime culture ("Respect," the Wolf boasts. "Respect for one's elders"), and in that of the rockabilly greaser, who will never get the respect of the squares, and would refuse it if he did (or says he would, anyway).

Jules, on the other hand, represents Tarantino's lifelong love of black pop culture and iconography. "I went to a mostly black school," Tarantino told Terry Gross. "You know, it wasn't all-black because I was there, but it was mostly black." He grew up listening to soul music and watching "urban" movies, and if Jules falls into the archetype of the tough, commanding heroes of those films, he also seems to personify something that Tarantino always wanted to be but couldn't, by sheer virtue of his being white. It wasn't for lack of trying; from his sporting of Kangol hats to match his *Jackie Brown* costars to his controversial use of the word "nigger" throughout his scripts (most problematically in *Pulp Fiction*, when Jimmy shouts it at Jules—an offense we're presumably to forgive since we've been assured Jules and Jimmy are friends),

Tarantino is firmly entrenched in a generation of misfits that looked to black culture for the street cred and the cool they were sorely lacking. But no matter what he does, Tarantino can never be as cool as Jules.

Then again, maybe the whole theory is bunk—maybe Butch is the real Tarantino avatar, from his Knoxville roots to his upbringing (with the television as babysitter, sitting in for an absentee father) to his predilection for fighting. And before the film's release, Tarantino mentioned in interviews how the sweetest thing a girl could say to him was that she liked his smell (as Fabienne says to Butch). And so it goes, on down the line. In a film with characters as rich as these, the filmmaker can't help but invest something of himself, until analysis and biography become one and the same.

"I don't smile in pictures." Jules (Samuel L. Jackson), Vincent (John Travolta), and The Wolf (Harvey Keitel) pose for Jimmie's photograph in a deleted scene. *Courtesy of Miramax*

PULP FICTION

When discussing Tarantino's body of work, there are many adjectives that come to mind: *meta*; *violent*; *labyrinthine*; *playful*; *stylized*. But of all the words used to describe the passionate director's oeuvre, perhaps the most encapsulating would have to be *cool*. From *Reservoir Dogs* to *Django Unchained*, Tarantino has been a purveyor of cool, his finger consistently on the pulse of the contemporary cultural landscape during the crafting of any given film, while simultaneously culling from the cultural zeitgeists that preceded him.

One such cultural touchstone he has returned to over the course of his career has been the short-lived blaxploitation genre, and it's easy to see why. When you think of *Shaft*, *Coffy*, or *Super Fly*, what do you think of? Cool. They were subversively so, movies meant to speak to a black audience routinely ignored by predominantly white Hollywood, working against The Man. And Tarantino revels in cool—in numerous interviews he's used the word when passionately discussing the movies he loves. He's always been forthcoming about his multitude of wildly eclectic influences, including blaxploitation—he idolizes Pam Grier (she's referenced directly or indirectly in at least three of his films), cites *Shaft* as one of his favorites, and frequently incorporates old-school soul music into his soundtracks.

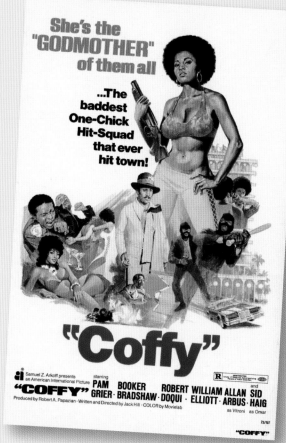

© *Moviestore Collection Ltd / Alamy*

Pulp Fiction is primarily a neo-noir/crime film featuring hit men Vincent Vega, Jules Winnfield, and other familiar characters and archetypes. But no Tarantino film is anything less than a panoply of various cinematic expressions, and the tony, witty barbs traded by Vincent and Jules on their way to a job—"Royale with Cheese"; "I'm the foot-fucking-master. . . . Got my technique down and everything, I don't be tickling or nothing"—are just as much an exercise in black cool as they are crime movie tropes.

AND THE BLACK COOL

By Aisha Harris

What is it about blaxploitation films—and black culture in general—that exudes, as art historian Robert Farris Thompson has dubbed it, an "aesthetic of the cool"? What exactly *is* that cool? In the seventies it could be both the deep, sexy bass of Isaac Hayes and the soft falsetto of Curtis Mayfield. As Thompson has pointed out, the West African definition connotes a certain mannerism conveyed through artistic performance. It also refers to an exuding of nonchalance and stoicism in moments of high pressure and excitement—what we see, for instance, when Priest, a cocaine dealer trying to get out of the game in *Super Fly*, is confronted by a couple of black militants and in a composed, yet badass manner, rejects their call to arms and sends them on their way.

It's easy to trace these characters of a particular male, urban essence directly to Jules; he strikes just the right balance between intimidating composure and intimidating anger, shifting between both states of being fluidly. When Brett sees an opportunity to try to leverage the situation in the apartment scene—in his unhip way—Jules never loses control. Rather, the slow buildup to a burst of anger and a Bible recitation seems to be a calculated part of his performance. A subtle-yet-firm wave of the hand, and Brad is sitting back down at his command; a swift gunshot to Brett's partner on the couch (without ever taking his stare off Brett), and Jules is rendered even more frightening to his remaining targets—and cooler to us, the audience.

It's not just his saunter that recalls the black heroes of the cinematic past. The ridiculous Jheri-curl wig Jackson sports, while not quite of the era in which blaxploitation lived and died, is nonetheless an ostentatious use of sartorial display that effectively marks him as unique from everyone else (white and black) around him, just like Priest's pimplike permed hair and flamboyantly bell-bottomed suits with matching

The epitome of cool.
Photo by John D. Kisch / Separate Cinema Archive / Getty Images

fedoras. From a purely visual perspective, it may seem laughable to modern-day audiences that anyone dressed like those two men could be taken seriously or seen as any kind of threat. But the power lay in the distinctly black aesthetic of their particular cultural moments and stylized performances of male masculinity.

Tarantino plays with this notion of black cool in the final scene, when Jules encounters the would-be diner robbers. Recalling many a blaxploitation film in which a potentially violent situation is diffused by the calm, self-assured command of a character, Jules uses his composure to his benefit. In his exchange with the dim, fumbling Yolanda and Ringo, Jules is even cooler than before; having miraculously survived being shot at, he's acquired a Zenlike state that

Across 110th Street,
1973. Q. T. lifted its
theme song for the
opening credits of
Jackie Brown. Photo
by Keystone-France /
Gamma-Keystone via
Getty Images

leaves him virtually unfazed by having another gun pointed at his head. When he deftly seizes the gun from Ringo, he notes, ironically, "We're all gonna be like three little Fonzies here, and what's Fonzie like?" "Cool," sputters Yolanda.

Of course, the iconic *Happy Days* character evoked by Jules represents a different kind of cool—the kind with its own catchphrase and supposedly Italian machismo (despite Henry Winkler being quite Jewish in real life). But that's part of what makes the statement so caustic, and such an interesting choice for Tarantino to make. Why doesn't Jules suggest they try to be chill like Shaft? Perhaps it would be too on the nose—though, as we see when it's revealed that his wallet is embroidered "bad motherfucker," the director's not above being so overt. More likely, it's Jules' subversive way of pandering to the white (and foreign) characters—surely they know who Arthur Fonzarelli is, though they may not have heard of "the man that would risk his neck for his brother man." And even if they had, it would be impossible for them to embody such cool in the same way that Jules can and does.

On the other end of the cool spectrum, Vincent fulfills in body and spirit the role that Tarantino plays behind the camera by adopting a white male hipness that feels informed by black culture. Part of this characterization stems from the persona of Travolta himself, carved out since his classic roles as the charming, suave Italian-American in *Saturday Night*

Fever and *Grease*. With the latter, he traded on an Elvis aesthetic—the slicked back hair, black jeans and tee, and the seductive singing voice and swiveled hips (which were in turn, of course, informed by black performers to some extent). Even more so, it's hard not to look at the opening credits of *Saturday Night Fever*, during which his character Tony confidently struts about New York City with a solid stare, and not see some trace of *Shaft*'s own opening credits.

Despite this differing of cool, there's no apparent racial tension between Vincent and Jules, unlike in *Across 110th Street*, a black-white cop crime film often associated with the blaxploitation genre, and rich with racial tension. Instead, Vincent is pretty much down with Jules, his inflections connoting a tint of blackness, though he exudes a more consistently relaxed demeanor than his partner. (It is Vincent, after all, who lingers in the background, barely saying a word as Jules employs his vengeance with reverence.)

Pulp Fiction's handlings of race, both implicit and explicit, echo some blaxploitation films, in which the urban landscapes and characters portrayed a black way of life as well as a stark commentary on the effects of white patriarchy. It lies under the surface with Jules and Vincent.

But black-white tensions burst through in other unexpected moments, as when an argument between Marcellus and Butch turns into a traumatizing attack on black manhood, and a temporary loss of Marcellus' cool. Like Priest, who struggles to get out from under corrupt cops, the power he's attained is consistently threatened by white outside forces. Once Marcellus is free from his rapist, his composure has been effectively jarred yet it still remains, as Marcellus calmly notes that he's "gonna call a couple of hard pipe-hittin' niggas to go to work on the homes here."

Other blaxploitation influences are notable within the dialogue, particularly in Jules' and Marcellus' casual employment of *nigga*, lending the word an air familiar to black culture. Tarantino's one misstep in taking from the genre is his controversial "dead nigger storage" moment, which feels unnecessary by modern standards. The word was used often by both blacks and whites in those earlier films, though those white characters who used it tended to be vilified by the story; but with Tarantino's scene—which to this day doesn't sit well with some black viewers, Spike Lee most famously—it appears to be his miscalculated way of echoing even further that brief period in Hollywood history when writers could more or less get away with such things (as in the titillating title *The Legend of Nigger Charley*).

Tarantino, the movie geek who spent his young adulthood educating himself in a video store, has mastered the art of adopting the cool from multiple cultures apart from his own. In the Kill Bill films, it's the stylized choreography and camera movement of Japanese samurai flicks. In *Inglourious Basterds*, it's the machismo of World War II movies. But perhaps his greatest source of hipness is the blaxploitation world, where cool was maintained by the hip, black super fly men and foxy ladies who kicked ass, spoke street slang, and challenged Hollywood conventions.

Aisha Harris is an assistant with the cultural blog for Slate Magazine.

PART V

The Release and Aftermath

Cannes

Tarantino's 1994 trip to the Cannes Film Festival did not get off to an auspicious start. First, he lost his room—the hotel had given it to someone else. Then he lost his bag and had to hit up Bruce Willis for a change of clothes. (Willis also gave him some promotional swag for his flaccid erotic thriller *Color of Night*, which was also screening at the festival.) Unshaven and exhausted, he'd finished the film only a few days before departing for France—only to discover, just before their pre-premiere screening for critics of note (Ebert, David Denby, Richard Schickel), that the dialogue was somehow out of sync for two full minutes.

Bump Fiction, by Juan Vega Martínez. 2011. *Courtesy of the artist.* www.domestika.org/ portfolios/juan_vega_ diseno_grafico_y_ creatividad

Q. T. and Willis
at Cannes.
*Patrick Hertzog / AFP /
Getty Images*

But all of that was forgotten by the time the film screened late in the festival, at 12:30 a.m. on Saturday, May 21. The critics were ecstatic. "*Pulp Fiction* remains bracingly off-kilter as it mixes lurid, outrageous elements with sweetly appealing ones, to the point where the viewer never has the faintest idea what to expect," wrote the *New York Times*' Janet Maslin. "Tarantino's perversely inventive humor, his randy dialogue,

and some sensational tongue-in-cheek performances give you little chance to regret your laughter," noted *Newsday*'s Jack Day. The panel at the forty-five-minute postpremiere press conference included Travolta, Willis, Thurman, Jackson, and de Medeiros, but every single question was directed at Tarantino, who gave quotes nearly as juicy as his movie. Explaining the picture's appeal, he noted immodestly (if accurately), "The thing about this movie is that it's just a great fucking movie."

The Cannes jury, led by Clint Eastwood, agreed. Quentin, still smarting from awards snubs during *Reservoir Dogs'* festival run, didn't want to go to the closing ceremony at all. But programmer Gilles Jacob told Miramax head Harvey Weinstein that it would be worth their

Cannes. *Photo by Pool
Benainous / DUCLOS /
Gamma-Rapho via
Getty Images*

[Palme d'Or]

The Palme d'Or is the grand prize of the Cannes Film Festival—its equivalent to the Oscars' Best Picture. Notable previous winners include *MASH*; *The Conversation*; *Apocalypse Now*; *Blow-Up*; *sex, lies, and videotape*; and *Taxi Driver*.

while to attend. Tarantino figured he might nab the screenplay or director prize, assuming Krzystof Kieslowski's *Three Colors: Red* had the Palme d'Or locked up. Weinstein thought the same, but as those awards went to other pictures (Cannes is famously reluctant to hand films more than one honor), he turned to Quentin and said the unthinkable: "I think we're going to get the big one!"

They did. The jury awarded *Pulp Fiction* the Palme d'Or; rumor had it their initial voting also gave Best Actor to Travolta, but the prize went elsewhere on the second poll, in order to spread the wealth. Not that anyone cared that night. The *Fiction* contingent went back to the Hotel du Cap and threw a victory party that went until the break of dawn (with Willis picking up the $100,000 tab).

Once he was back on American soil, Tarantino was introspective about the win. "It hasn't changed my stature in the industry," he

The Palme d'Or, Cannes, 1994. When *Pulp Fiction* was announced as the award's winner, a woman in the crowd started shouting angrily in French, to which Tarantino calmly responded, "I don't make the kind of movies that bring people together. . . . I kinda make movies that split people apart." *Patrick Hertzog / AFP / Getty Images*

shrugged, "because my stature in the industry couldn't be better. But it has given me the Good Housekeeping Seal of Approval, so if you don't like my work now, it has to do with your own taste and not my material." The boys at Miramax had their own read on the win: it had transformed their late-summer counter-programming movie into a fall prestige picture. At Bob Weinstein's suggestion, *Pulp Fiction* was pushed back from its original August release date into an October slot, with a U.S. premiere at the New York Film Festival (NYFF) paving the way for, of all things, an Oscar campaign.

An Indie Smash

September 23, 1994. It is opening night of the New York Film Festival, and *Pulp Fiction* is unspooling at Lincoln Center's Avery Fisher Hall. Everything's tip-top; the audience is laughing and applauding and eating up the festival's most-buzzed selection. Mia Wallace is laid out on Lance's floor, her host and her date arguing over who will administer a shot of adrenaline to her heart. Vincent Vega raises the syringe, Lance counts to three . . . and a man down front keels over, in a dead faint. People scream. The movie stops. The lights come up. Harvey Weinstein, his concert promoter's instincts kicking in, is at the stricken man's side in seconds. Ten minutes later, an announcer assures the audience that "the victim is okay" (The *victim!* Of a *movie!*), and the film resumes, to cheers.

Some audience members were skeptical of the authenticity of the incident. ("I was sitting behind that guy, and you could practically see the SAG card sticking out of his pocket," grumbled one.) But, as Samuel L. Jackson later said, "It was one of those things where people said, 'I've gotta see this movie!'" The Miramax hype machine was cranking full blast, in anticipation of what would be their first wide release.

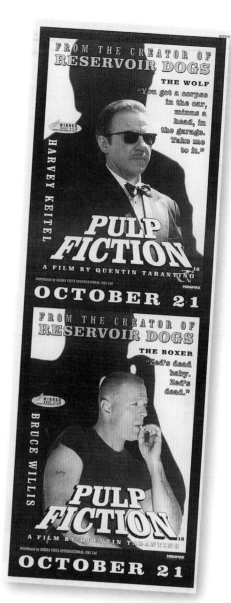

1994 ad for the movie, from a British newspaper.

The boutique label was more accustomed to a platform rollout: a few screens in major markets, to accumulate good reviews and build buzz, before slowly expanding to additional cities. But this time, they employed what Harvey Weinstein dubbed an "Iron Curtain strategy": only one press and one public screening at Cannes, and then nothing until NYFF in September. Miramax would then open the film across the country all at once, like the big boys did. The reasoning was twofold: they had a product they believed in, a movie they thought had the ability to cross over to the mainstream in a big way. And they

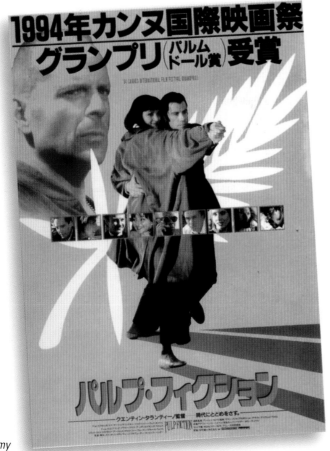

Japanese poster.
© Photos 12 / Alamy

Director Kevin Smith, who had seen the film at Cannes (where his own chatty debut, *Clerks,* also screened), recalled initially thinking, "It's great, but who's gonna see this besides the five people who saw *Reservoir Dogs*? When Miramax said they were going to go out on a thousand screens—which at that time was unheard of for an arthouse film—people were giggling, 'Oh my God, they're going up against a Stallone movie too, *The Specialist*.'"

That film—which costarred the equally bankable Sharon Stone—was going out on nearly twice as many screens: 2,500 to *Pulp's* 1,300. Everyone expected Miramax's little movie to get clobbered, but when the tickets and

also had considerably deeper pockets, now that Disney was signing the checks.

No one was worried about its critical success; as reviews rolled in before its October opening, the critics were as rhapsodic as they'd been at Cannes. "The proudly disreputable *Pulp Fiction* (cost: a measly $8 million) is the new King Kong of crime movies," Peter Travers wrote in *Rolling Stone,* calling it "ferocious fun without a trace of caution, complacency, or political correctness to inhibit its 154 deliciously lurid minutes." The *San Francisco Chronicle's* Mick LaSalle raved, "It's the movie equivalent of that rare sort of novel where you find yourself checking to see how many pages are left and hoping there are more, not fewer." And *Entertainment Weekly's* Owen Gleiberman called it "nothing less than the reinvention of mainstream American cinema."

PULP FACT 27

Miramax's deal with Disney granted them autonomy to make whatever movies they wanted to make, without Disney's approval, provided they stayed within certain perimeters of budget and MPAA rating. But Harvey Weinstein did send a copy of the *Fiction* script to studio chief Jeffrey Katzenberg, as a courtesy, after they purchased it. "Holy shit, this fucking thing," Katzenberg said, after reading it. "It's brilliantly written, but you're out of your mind." Tarantino was less concerned about making his film under the Disney banner: "I think Walt'd probably get a big kick out of it," he laughed.

The Critics Who Got It WRONG

It is easy to forget, from this perch of immortality, that not everyone was wild about *Pulp Fiction*. "It is possibly the most unpopular movie ever to gross one hundred million dollars at the American box office," Ebert wrote. "I've received mail from those who hate the movie. They say it is too violent, too graphic, too obscene, or 'makes no sense.' Many say they walked out after twenty, thirty, or sixty minutes." And it wasn't just casual moviegoers who were pushing back on *Pulp*; though reviews were overwhelmingly positive, there were a few that went against the tide.

- "The word *tedious* has not been much used in describing *Pulp Fiction*, but there are extended moments when it fits rather too well," wrote Kenneth Turan of the *Los Angeles Times*. "Because *Pulp Fiction* is sporadically effective, the temptation to embrace the entire two hours and twenty-nine minutes of Tarantiniana is strong. But in truth this is a noticeably uneven film, both too inward-looking and self-centered in its concerns and too outward-bound in the way it strains to outrage an audience, to be successful across the board."

- "The way that this picture has been so widely ravened up and drooled over verges on the disgusting," proclaimed The *New Republic*'s Stanley Kauffmann. "*Pulp Fiction* nourishes, abets, cultural slumming."

- Lee Krenis More of the *Rochester Democrat and Chronicle* also advised viewers to resist the critical hype, since "the movie they're bubbling over may not be the same one you end up fidgeting through."

- *USA Today*'s Joe Urschel was unamused and disturbed by the picture. "It has no redeeming value in itself; it's just a joke on violence, on life. . . . It's the absolute essence of amorality."

- M. V. Moorhead of the *Phoenix New Times* was more succinct: "*Pulp Fiction* is rubbish about scum."

Pulp Fiction,
by Chris Marlow.
Digital print, 2011.
Courtesy of the artist

dollars were counted at the end of the October 14 weekend, *Pulp* was on top. Bolstered by a promotional budget that surpassed its production costs, *Pulp Fiction* came in at number one for the weekend, with a weekend gross of $9.3 million (to *The Specialist*'s $8.9 million). It would stay there the following weekend and remain in the top ten for six weeks. Even more impressively, it stayed in the top twenty until April of 1995, eventually playing nearly a full year in first- and second-run houses on the way to a total domestic gross of $107 million. (It took in another $106 million overseas.)

It wasn't just that a scrappy indie had toppled a piece of Stallone-Stone "product." A new bar had been cleared: *Pulp* was the first independent film to break the $100 million mark, becoming, in *Down and Dirty Pictures* author Peter Biskind's assessment, "the *Star Wars* of independents, exploding expectations for what an indie film could do at the box office." By creating the first "indie blockbuster," Tarantino had done to the industry what his leading man did to Mia Wallace: he gave it a shot of adrenaline straight to the heart. Two years later, surveying the events that would follow, the filmmaker mused, "The movies that used to be making $100 million are barely making $20 million or they're not even making that. I think right now is the most exciting time in Hollywood since 1971. Because Hollywood is never more exciting than when you don't know."

The Oscars

As 1994 rolled into 1995, *Pulp Fiction* vacuumed up awards from every critics' organization and award-bestowing body in sight—the National Board of Review, the New York Film Critics Circle, the Los Angeles Film Critics Circle, the British Academy of Film and Television Arts (BAFTA), the Independent Spirit Awards. But those were all a warmup for the big kahuna: the Academy Awards.

The Academy of Motion Picture Arts and Sciences (AMPAS) was a different beast altogether. While the critics and specialty awards were given out by institutions that appreciated *Pulp*'s edgy sensibility, the AMPAS had an older membership, one less prone to embrace the film's casual drug use, nonstop profanity, lurid

The Wolf and Jimmie reunite at the Independent Spirit Awards, March 2003. *George Pimentel / WireImage / Getty Images*

Vincent and Jules, reunited at the rehearsal for the Oscars. *Lois Bernstein / Associated Press*

violence, and anal rape. They were more likely to line up with the summer smash *Forrest Gump*, a nostalgia-laced PG-13 comedy-drama that tugged their heartstrings and had them quoting dialogue about boxes of chocolates—slightly more sentimental than Royales with Cheese.

Making matters worse, Miramax initially resisted the urge to send out "screener" videotapes, by then a standard practice for getting movies in front of voters unlikely to trudge out to theaters and screening rooms. Trade papers reported that it was Tarantino's call—he wanted to make sure his widescreen epic was seen under the best possible circumstances.

But within days, the company backtracked, sending out not only videotapes but a slick black-and-white booklet with a scholarly essay by University of Texas at Austin professor Thomas Schatz, assuring voters that *Pulp* was serious, award-worthy stuff. Just to be safe, though, the AMPAS screener tapes subtly lowered the volume on the film's scenes of gunplay, lest the loud blasts send any older viewers into cardiac arrest.

For his part, Tarantino made himself as Oscar-friendly as he could. "Believe me, I've always been Mr. Kick the Academy and everything because I never agreed with a lot of the stuff that they chose," he admitted. "But lately it's actually been a little different. I mean, I really loved *Unforgiven,* you know, and *Silence of the Lambs.*" His schmoozing—and, presumably, the $350,000 or so Miramax spent campaigning—helped land the film seven Academy Award nominations: Best Editing, Best Original Screenplay, Best Supporting Actress (for Thurman), Best Supporting Actor (for Jackson), Best Actor (for Travolta), Best Director, and Best Picture.

Tarantino and Avary accept the Oscar for Best Original Screenplay, March 1995. *Photo by Don Emmert / AFP / Getty Images*

But *Gump*, with nearly twice as many nominations (and twice the Oscar campaign budget), steamrolled through the spring as the clear favorite. In a dual interview with Zemeckis shortly before the ceremony, Quentin carefully downplayed the rivalry ("I don't see them as being as drastically different or right and left. If you're familiar with Bob's work, actually there's a tremendous amount of acid running through it. I think it [*Gump*] is a black comedy"). But the writing was on the wall. "*Pulp Fiction* won't win the best picture Oscar on Monday," Jay Carr predicted in *The Boston Globe.* "It's fresh, surprising, and entertaining, the most dazzling and exhilarating reinvention of the gangster movie since Scorsese's *GoodFellas.* This, of course, amounts to the kiss of death in an Oscar race."

On March 27, 1995, *Forrest Gump* swept the Academy Awards, collecting six trophies, including Best Actor, Best Director, and Best Picture. *Pulp Fiction* won a single prize, for Best Original Screenplay (one of the few in which it wasn't up against *Gump*, an adaptation). Tarantino and Avary went to the podium to collect their Oscars.

"This has been a very strange year," Tarantino mused, before turning prognosticator. "I think this is the only award I'm going to win here tonight, so I was trying to think, maybe I should say a whole lot of stuff, right here, right now, just get it out of my system, you know, all year long, everything rolling up and everything, just blow it all, just tonight, just say everything!" He smiled, and paused. "But I'm not. Thanks!"

Avary was even briefer. After thanking his wife, he made what some took as a tasteless joke, but was actually a rough quote from both their film and the one that beat them: "I really have to take a pee right now so I'm gonna go. Thank you."

After the ceremony, the Miramax crew headed to their post-Oscar bash at Chasen's, the dining establishment that was part of Hollywood folklore—but not for much longer, since the Miramax party marked the restaurant's last night standing. It was being demolished for a shopping mall. The symbolism was eerie; though *Pulp Fiction* had lost the golden boy to a largely conventional feel-good studio picture, it still felt like the end of an era, and the start of something new.

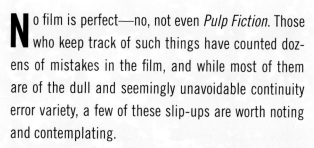

GAFFES

No film is perfect—no, not even *Pulp Fiction*. Those who keep track of such things have counted dozens of mistakes in the film, and while most of them are of the dull and seemingly unavoidable continuity error variety, a few of these slip-ups are worth noting and contemplating.

★ At the end of the post-title "morning hit" sequence, when Jules and Vincent shoot Brett, Jules clearly and audibly empties his pistol. But when we return to the scene at the beginning of "The Bonnie Situation," his gun isn't empty—since he's able to raise it and shoot down the "fourth man" who emerges from the bathroom.

★ Also in that scene: look closely at the wall behind Jules and Vincent as they talk to Marvin, before the "fourth man" emerges. It is already riddled with holes from the bullets he has not yet fired at them. Divine intervention is one thing, but this is probably something else.

★ A continuity error, but a major one: after Mia gets her shot to the heart and roars back to life, the all-important Magic Marker dot that marked the spot where Vincent injected her has disappeared completely.

★ Mia's "don't be a . . ." pantomime is such a charming moment that few people notice that she outlines not a square, but a rectangle. Don't be a rectangle?

★ The most controversial possible goof in the movie concerns Honey Bunny's threat to the diner patrons. At the end of the prologue, immediately before "Misirlou" and the opening credits, she screams, "Any of you fucking pricks move, and I'll execute every motherfucking last one of you!" But when we return to the scene of the crime during "The Bonnie Situation," she screams, "Any of you fucking pricks move, and I'll execute every one of you motherfuckers!" Since we cut to an alternate angle midway through the line the second time around, it appears to be a simple editing (or acting) mistake. But Tarantino has pushed back against this, claiming that the disparity (which exists in the published version of the screenplay) is purposeful, as a commentary on how different people remember different events. If the prologue is from Pumpkin and Honey Bunny's perspective, we see their robbery from the point-of-view of Jules the second time around—and if that's the case, he remembers her threat in language much closer to his own.

The Director As Celebrity

"Rarely in our years on the movie beat has a director got as hot as fast as Quentin Tarantino," opined Roger Ebert during the introduction of a special *Siskel and Ebert* episode dubbed "The Tarantino Generation." By the time that show aired, in spring of 1995, Tarantino had become more than the director behind the hot movie of the moment. He had become something closer to a rock star, a Gen-X hero, instantly recognizable and as identified with his film as the movie stars who fronted it.

There was a precedent for this kind of thing. Alfred Hitchcock, for one, had turned himself into a brand in the 1950s via his cameos in his films, his introductions to his television anthology show, and the mystery magazines that bore his name and distinctive silhouette. And Tarantino was aware of other precedents: "What's happening recently is that the people who work in the crime genre now, the directors, are kind of becoming the stars of the movies," Tarantino said in 1994, drawing a parallel to the horror auteurs of the 1970s (Carpenter, Romero, and the like) who became the draw for genre fans. Their mainstream contemporaries, the Scorseses and Spielbergs and Coppolas, had similarly become names above the titles, objects of seventies cinematic idolatry. But there was more to it than that. "Quentin became the face of *Pulp Fiction*," said Kevin Smith, "more so than Bruce fuckin' Willis, or Uma Thurman, or Travolta. When you see a director hosting *Saturday Night Live*, you're like, My God, what happened here? Something huge."

Director Alexandre Rockwell, whose *In the Soup* won Sundance over *Reservoir Dogs* and who was collaborating with Tarantino on the omnibus film *Four Rooms* during this period, put a finer point on it. "Quentin is a video-geek-type character who woke up in a candy store," he said. "All of a sudden, these women are interested in him who didn't even want to rent videos from him before. It was like wildfire."

Looking back on that period, Tarantino admitted, "There was a lot of making up for lost time." It began before *Pulp Fiction*, while escorting *Reservoir Dogs* to film festivals. "I felt like Elvis when I was meeting girls on the festival

Tarantino as the host of *Saturday Night Live,* with Molly Shannon and Cheri Oteri, November 1995. (The Smashing Pumpkins were the musical guest.) *Photo by Al Levine / NBC / NBCU Photo Bank via Getty Images*

Four Rooms.
© Moviestore
Collection Ltd / Alamy

In February of 1995, Miramax announced that they were handing Tarantino his own specialty distribution label, Rolling Thunder. Quentin would handpick foreign films and obscurities that he wanted to spotlight, and Miramax would release them in theaters—like his Video Archives days, but on a national scale. ("I don't think this is going to be a highly profitable venture, to say the least," Weinstein chuckled, and he was right; over its three active years, only one of Rolling Thunder's five releases hit a six-figure gross.) Miramax also bought the rights to four novels by Tarantino's favorite author, Elmore Leonard; one of them was *Rum Punch*, which would become his next feature, *Jackie Brown*.

Tarantino's newfound celebrity and friendships with fellow directors also landed him supporting roles in *Desperado, Destiny Turns on the*

circuit. I went crazy for a little bit. . . . What handsome guys did in their twenties, I did in my thirties. When you become famous, it's cool."

Once *Pulp Fiction* became an international phenomenon, it wasn't just festival groupies who were recognizing him. "One of the bummers is, I like to walk," he said in 1996. "And the neighborhood that I live in, West Hollywood, is one of the few areas that is sort of villagelike, you can actually walk. And I find that I make less eye contact with people on the street. Basically everyone turns into a homeless person."

There were consolations. Before *Pulp* was even released, he picked up $200,000 for a two-week dialogue polish on *Crimson Tide*, the new film from *True Romance* director Scott. (His contributions are hard to miss: they include the stuff about Silver Surfer comics.) The following spring, he was invited to direct an episode of TV's hottest drama, *ER*. He brought along Angela Jones (aka Esmerelda Villalobos) to play a small role. (Coincidentally, the script—written before Tarantino signed on—featured a patient with a severed ear.)

Tarantino directing *ER*, 1995. *NBC via Getty Images*

Radio, and *Somebody to Love*. The reviews were unkind. "They're not gonna give me a break for another couple of years on this," he said at the time. "They almost resent the fact that I want to act. Until I keep doing it and doing it and shoving it down their throats, then maybe they'll look at it for what it is." The work was often aboveboard—he basically plays himself in *Sleep with Me*, entertainingly, and Rodriguez got a solid, calm performance out of him in *From Dusk Till Dawn*—but when critics roasted his Broadway debut in a 1998 revival of *Wait Until Dark* ("Tarantino has become the Madonna of

male thespian wannabes," jeered *Entertainment Weekly*), he finally let go of his leading-man aspirations and settled on the occasional cameo.

Nonetheless, it's hard not to acknowledge the downside of such unexpected and sudden fame. "I just got through reading three, count 'em, three biographies of my life," Tarantino said in 1995. "It's a peyotelike experience." Some were gossipy, airing dirty laundry about broken friendships with Avary and other old pals. By the following year, Tarantino was introspective: "As far as fame is concerned, if it had an on-and-off button, it would be the greatest thing in the world." He had steeled himself for the backlash ("It's natural, it's gonna happen"). What he might not have been prepared for were the dozens of copycats waiting in the wings.

Wait Until Dark, Tarantino's one foray into Broadway acting (opposite Marisa Tomei). *Everett Collection*

The basis of *Jackie Brown,* by one of Tarantino's favorite novelists.

A Handy Guide to *Pulp Fiction*'s Influence on Post-1994 Cinema

Pulp Fiction is likely to be the most influential film of the next five years," wrote Ebert in 1995, "and for that we can be thankful, because it may have freed us from uncounted predictable formula films." Ha ha, joke was on him; instead, it led to a glut of predictable films that merely borrowed the formula of *Pulp Fiction*.

"There's always been imitation," said Miramax development head Jack Lechner, "But I didn't see a lot of people imitating *sex, lies, and videotape*. Because there wasn't yet that perception that this is a way to get rich, this is a way to gain fame and fortune. It really became rampant after *Pulp Fiction*." And how:

TITLE	DIRECTOR, YEAR	TARANTINO-ESQUE ELEMENTS	DOMESTIC GROSS
Things to Do in Denver When You're Dead	Gary Fleder, 1995	Crew of eccentric criminals; peculiar nicknames; deadpan violence; Steve Buscemi and Christopher Walken in supporting roles.	$529,766
The Usual Suspects	Bryan Singer, 1995	Nonlinear structure; crew of eccentric criminals; peculiar nicknames.	$23 million
Coldblooded	Wallace Wolodarsky, 1995	Sympathetic hit man protagonist; deadpan violence.	$16,198
2 Days in the Valley	John Herzfeld, 1996	Crew of eccentric criminals; seemingly unrelated stories intersect unexpectedly; Eric Stoltz in a supporting role.	$11 million
American Strays	Michael Covert, 1996	Crew of eccentric criminals; seemingly unrelated stories intersect unexpectedly; comically unrelated small-talk dialogue.	$1,910
Grosse Pointe Blank	George Armitage, 1997	Sympathetic hit man protagonist; deadpan violence; esoteric soundtrack.	$28 million
8 Heads in a Duffel Bag	Tom Schulman, 1997	Sympathetic hit man protagonist; deadpan violence; comically unrelated small-talk dialogue; dismembered bodies as plot point.	$3.6 million
Lock, Stock, and Two Smoking Barrels	Guy Ritchie, 1998	Crew of eccentric criminals; peculiar nicknames; deadpan violence; comically unrelated small-talk dialogue; esoteric soundtrack.	$3.7 million
Out of Sight	Steven Soderbergh, 1998	Nonlinear structure; comically unrelated small-talk dialogue; crew of eccentric criminals; Ving Rhames, Paul Calderón, and Samuel L. Jackson in supporting roles.	$37 million
The Boondock Saints	Troy Duffy, 1999	Sympathetic hit men protagonists; religious overtones.	$30,471
Go	Doug Liman, 1999	Three-story nonlinear construction; seemingly unrelated stories intersect unexpectedly; deadpan violence; comically unrelated small-talk dialogue.	$16.9 million
The Way of the Gun	Christopher McQuarrie, 2000	Crew of eccentric criminals; deadpan violence; buddy criminals.	$6 million
Swordfish	Dominic Sena, 2001	Crew of eccentric criminals; meta-movie commentary; John Travolta in leading role.	$69 million

Video, Books, and Other Afterlife

Pulp Fiction was released on VHS on September 12, 1995, eleven months after its theatrical debut—a remarkable feat, considering that the average theatrical-to-video release window was usually half that. The delay was partly business-related; people kept going to see it, first pushed by word-of-mouth, then by year-end and Oscar recognition. Part of the delay was deliberate. According to Tarantino, "The video guys were making their plans when I said, 'Hey, we've kinda got a cult thing going here, and the quickest way to kill a cult is to make it easily accessible.' I thought we should hold off a whole year before releasing it on video. The video people said to strike while the iron's hot, but it goes back to something I observed at Video Archives. The video customers *know* when a video should be available, and they're going to be coming into video stores in droves looking for *Pulp Fiction*."

While they waited for the video release, the filmmaker was happy to offer other ways for them to get their *Pulp* fix. The Weinsteins had been working with Disney's publishing arm, Hyperion Books, to develop a Miramax Books imprint. Their first release was the screenplay for *Pulp Fiction*, unveiled at the Frankfurt Book Fair the same month as the film's release. Quentin's advance was in the neighborhood of $200,000. It hit shelves in December of 1994 and went on to sell over seventy thousand copies, allowing amateur actors across the world to recreate the "Royale with Cheese" scene in their dens and dorms.

Or they could listen to the real thing

The script of *Death Proof* on sale in London. The *Pulp Fiction* screenplay was a bestseller in the UK.
© bruciebonus / Alamy

on their stereos. The *Pulp Fiction* soundtrack album, released in September 1994, combined songs from the movie with snippets of dialogue, allowing listeners to enjoy uninterrupted versions of "Misirlou" or "Jungle Boogie," barely-heard background tracks like Maria McKee's "If Love is a Red Dress (Hang Me in Rags)," and movie excerpts, including the full "Royale with Cheese" discussion, Jackson's recitation of Ezekiel 25:17, and Zed's sinister directive to "Bring out the Gimp." It would reach number twenty-one on the *Billboard* album charts, and by the following spring it had sold three hundred thousand copies. The album also helped put Urge Overkill's "Girl, You'll Be a Woman Soon" on the singles chart (it peaked at number fifty-nine), and it revived the career of fifty-seven-year-old Dick Dale, who suddenly found his concerts populated by college kids screaming for "Misirlou."

When *Pulp Fiction* finally hit video stores in September of '95, Tarantino broke the mold

>>>> *Frame of Reference* <<<<

[Pan and Scan]

Pan and scan is the process of placing a rectangular image into the square confines of a television screen by lopping off the sides of the original picture and panning to show action, when necessary. Some directors and labels circumvented this process by presenting letterboxed versions of their films, which preserved the original widescreen image by placing the full rectangle within the square of a television with black bars at the top and bottom of the image.

PULP FACT 28

One of the deleted scenes finds Thurman asking Travolta if he's ever fantasized about being beaten up by a girl. He says yes—"Emma Peel on *The Avengers*." In 1998, Thurman would play Emma Peel in the ill-fated film version of *The Avengers*.

by insisting that Miramax release it in both widescreen and pan-and-scan versions. In that pre–high definition era, when most televisions were still square, pan and scan was the default for VHS releases; with a few exceptions, letterboxed widescreen was purely the domain of specialty releases and LaserDiscs. But he also personally supervised the pan-and-scan process and bragged, "In a weird way, I like my pan-and-scan version."

The following spring, Miramax released a "special collector's edition" VHS, featuring the widescreen presentation along with two deleted scenes, introduced by Tarantino. The company has released the film five more times on home video: a bare-bones, movie-only DVD in 1998; a two-disc collector's edition in 2002; an "award-winning edition" reissue in 2011; a Blu-ray disc that same year; and as part of the giant "Tarantino XX" box set in 2012. It seems that, for both viewers and distributors, *Pulp Fiction* is the gift that keeps on giving.

Deleted Scenes

Pulp Fiction's five major deleted or extended scenes dribbled out slowly in the years after its release—a couple on early VHS editions, a couple more on the Canadian DVD, and finally all on the 2002 collector's edition DVD and 2011 Blu-ray. In his introduction, Tarantino stresses that he didn't reinsert them into a "director's cut" because "I made the movie I wanted to make in the first place," and says that most of them were cut for overall pacing purposes. They are:

- **Lance's monologue:** After his dialogue with Vincent about the keying of the Malibu, Lance talks about getting lost on his way to "Panorama City" and a guy at a gas station giving him false directions. "What kind of a world do we live in where people give other people the wrong directions on purpose?"

- **The Vincent-Mia interview:** At the beginning of their "date," Mia comes out behind a Hi8 video camera. "Pretend I'm Barbara Walters," she says, and proceeds to interview him about his personality and pop-culture preferences. In his introduction to the scene, Tarantino says that "it sounds more like someone trying to *write like* me than me, with all the references in there," and he's right, frankly. But there is one important line: one of her questions for Vincent is whether he's an "Elvis man" or a "Beatles man" ("Nobody likes them both equally. Somewhere you have to make a choice"); without that interchange, her pegging of him as an "Elvis man" in the parking lot of Jackrabbit Slim's seems like just a guess, albeit a safe one.

- **Extended Vincent-Mia date:** After Vincent gives Mia her hand-rolled cigarette, we get a more dramatic version of the faux Marilyn Monroe subway grate moment followed by Mia and Vincent discussing their favorite Amsterdam hash bar. They then go into their conversation about *Fox Force Five*, with some additional dialogue about Mia's character, Raven McCoy.

- **Extended Esmerelda-Butch cab scene:** Tarantino has noted that he loves this longer version of their dialogue scene, but it was just too long at a key point in the narrative. This one is a little more loosely paced, with a bit more discussion of Esmerelda's name and a long chunk of dialogue for Butch at the end, in which he explains that his indifference toward Floyd's death is par for the course, "'cause I'm a boxer."

- **Monster Joe and Raquel:** Originally falling before the Wolf and Raquel bid farewell to Vincent and Jules, this scene finds Monster Joe (Corman favorite Dick Miller) and the Wolf discussing business, the Wolf and Raquel making their breakfast date, and Jules and Vincent "having a moment" of reconciliation.

Legacy: From the Multiplex to the Art House—and Back Again

In the fall of 2012, *Salon* film critic Andrew O'Hehir wrote an essay on the state of cinema, provocatively titled "Is Movie Culture Dead?" The trope was an established and rather exhausted one, trotted out every few months by film writers bemoaning the current state of the form. In it, O'Hehir despairs for what he dubs "the Susan Sontag era," during which "discussion and debate about movies was often perceived as the icy-cool cutting edge of American intellectual life"; Bergman, Truffaut, Fellini, and Kurosawa are invoked. Nothing new there. But what is particularly odd about O'Hehir's treatise is a throwaway sideswipe halfway through. "Film culture—in my now-defunct Susan Sontag sense—has a history," O'Hehir writes, "and I think it pretty much ended with *Pulp Fiction*, the brief indie-film boom of the late nineties, and the rise of the Internet. It's just taken us a while to realize it."

The argument is anomalous; he sees *Fiction* and the "indie-film boom" it wrought as an extension of eighties-era "machine-made production units," rather than as a rebuke to it. If you parse O'Hehir's words carefully enough, though, perhaps it's not such a slight: maybe *his* sense of film culture died with *Pulp Fiction*. But for a generation of moviegoers and moviemakers that came of age at the time of its release or in the aftermath of it, for Gen-Xers and Millennials, Tarantino's film was the exact opposite: it was the moment when film culture *began*.

"In the eighties, the studios could predict what worked and what didn't," Tarantino said in 1992. "And that's what the eighties were—one movie you'd already seen after another. Suddenly, that's not working anymore. . . . When the audience is fed up with the standard stuff and crying out for something different is when exciting things happen in Hollywood." You could feel that restlessness in audiences during the decade previous to Tarantino's ascension, an era that gave us precious few films that were genuinely exciting, enlightening, or arousing. And it was that charge of "something different" that made *Pulp Fiction* so electrifying—at those first screenings, when Plummer screamed her threat in that diner and the frame froze on the two of them with their guns drawn and that opening riff of "Misirlou" kicked in, it was like a fuse being lit on a stick of dynamite that kept exploding for two and a half hours.

Greil Marcus wrote of Bob Dylan's 1965 classic, "Nothing as singular as 'Like a Rolling Stone' ever influences anything in its medium as form or content—its only influence is the line that it draws." And so it is with *Pulp Fiction*, which is as much a demarcation line in modern cinema as *Bonnie and Clyde* was twenty-seven years before. Like Arthur Penn's New Hollywood powerhouse, *Pulp Fiction* played like a rejoinder to years of rotting, ponderous, tacky Hollywood bullshit. Here was a movie that was frisky, bracing, raw, and alive; here was a film that made you pick sides and join in the fight. For those on Team Tarantino, it wasn't just that independent cinema no longer had to mean dull, drab, navel-gazing, Sundance-friendly tales of familial discord and sexual dysfunction. It was that the instruments of conventional cinema had been reappropriated and reinvigorated, and the mainstream was going to have to readjust if it wanted to keep pace.

The B movies of Hollywood's golden age (the thirties and forties, particularly) were second-tier and even a little disreputable, but they weren't stupid. Crime movies had a grit and wit and intelligence all their own, Westerns were formulaic and businesslike but stylish and tough, and even dopey sci-fi and horror pictures were done with a knowing wink. In the 1970s, when Hollywood's biggest-grossing movies were a gangster flick, a horror movie about a shark, and a sci-fi swashbuckler, the B movies became the A movies. However, over the course of the ensuing decade, those B-turned-A movies were dumbed down and plucked of eccentricities to appeal to the widest possible audience.

Pulp Fiction was a reclaiming of the tropes and types of the B movie, an exuberant yet insistent reminder (from a cinephile who'd seen it all) of how this kind of thing was supposed to be done, and a dare to anyone flatfooted enough to keep doing it wrong. The action stars stumbled; Willis was wise enough to hitch himself to Tarantino's wagon (and to bring along Jackson for his next *Die Hard* movie), but Schwarzenegger's star was falling fast, Stallone's even faster (he would attempt a Travolta-style comeback three years later, with a small Miramax drama called *Cop Land*).

Above all else, Tarantino's film tore down the wall between independent and mainstream

The Olympic Village, Munich. © *Dave Williams / Alamy*

Q. T./*PF*'s international popularity. The Tarantino bar-club in Vilnius, Lithuania. © *Tim E. White / Alamy*

cinema, crossbreeding and zigzagging them, and irrevocably altering both in the process. "I don't want to be this little arthouse guy who does a particular kind of picture for a particular audience," Tarantino said in 1994. "That's just as much of a talent-strangling road as becoming a hack and doing every picture that comes along."

Instead, he forged a new road. Multiplex audiences, drawn by marquee stars and violence and sex, had their minds blown by *Pulp Fiction*'s brainy dialogue and structural ornamentation and anything-goes storytelling. Arthouse audiences, drawn by the rapturous reviews and film festival kudos, were reminded of what it was to have a great time at the movies, to be rocked

by gunplay and car crashes and cool cats in sharp suits. Or, as Willis summarized, "You can say the most intellectual thing about *Pulp Fiction* and be right. But it also works for the trailer-park kids."

There's no question that *Pulp Fiction* changed the business of independent film—Harvey Weinstein, who should know, would call it "the first independent movie that broke all the rules. It set a new dial on the movie clock." Its $200 million-plus gross on an $8.5 million budget proved how profitable indies, with their low budgets and low risks, could be, and studios scrambled to set up "classic" and specialty divisions—their own Miramaxes—in *Fiction*'s wake.

But it also changed the aesthetics of independent film, sneakily blurring the line between the fringe and the mainstream, just as Nirvana's *Nevermind* had for popular music three years prior. Although *independent film* became a buzz phrase, it became harder to define—the question was less about tangible distinctions than an overall sensibility.

"I didn't watch *Boogie Nights* or *Spanking the Monkey* and see cause-effect," Tarantino later said, "but the thing is, I do feel part of an exciting community. Which has always been my dream—it's always been my dream to be part of a community of artists, a community of filmmakers and directors and actors. Every generation needs its young, exciting auteurs."

Street art, Dusseldorf, Germany. © *David Crausby / Alamy*

PART VI

The Tarantinoverse

Quentin Tarantino: To me they're all living inside of this one universe.

Gavin Smith: And it isn't [pointing out the window] out there.

Quentin Tarantino: Well, it's a little bit out there, and it's also there too [points at his TV], in the movies, and it's also in here [points to his head]. It's all three.
—*Film Comment* interview, 1994

As the cult of Tarantino grew in the aftermath of *Pulp Fiction*, sharp-eared fans began to pick up on certain commonalities among his films. Most had already noticed that Travolta's character shared the same surname as Vic Vega, aka Mr. Blonde, from *Reservoir Dogs*. They also may have noted that Big Joe Cabot and Mr. White discuss a fellow criminal named Marsellus. Was this the same Marsellus as in *Pulp Fiction*? And what about the woman named Alabama that Joe asks after? Is she the Alabama who fell for Clarence in *True Romance*? And what about "that Scagnetti fuck" who's on Vic Vega's back? Is he the same crooked cop that Tom Sizemore plays in *Natural Born Killers*?

The answer to all of those questions, too often overlooked in fans' feverish discussions of Tarantino's world, is "no." The ice dealer mentioned in *Reservoir Dogs* is Marsellus Spivey, not Wallace. (Spivey, by the way, is the last name of the vicious pimp Oldman plays in *True Romance*.) *Romance*'s Alabama Worley is a short-term call girl, not a professional thief, and whichever ending you prefer to that film, it doesn't include her going off and "pulling jobs" with Mr. White. And Vic Vega's headaches are provided by Seymour Scagnetti, parole officer, not Jack Scagnetti, author and supercop.

So why do these names recur in those early scripts? For the same reason that, as suggested elsewhere, certain scenes and ideas reappear as well: because they were written roughly concurrently, with no guarantee that any of them were going to be made, and Tarantino wasn't letting anything go to waste. The ubiquity of these Alabama and Marsellus and Scagnetti characters is a lot less likely than the possibility that they were just cool names that Tarantino liked and used more than once.

Still, it became something of a viewer's sport, spotting the persistent brands and lineages. By the time he made the *Kill Bill* movies, Tarantino had not only embraced the fan theory of a "Tarantinoverse," but also had chopped it up into three subdivisions. There was the "movie

FICTION

PULP

Tarantino may not have made a traditional sequel to *Pulp Fiction*, but that hasn't prevented its actors from reuniting in other, non-Tarantino projects.

➤ **Bruce Willis** and **Samuel L. Jackson** reteamed twice after *Pulp Fiction*, playing reluctant partners in *Die Hard with a Vengeance* and would-be foes in *Unbreakable*.

➤ **John Travolta** and **Samuel L. Jackson** faced off in John McTiernan's forgettable 2003 military thriller *Basic*.

➤ **Samuel L. Jackson**, **Ving Rhames**, and **Paul Calderón** all turn up in the 1995 David Caruso vehicle *Kiss of Death*, which most critics dismissed as a *Fiction* wannabe (though it was in the can well before Tarantino's film was released), and in Steven Soderbergh's *Pulp*-y 1998 adaptation of Elmore Leonard's *Out of Sight*.

➤ **Samuel L. Jackson** played a small supporting role in **Steve Buscemi**'s 1996 directorial debut *Trees Lounge*.

➤ **Ving Rhames** and **Buscemi** are among the criminal passengers of the 1997 action flick *Con Air*.

➤ **Steve Buscemi** played a supporting role in the 2001 **John Travolta** flop *Domestic Disturbance*.

➤ **John Travolta** and **Uma Thurman** reunited— and danced again—in *Be Cool*, the sequel to Travolta's *Pulp Fiction* follow-up *Get Shorty*. **Harvey Keitel** also appeared, as did *Pulp* coproducer **Danny DeVito**. Travolta and Thurman were to costar again in Oliver Stone's *Savages*, but Thurman's scenes didn't make the final cut.

Reunions

➤ **Amanda Plummer** and an uncredited **Tim Roth** both appeared in the 2000 Mel Gibson–produced oddity *The Million Dollar Hotel*.

➤ **Harvey Keitel** and **Quentin Tarantino** both turned up in the 2000 Adam Sandler misfire *Little Nicky* and in the 1994 Alexandre Rockwell film *Somebody to Love* (alongside **Steve Buscemi**).

➤ *Pulp* was already a reunion for **Tim Roth** and **Eric Stoltz**, who starred in the 1993 film *Bodies, Rest and Motion* alongside future *Jackie Brown* costar Bridget Fonda.

Roth and Stoltz (with Fonda and Phoebe Cates) in the drama *Bodies, Rest and Motion*.
© *Moviestore Collection Ltd / Alamy*

➤ As previously mentioned, **Eric Stoltz** agreed to appear in *Pulp* and *Killing Zoe* if **Quentin Tarantino** would appear in Stoltz's film *Sleep with Me*—which Tarantino did, performing a comic riff on *Top Gun* that he and Roger Avary used to do at Video Archives and at parties.

The Tarantino Brand

The most identifiable elements of the Tarantinoverse are the brands and restaurants that reappear in his films. Here's a brief summary of what you'll find, and where.

Red Apple Cigarettes: Tarantino's favorite smokes first appear in *Pulp Fiction*, in which Butch asks for them by name. Packs of Red Apples are later seen by the hotel switchboard in *Four Rooms*, on the dashboard of the Gecko brothers' car in *From Dusk Till Dawn*, and on Esteban's table in *Kill Bill Volume 2*. Abernathy asks for a pack of Red Apple Tans in *Death Proof*, and The Bride strolls past a Japanese billboard for the brand in *Kill Bill Volume 1*. (A billboard also appears in *Romy and Michelle's High School Reunion*, the 1997 comedy starring Tarantino's then-girlfriend Mira Sorvino.)

Big Kahuna Burger: "That Hawaiian burger joint" also makes its first appearance in *Pulp Fiction*, though some insist Mr. Blonde makes his fast food stop there on the way to the rendezvous in *Reservoir Dogs*. (It's never mentioned, and he sips from a generic, unmarked cup.) Seth Gecko brings Big Kahuna Burgers back to their motel room in *From Dusk Till Dawn*, and a Big Kahuna soda cup can be seen on the bar in Tarantino's segment of *Four Rooms*. (A Big Kahuna bag can be glimpsed in the background of *Romy and Michelle* as well—and in an amusing coincidence, *Pulp Fiction* producer DeVito would later costar in a 1999 film called *The Big Kahuna*.)

Teriyaki Donut: Marsellus is returning from a run to this presumably Eastern-influenced doughnut shop when he crosses the street in front of Butch in *Pulp Fiction*. It is also Jackie Brown's favorite Del Amo food court restaurant in the film that bears her name.

Jackrabbit Slim's: Most *Fiction* fans have noticed that a snippet of a radio ad for Mia Wallace's favorite restaurant can be heard later in the film, drifting through a window that Butch passes while taking the back route to his apartment. Fewer are aware that the same ad is heard in *Reservoir Dogs*; it plays on K-BILLY just after "Stuck in the Middle with You," and can be heard (barely, in the background) as the camera pans across the warehouse from Mr. Orange to Mr. Blonde, whom he's just shot dead.

Acuña Boys: The Bride's voice-over in *Kill Bill Volume 2* explains the history of the Acuña Boys, the gang run by Esteban and composed of the bastard sons of his "girls." (It's also the name of the villainous gang in the Tarantino favorite *Rolling Thunder*.) The crew apparently diversified into fast food: Acuña Boys Authentic Tex-Mex Food has an intermission bumper ad in *Grindhouse*. Arlene also drinks from one of their soda containers in *Death Proof*, and Sharonda partakes of their food court fodder in *Jackie Brown*.

G.O. Juice: This Japanese energy drink first appears on a billboard in *Kill Bill: Volume 1*. It has apparently made its way to the States by the time of *Death Proof*, in which Abernathy consumes a can at the convenience store.

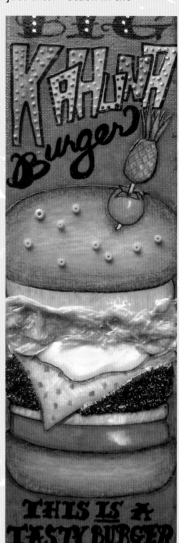

"Big Kahuna" burger, by Angie Cornelius of Lonesome Road Studio. Mixed media / marker art. *Courtesy of the artist*

universe," where films like *True Romance, Reservoir Dogs*, and *Pulp Fiction* took place ("That universe is realer than real life," he told *Entertainment Weekly*); there were those films set in the "movie movie universe," which were the pictures that those other characters would go see (like *Kill Bill, From Dusk Till Dawn*, and *Natural Born Killers*); and then there's the Elmore Leonard universe, with that author's own running characters and situations, which *Jackie Brown* fits into (as would Soderbergh's *Out of Sight*, in which Michael Keaton reprises the role of Ray Nicolet).

Intriguing, sure, but ultimately as silly and nonsensical as the name-chasing. Where, for example, does Earl McGraw fit in? Michael Parks' low-muttering Texas Ranger appears in the opening scene of *From Dusk Till Dawn*, when he's murdered by the Gecko brothers, but subsequently appears in *Kill Bill Volume 1* and both halves of *Grindhouse*. How does he traverse the line between movie universe and movie movie universe? And how does he come back to life after *Dusk*—or is that just some actor dramatizing the real Earl McGraw's fictional death? Or are those other films all prequels to it? The mind boggles.

Theorizing and analysis of that sort are child's play next to the hypotheses worked up by Internet fans after *Inglourious Basterds*, Tarantino's 2009 World War II picture, which ends with the sublimely satisfying assassination of Adolf Hitler in a French cinema. One of the film's titular heroes, the tough "Bear Jew" played by *Hostel* filmmaker Eli Roth, is named Donnie Donowitz. At a Q and A, Tarantino admitted that he intended the character to be the father of Lee Donowitz, the big-shot Hollywood producer played by Saul Rubinek in *True Romance*.

But wait—if *Inglourious Basterds* had a familial connection to *True Romance*, that would make it part of Tarantino's movie universe, which would mean that this was a universe where *that* was how World War II ended. And thus was given birth a new theory, first postulated by Reddit user "UOLATSC": "Because World War II ended in a movie theater, everybody lends greater significance to pop culture. . . . Likewise, because America won World War II in one concentrated act of hyperviolent slaughter, Americans as a whole are more desensitized to that sort of thing. Hence why Butch is unfazed by killing two people, Mr. White and Mr. Pink take a pragmatic approach to killing in their line of work, Esmerelda the cab driver is obsessed with death, etc." Further, the user theorized, this explains why Tarantino's movie movies are so

(continued on page 192)

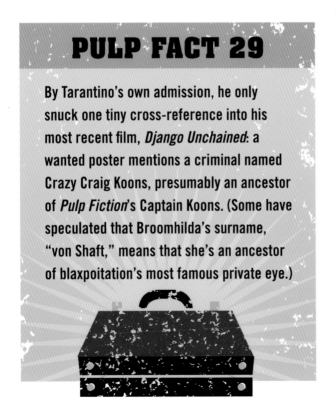

PULP FACT 29

By Tarantino's own admission, he only snuck one tiny cross-reference into his most recent film, *Django Unchained*: a wanted poster mentions a criminal named Crazy Craig Koons, presumably an ancestor of *Pulp Fiction*'s Captain Koons. (Some have speculated that Broomhilda's surname, "von Shaft," means that she's an ancestor of blaxpoitation's most famous private eye.)

The Tarantino Rep Company

Throughout cinema history, directors have forged relationships with favorite actors, reteaming on multiple occasions and taking advantage of a shorthand and ease of collaboration: John Ford and John Wayne, Josef von Sternberg and Marlene Dietrich, Martin Scorsese and Robert De Niro, Akira Kurosawa and Toshiro Mifune. Tarantino is no exception; actors love to say his words nearly as much as he delights in finding actors who can say them well. Here are a few of the actors who have appeared in two or more films directed and/or written by Tarantino:

Samuel L. Jackson
in

True Romance
Pulp Fiction
Jackie Brown
Kill Bill Volume 2
Inglourious Basterds
(voice only)
Django Unchained

Harvey Keitel
in

Reservoir Dogs
Pulp Fiction
From Dusk Till Dawn
Inglourious Basterds
(voice only)

Michael Parks
in

From Dusk Till Dawn
Kill Bill Volume 1
Kill Bill Volume 2
Death Proof
Django Unchained

Uma Thurman
in

Pulp Fiction
Kill Bill Volume 1
Kill Bill Volume 2

Michael Madsen
in

Reservoir Dogs
Kill Bill Volume 1
Kill Bill Volume 2

Tim Roth
in

Reservoir Dogs
Pulp Fiction
Four Rooms

The **Tarantino Rep Company**

Christoph Waltz
in
Inglourious Basterds
Django Unchained

Brad Pitt
in
True Romance
Inglourious Basterds

Bruce Willis
in
Pulp Fiction
Four Rooms

Steve Buscemi
in
Reservoir Dogs
Pulp Fiction

Paul Calderón
in
Pulp Fiction
Four Rooms

Eli Roth
in
Death Proof
Inglourious Basterds

Chris Penn
in
Reservoir Dogs
True Romance

Frank Whaley
in
Natural Born Killers
Pulp Fiction

Tom Sizemore
in
True Romance
Natural Born Killers

Juliette Lewis
in
Natural Born Killers
From Dusk Till Dawn

Michael Bowen
in
Jackie Brown
Kill Bill Volume 1

Sid Haig
in
Jackie Brown
Kill Bill Volume 2

(continued from page 189)

much more violent than not only the rest of his films, but movies in general: because they are intended for the consumption of an immeasurably more violent society.

It's an interesting theory, and fun to explore. But it, too, is poppycock. It provides false explanations for essential truths about Tarantino's work. His movie movies are violent, sure, but not so much as to fit less than snugly into a world that has made itself plenty violent without that particular resolution to World War II.

But more importantly, this generation didn't need an historical excuse to become obsessed with the minutiae of popular culture. It happened anyway, for any number of reasons (advances in technology, the hyperspecialization of the Internet, the conclusion of the Cold War). When we watch Vincent frame an argument with a reference to *Cops*, or Jules explain the particulars of pilot season to Vincent, or the two of them joke about the pet pig on *Green Acres*, it's not some sort of science fiction scene from a universe parallel to our own. It's *us*. It's what makes us relate to Tarantino's killers and junkies and thieves: they watch the same TV shows and go to the same movies and live lives that aren't that far removed from our own. There is no separate Tarantinoverse. We love Quentin Tarantino's movies because he lives in our world—and we in his.

"I think this just might be my masterpiece." Donnie Donowitz (Eli Roth) and Aldo Raine (Brad Pitt) in *Inglorious Basterds.* © *AF Archive / Alamy*

Jules 1, by Greg Gossel. Mixed media on canvas. *Courtesy of the artist*

Bibliography

Ashley, Mike. "The Golden Age of Pulp Fiction." *The Pulp Magazines Project*. Originally published in *Rare Book Review* 32:4 (May 2005). http://www.pulpmags.org/history_page.html.

Barlow, Aaron. *Quentin Tarantino: Life at the Extremes*. Santa Barbara: Praeger, 2010.

Barnes, Alan, and Marcus Hearn. *Tarantino, A to Zed*. London: B. T. Batsford, 1999.

Bernard, Jami. *Quentin Tarantino: The Man and His Movies*. New York: HarperPerennial, 1995.

Biskind, Peter. *Down and Dirty Pictures: Miramax, Sundance, and the Rise of Independent Film*. New York: Simon & Schuster, 2004.

Bloom, Clive. *Cult Fiction: Popular Reading and Pulp Theory*. New York: Palgrave Macmillan, June 1998.

Bordwell, David. "Intensified Continuity: Visual Style in Contemporary Film." *Film Quarterly* 55, no. 3 (2002): 16–28.

Box Office Mojo. Accessed January 31, 2013. http://www.boxofficemojo.com.

Canby, Vincent. "A Caper Goes Wrong, Resoundingly." *New York Times*. October 23, 1992. http://movies.nytimes.com/movie/review?res=9E0CE6DD113EF930A15753C1A964958260.

Clarkson, Wensley. *Quentin Tarantino: Shooting from the Hip*. Woodstock: The Overlook Press, 1995.

Dawson, Jeff. *Quentin Tarantino: The Cinema of Cool*. New York: Applause Books, 1995.

Ebert, Roger. *Questions for the Movie Answer Man*. Kansas City: Andrews and McMeel Publishing, 1997.

——. *Roger Ebert's Video Companion: 1996 Edition*. Kansas City: Andrews and McMeel Publishing, 1995.

Fields, Syd. *Screenplay: The Foundations of Screenwriting*. New York: Dell Publishing, 1984.

Fleming, Michael. "Playboy Interview: Quentin Tarantino." *Playboy*, November 2003: 59–62, 140–142.

——. "Playboy Interview: Quentin Tarantino." *Playboy*, December 2012: 67–70, 178–179.

Fox, David Jesse. "*Django Unchained–Pulp Fiction* Connection Found." *Vulture.com*, January 22, 2013. http://www.vulture.com/2013/01/pulp-fiction-connection-found.html

Gallafent, Edward. *Quentin Tarantino*. Essex, NJ: Pearson Education Limited, 2006.

Gleiberman, Owen. "Reservoir Dogs." *EW.com*. October 30, 1992. http://www.ew.com/ew/article/0,,312190,00.html.

——. "Wait Until Dark." *EW.com*. April 17, 1998. http://www.ew.com/ew/article/0,,282703,00.html.

Gray, Ali. "The Intricate, Expansive Universe of Quentin Tarantino." *IGN*. January 17, 2013. http://www.ign.com/articles/2013/01/17/the-intricate-expansive-universe-of-quentin-tarantino.

Greene, Richard, and K. Silem Mohammad. *Quentin Tarantino and Philosophy*. Chicago: Open Court, 2007.

Gross, Terry. "Quentin Tarantino, 'Unchained' and Unruly." *NPR*. January 2, 2013. http://www.npr.org/templates/transcript/transcript.php?storyId=168200139.

Haining, Peter. *The Classic Era of American Pulp Magazines*. Chicago: Chicago Review Press, 2001.

Hill, Jack. *Switchblade Sisters*. (DVD) Santa Monica: Miramax Home Video, 2000.

IMDb.com: "Pulp Fiction." *IMDb.com*. Accessed November 26, 2012. http://www.imdb.com/title/tt0110912/reference.

——. "Quentin Tarantino." *IMDb.com*. Accessed November 26, 2012. http://www.imdb.com/name/nm0000233/.

——. "Roger Avary." *IMDb.com*. Accessed January 7, 2013. http://www.imdb.com/name/nm0000812/.

Kael, Pauline. (1966) "Are Movies Falling Apart?" in *Film: A Montage of Theories*, edited by Richard Dyer MacCann, 341–54. New York: E. P. Dutton.

——. "Raising Kane." In *The Citizen Kane Book*, 3-84. Boston: Little, Brown and Company, 1971.

Knowles, Harry. "Harry Talks to Quentin Tarantino about *Kill Bill, Glorious Bastards* and QTV!!!" *Ain't It Cool News*. August 10, 2001. http://www.aintitcool.com/node/9830.

LaSalle, Mick. "'*Pulp*' Grabs You Like a Novel." *SFGate*. September 15, 1995. http://www.sfgate.com/movies/article/FILM-REVIEW-Pulp-Grabs-You-Like-a-Novel-3024865.php.

Marcus, Greil. *Like a Rolling Stone: Bob Dylan at the Crossroads*. New York: Public Affairs, 2006.

Maslin, Janet. "Quentin Tarantino's Wild Ride on Life's Dangerous Road." *New York Times*. September 23, 1994. http://movies.nytimes.com/movie/review?res=9B0DE5DA143AF930A1575AC0A962958260.

Matthews, Jack. "Can 200 Critics Be Wrong? (Maybe.)" *Los Angeles Times*. December 26, 1994. http://articles.latimes.com/1994-12-26/entertainment/ca-13157_1_pulp-fiction.

McGrath, Charles. "Quentin's World." *New York Times*. December 19, 2012. http://www.nytimes.com/2012/12/23/movies/how-quentin-tarantino-concocted-a-genre-of-his-own.html.

Mitchell, Elvis. "Quentin Tarantino," *Elvis Mitchell Under the Influence*. Turner Classic Movies. July 28, 2008.

Mottram, James. *The Sundance Kids: How the Mavericks Took Back Hollywood*. New York: Faber and Faber, 2006.

O'Hehir, Andrew. "Is Movie Culture Dead?" *Salon*. September 28, 2012. http://www.salon.com/2012/09/28/is_movie_culture_dead.

Peary, Gerald, ed. *Quentin Tarantino Interviews*. Jackson: University Press of Mississippi, 1998.

Penzler, Otto, ed. *The Black Lizard Big Book of Black Mask Stories*. New York: Vintage, 2010.

Perez, Rodrigo. "The Tarantino Movie Universe Connection." *The Playlist*. August 16, 2009. http://theplaylist.blogspot.com/2009/08/tarantino-movie-universe-connection.html.

Quentin Tarantino Archives. Accessed January 7, 2013. http://wiki.tarantino.info/index.php/Main_Page.

Rosenbaum, Jonathan. "Reservoir Dogs." *Chicago Reader*. 1992. http://www.chicagoreader.com/chicago/reservoir-dogs/Film?oid=2035159.

Smith, Jim. *Virgin Film: Tarantino*. London: Virgin Books, 2005.

Stern, Howard. "Quentin Tarantino Interview." *The Howard Stern Show*. December 5, 2012. http://www.openculture.com/2012/12/quentin_tarantinos_75_minute_interview_with_howard_stern.html.

Takamori, Tatsuichi. "Sonny Chiba—The Bodyguard." *YouTube*. December 7, 2005. http://www.youtube.com/watch?v=8LYT4JC2dd4.

Tarantino, Quentin. "*My Best Friend's Birthday*, Quentin Tarantino's 1987 Debut Film." *Open Culture*. April 10, 2012. http://www.openculture.com/2012/04/imy_best_friends_birthdayi_quentin_tarantinos_1987_rockabilly_debut.html.

———. *Natural Born Killers: The Original Screenplay*. New York: Grove Press, 1995.

———. *Pulp Fiction*. Blu-ray. Santa Monica: Lionsgate, 2011.

———. *Pulp Fiction: A Quentin Tarantino Screenplay*. New York: Miramax Books, 1994.

———"Quentin Tarantino Tackles Old Dixie by Way of the Old West (by Way of Italy." *New York Times*. September 27, 2012. http://www.nytimes.com/2012/09/30/magazine/quentin-tarantino-django.html?smid=pl-share

———. *Reservoir Dogs/True Romance: Screenplays by Quentin Tarantino*. New York: Grove Press, 1994.

———. *Truth and Fiction*. Santa Monica: MCA Records, 1994.

Thompson, Kristin. *Storytelling in the New Hollywood*. Cambridge, MA: Harvard University Press, 1999.

Thompson, Robert Farris. "An Aesthetic of the Cool." *African Arts* 7, no. 1 (1973): 41. http://www.jstor.org/discover/10.2307/3334749?uid=3739736&uid=2&uid=4&uid=3739256&sid=21101768518273.

Travers, Peter. "Pulp Fiction." *Rolling Stone*. October 14, 1994. http://www.rollingstone.com/movies/reviews/pulp-fiction-19941014.

Turan, Kenneth. "Quentin Tarantino's Gangster Rap: Sure, the Director Can Write. But Does He Deserve All the Hype?" *Los Angeles Times*. October 14, 1994. http://articles.latimes.com/1994-10-14/entertainment/ca-50020_1_pulp-fiction.

UOLATSC. "What 'Fan Theories' Have Blown Your Mind with Their Devastating Logic?" *Reddit*. May 29, 2012. http://www.reddit.com/r/AskReddit/comments/ubaqq/what_fan_theories_have_blown_your_mind_with_their/c4tzvnn.

Watercutter, Angela. "The Unified Tarantino Film Theory and *Django Unchained*." *Wired*. December 19, 2012. http://www.wired.com/underwire/2012/12/django-unchained-tarantino-universe.

Waxman, Sharon. *Rebels on the Backlot: Seven Maverick Directors and How They Conquered the Hollywood Studio System*. New York: HarperEnterainment, 2005.

Woods, Paul A. *King Pulp: The Wild World of Quentin Tarantino*. London: Plexus, 1998.

———, ed. *Quentin Tarantino: The Film Geek Files*. London: Plexus, 2005.

Index

Acknowledgments

This book came to me quickly and unexpectedly, as the best things so often do. First and foremost, I must thank my terrific editor Grace Labatt, who took a chance on a first-time author and offered up insight, encouragement, and a judicious yet kind hand throughout. (Sorry again about all the semicolons). My name would have never made its way to her were it not for Spencer Kornhaber, my wonderful editor at the *Atlantic*, who sent me one of the greatest e-mails I've ever received: "Uhhh, wanna write a book about *Pulp Fiction*?" Spencer thought of me because I'd just written a piece that mounted a case for the film against that weird attack from Andrew O'Hehir, so I guess I owe him a thanks as well; Andrew, I still think you're wrong about *Pulp Fiction*, but I owe you a beer for indirectly helping me land my dream book.

Every draft was first read by Rebekah Dryden, who is not only the best wife on the planet, but the best editor as well; sweetie, I love you and I like you. Mike Hull and Judy Berman also read the book prior to its submission and offered up tremendous feedback and suggestions. And thanks to everyone who watched *Fiction* with me and let me steal your insights during the months I was working on the book; particular thanks to Amy Hughey, Mike Hull, and Andrew Schaper, who chatted and e-mailed with me at length about the ideas that made their way into the analytical essays, and to Lonny Quattlebaum, who explained the jump from "The Gold Watch" to "The Bonnie Situation" to me clear back in 1995.

Thanks of course to Drew McWeeny, Aisha Harris, Adam Rosen, Mark Peters, and Gary Graff for adding their voices and expertise to the volume, and to the many artists who were inspired by the film to create works of their own. Thanks to my instructors at New York University (particularly Dennis Lim, Charles Taylor, Susie Linfield, and Ben Ratliff) and my editors at Flavorwire (Caroline Stanley and Judy Berman), who all did their best to make me a better writer.

And finally, thanks to Quentin Tarantino, who made a movie not only rich enough to warrant this kind of examination, but entertaining enough that—even after living with it for several months and watching it six *more* times—I'd still drop everything right now to go run it again.

About the Author

Jason Bailey is a graduate of the Cultural Reporting and Criticism program at New York University's Arthur L. Carter Journalism Institute. His writing has appeared at the pop culture blog Flavorwire, as well as the *Atlantic*, *Slate*, *Salon*, and the *Village Voice*. He's also done stints in TV news and (surprise, surprise) video stores, as well as writing and directing eleven feature films in his hometown of Wichita, Kansas. He now lives in New York with his wife, Rebekah, where he sees too many movies and tweets too much (@jasondashbailey).